THE KGB

Books by Harry Rositzke

The Peterborough Chronicle
The U.S.S.R. Today
Left On: The Glorious Bourgeois Cultural Revolution
The CIA's Secret Operations
The KGB: The Eyes of Russia

THE KGB:

THE EYES OF RUSSIA

Harry Rositzke

DOUBLEDAY & COMPANY, INC.
GARDEN CITY, NEW YORK
1981

Library of Congress Cataloging in Publication Data
Rositzke, Harry August.
The KGB: the eyes of Russia.
Includes index.
1. Russia (1923–   U.S.S.R.). Komitet gosudar-
stvennoy bezopasnosti. I. Title.
HV8225.R67   327.1'2'06047
ISBN 0-385-15390-2
Library of Congress Catalog Card Number 80–2063

For Barbara

CONTENTS

PREFACE

CHEKA, OGPU, NKVD, KGB.

To millions of people inside and outside the Soviet Union these acronyms have become the symbol of Soviet repression, brutal and murderous under Stalin, more selective and less bloody under his successors.

Today, the Soviet Committee of State Security, the KGB, is seen abroad as the secret arm of the Soviet state intent on stealing the secrets of Western governments, undermining the loyalty of their citizens, and plotting revolutionary actions in the Third World. The wholesale exposure of Soviet spies, the expulsion of Soviet diplomats for espionage, and the revelations of Soviet defectors fortify its threatening image.

In Moscow, meanwhile, where the KGB chief sits on the Politburo, a Soviet spy is honored on a postage stamp, KGB officials are rewarded for their exploits with high honors, and KGB anniversaries are publicly celebrated with patriotic fervor.

During my career on the operational side of the Central Intelligence Agency, I saw the KGB in action both at home and abroad. It operated against the agents we sent into the Soviet Union and against the base in Germany where we trained them. For five years in New Delhi I watched its modest programs against the Indian regime, and for three years in the late sixties I had a closeup look at its more vigorous efforts in New York City and Washington.

In the course of these years I gained great respect for the KGB's professional competence. It has, of course, the tremendous advantage of operating in the open societies of the West, but it goes about its business with energy and persistence. It is a straightforward secret service, even in its more devious and deceptive practices. I found no "wilderness of mirrors" to confuse the observer. More apt, in my view, is the remark a KGB officer made during his interrogation on a Soviet deception operation: "The problem with you Americans is that you always make things much too complicated. In the KGB everything we do is very simple. Take things at face value. They are what they appear to be."

Moscow looks upon its intelligence service as part of the Soviet defense establishment, and it receives the same generous handling as regards staffing and budget. It is an effective and well-disciplined instrument of the Party-State. It enjoys high prestige within the government, attracts the brightest college graduates to its ranks, and provides the best professional training of any intelligence service in the world.

The collection of secret intelligence in Moscow, as in Washington, rests on a triad: photographic and electronic coverage from space, the interception of coded communications from the air, and reports from secret agents on the ground.

These optical, acoustic, and electronic eyes have one failing in common: they cannot see into men's heads.

Moscow knows that satellite cameras cannot photograph what goes on under the roof of the Pentagon or within the research laboratories of Lockheed or Los Alamos.

There is no question in Moscow about the value of human agents even in this technological age.

The secrets of the Western powers, their capacities and intentions, are locked up in documents—not only wiring diagrams, missile performance records, and early warning procedures, but contingency plans, secret NATO negotiations, SALT position papers. It is from documents that Moscow can determine what an adversary can do with what he has, what he knows, what he is thinking, and what actions he is planning to take. For the acquisition of documents the human agent is indispensable.

The KGB is voracious in its appetite for classified documents. The Minox camera is its most powerful weapon.

Soviet intelligence operates on a large scale. It now has over a thousand operations officers under diplomatic cover in Europe, over four hundred in the United States, with at least three hundred in Manhattan alone. During the sixties more than two hundred Soviet diplomats were expelled for improper conduct from almost fifty countries. In West Germany, Soviet and East German agents arrested and convicted in the past thirty years are numbered not in the thousands but in the tens of thousands. Not a year goes by without the exposure of Soviet agents operating in high-security installations of the West.

The KGB works on a basic assumption that reflects its view of human, or at least capitalist, nature: every man can be had. General or sergeant, technician or businessman, executive or clerk—in the right circumstances each is vulnerable to recruitment as a spy.

By the same token no Western establishment is spy-proof. The most drastic security measures, the most efficient counter-espionage work, can reduce but not eliminate the chances for a successful penetration.

In the past ten years the reservoir of potential Soviet agents in the West has grown enormously. The expansion of Western bureaucracies engaged in sensitive undertakings has caused a quantum jump in the number of men and women who have access to classified documents: code clerks, typists and secretaries, junior officers and mid-level bureaucrats, top-secret laboratory workers and couriers, trainees and administrative personnel. Moreover, in Washington, Bonn, and Rome the activities of the national intelligence services have been brought under review by select and, inevitably, not so select legislative committees, whose members and expanding staffs become privy to the secrets of Western espionage and are therefore recruitment targets for the KGB.

As the reservoir of potential agents in the West has increased, Soviet access to them has become easier. With the enormous expansion of East-West contacts brought on by détente—exchanges, scientific conferences, diplomatic and trade negotiations—more Russians meet more Americans and Europeans both on business and around a dinner table. For the KGB the improved climate of East-West relations means a greater opportunity to make "purposeful acquaintances," to meet and size up potential agents. You cannot recruit an agent you have not met.

Here the scale of KGB operations pays off. The chances of successful recruitment are automatically enhanced. Human nature being what it is, a high volume of social contacts is bound to uncover, here and there, a susceptible candidate. The more approaches, the greater the number of agents recruited, however small the percentage of successes.

The wholesale Soviet espionage apparatus is wasteful to the same extent that a surplus of armaments is wasteful. There is more information and more firepower than are needed to pre-

serve the security of the nation. It is an insurance for which the
Russians are more than willing to pay.

The KGB has an insatiable greed for more and more agents. It
is a service totally devoted to its main business: recruiting men
and women to work for it. But it is neither the scale nor the vigor
of the KGB abroad that gives it the first place among contemporary intelligence services. What counts is the performance of
its best agents and the quality of the information they produce.

KGB agents have operated in almost every secret institution of
consequence in the capitalist world during the past generation. It
has been served by scientists and technicians in the wartime Allied atomic bomb research centers; by scores of officials in the
headquarters of the North Atlantic Treaty Organization; by
dozens of Western diplomats; by American field-grade officers
and noncoms with top-secret clearances; by a general and an admiral in the West German High Command; by generals in
Teheran and Tokyo; by bevies of secretaries in the West German
Foreign Office and Defense Ministry; by members of parliament
in London and Bonn; by a personal aide to former West German
Chancellor Willy Brandt.

In the most secret of our secret institutions, the Western intelligence services, the KGB has had agents in the heart of the British, French, and West German intelligence establishments for a
decade or more.

It has penetrated two of the highest security vaults of American military communications: the Armed Forces Courier Station
in Orly, France, and a CIA-controlled satellite communications
center in California.

From these operations it has obtained classified documents that
give Moscow an insight into the highest reaches of Western technology, contingency planning, military and political policy-making. The best have been brought right to the desk of the boss, for
Stalin, Khrushchev, and Brezhnev liked to read "raw" agent reports, and, perhaps, to gloat over the successful rifling of the
West's best secrets.

The tone of the KGB's approach is put most simply in an instruction sent to the stagnant KGB station in Australia in 1952:
"The work of recruitment should be carried out boldly, with fore-
thought and inventiveness. . . . The work of carrying into effect
the tasks that have been set should be conducted with active, aggressive methods."

The KGB is a bold service unhampered by bureaucratic timidity. It knows precisely what it wants out of the Western establishment, and it goes after its targets with simple directness: a clerk in an American Embassy, a secretary in a Foreign Office, a scientist in a research center, a worker in a defense plant. It weighs the risk in each attempted recruitment, and takes its chances. It is willing to pay the price when it loses; hundreds of Soviet intelligence officers have been caught red-handed in Western capitals and expelled. Thousands more of its agents have been arrested and imprisoned. But Moscow is not deterred by the factor of risk. It is not limited by a charter from the Supreme Soviet. Its oversight is confined to the Politburo. Its mistakes are not heralded in the Soviet press.

ACKNOWLEDGMENTS

I am grateful to those of my former colleagues who helped update my knowledge since I retired in 1970. I am especially indebted to Raymond Rocca, the most knowledgeable historian of Soviet intelligence I know of, and to Lawrence McWilliams, who devoted most of his twenty-seven years with the Federal Bureau of Investigation to countering Soviet intelligence operations in the United States. Errors of fact and of judgment are my own.

THE KGB

I

ROOM 2242 QUE

I met my first Russians some ten days after VE day, 1945. On leave from my OSS post at Wiesbaden, Germany, and with two partners, one a Russian-speaking lieutenant, I made an unofficial trip to Berlin to take a look at the Russians. To reach Berlin we had to traverse the Soviet occupation zone which was about to be sealed off from the West.

After talking our way past the border guard, we ended up at the headquarters of the Soviet 33rd Army and talked for several hours with its commanding general, a spare, handsome Russian in his fifties, flanked by two Mongolian officers, his deputy, and his chief of staff. The general was charming, friendly, loquacious. The two Mongolians were suspicious and terse: What are you doing in our zone?

During two more hours around a richly loaded buffet I talked mostly with an English-speaking major, who was obviously a security man instructed to find out what we were really up to. I maintained our cover story: we were going to Berlin to join in on the victory celebrations.

Next morning, after sleeping in warm beds recently evacuated by some Russian WACs, the major appeared to escort us back to the American zone. Our protests were of no use—Mongolian suspicions had carried the day.

Our adventure began. In our Jeep trailer, a prewar road map on our knees, followed by the major and his driver in a battered

Mercedes, we began to speed up, left him behind, and took a turn off the highway that eventually led us to Potsdam and Berlin.

We met other Russians along the way, but none to talk to. I still retain several sharp visual impressions of that rather tense day: farm wagons with thin horses led by short, sloppily dressed Russian soldiers, full of loot from featherbeds to baskets of door-knobs; a long column of German men in their sixties and boys in their teens being shepherded along the Ring Road around Berlin on the way to the East; a stream of Soviet soldiers carrying paint-ings, rugs, and sculptures out of Hermann Goering's villa in Berlin; fifty Studebaker flat-bed trucks at the Siemens-Halske fac-tory, each loaded with one or two large drill presses and lathes, their shiny steel surfaces reflecting the broken sunlight like mod-ernistic sculptures in a burnt-out slum.*

From that day I became preoccupied with Russia and the Rus-sians. Ten months later, in March 1946, still on terminal leave from the Army, I reported for duty with the Strategic Services unit of the War Department, the successor to the wartime Office of Strategic Services (OSS), which was still housed in a series of dilapidated World War I barracks along the Potomac. For almost two years with the OSS in London, Paris, and Germany, I had been, like the rest of my colleagues, preoccupied with the Ger-mans. Now I discovered that no one else had any interest in working on the Soviet Union. The main focus was still on matters German: the retrieval of German scientists, the ferreting out of SS and Gestapo personnel and files; the search for war criminals. Except for the Middle East desk, which was dealing with the Russians in Azerbaijan and the Tudeh (Communist) Party in Iran, Moscow was a distant prospect. The Soviet Union was still our ally. Suspicion at the top in Washington had not yet hard-ened into hostility. No directives were coming down on Soviet requirements.

I asked for, and was given, carte blanche to learn what I could about the Russians from our wartime files.

For the next two months I sat at a table outside the wartime registry scanning stacks of manila folders containing captured German and Japanese documents on the Soviet Union, on Soviet prewar and wartime intelligence, and on the covert operations of the Third Communist International, or Comintern. Allied inter-rogations of former German and Japanese intelligence officials

---

* A brief and somewhat garbled version of this episode is enshrined in the Final Report of the Senate Intelligence Committee, Book I, 1976, pp. 19–20.

were beginning to come in. The German documents were the richest: interrogation reports of captured Soviet agents, Gestapo investigations of Soviet and Communist suspects, studies on the bureaucratic structure of the intelligence services in Moscow.

After four years of the war—in a dull, Miami Beach basic training center, a blacked-out London, a chilblain-infested Paris, and an empty champagne factory near Wiesbaden in Germany— the quiet surroundings of the registry gave me some of the same solitude and room for thought that I had enjoyed for four years in the Widener Library at Harvard. There I had tried to find out something new about the origins of language, the sources of *The Canterbury Tales,* the length of vowels in American English.

Now I had a new subject: what makes the Russians tick? I worked undisturbed. There were few calls for registry files from the regional desks bogged down in the administrative business of dismantling the complex OSS structure that had mushroomed during the war.

My daily companion was the head of registry, a bright dignified, precisely articulate lady who smoked cigars. She combed the files for captured documents that might conceivably be useful to me. I quizzed some of the late returnees from Europe and the Far East on Soviet activities in their areas: nothing was going on. I talked to intelligence officers at the Pentagon and the Department of State: they had seen live Soviet officials at diplomatic conferences and at meetings of the Allied High Commission, but knew nothing of any unofficial Soviet activities. I went back to my files, segregating the nuggets for further study.

In May 1946 I was given a title: Chief SPD/S (Special Projects Division/Soviet), an assistant for its Soviet Intelligence Section (the other two sections were the Soviet Union and International Communism), and an office.

Room 2242 was located on the second floor at the end of a side wing off the long central corridor of Que Building. It was a dismal office. The walls were pockmarked with holes and the ceiling smudged with stains from the rain and snow that leaked through the fragile roof. It had no carpet. It was furnished with one antique green desk, a green four-drawer file cabinet with a combination lock, a green government clock on the wall, and a government "executive" calendar on the desk (my secretary quickly circled the Friday paydays in red).

The view was equally dismal: a brewery and a roller-skating rink. The cafeteria was only slightly less depressing—a cavernous room in nearby M Building in which the polyglot accents of the OSS diehards mingled in the clatter with the bland midwestern speech of the earnest, balding high-school teachers who worked for the Commissioner of Education in M.

The German and Japanese documents on wartime Soviet intelligence operations were a revelation. Here, for the first time, we saw the Russians at work in a Europe dominated by Hitler's counterespionage organs and against a tightly knit Japanese military bureaucracy allergic to white men. Here were the details on how Moscow went about its field operations: what kind of men were recruited, how they were paid, how these men communicated with headquarters, how they carried out the intelligence tasks assigned to them. And, closer to our job, how the German and Japanese security services went about hunting down the Soviet agents operating under their noses. In graphic detail we read the records of agent meetings, contacts exploited, narrow escapes, arrest and torture, and the agent reports—hard intelligence in cables and on microfilm. Here was the evidence for the extraordinary role Soviet intelligence had played in helping Stalin win the Great Patriotic War.

There was a major difference between the intelligence efforts on the Eastern and Western fronts in Europe during World War II. The Russians worked with men, the British with machines. For the Western allies the vital intelligence was Ultra, the almost instantaneous decipherment of the top German military coded communications.

These communications were enciphered by an electronic coding machine, the Enigma, which the Germans had perfected into a highly complex and "unbreakable" system from a commercial device constructed in the twenties. Its virtue lay in its complexity. A series of electrical circuits converted the plain-text into coded text through a precise setting of the machine that was changed every twenty-four hours. Without the key to these settings the messages could not be broken.

Both the French and Polish intelligence services made some headway in working out the keys used, but it was the British, with a sample Enigma machine from Poland, who constructed a counter-machine that could unscramble or "unbutton" the Enigma ciphers by matching the Enigma's internal circuitry and determining the daily settings.

From April 1940 to the end of the European war, Ultra intelligence, the unscrambled Enigma radio traffic, gave the British and

American high commands a microscopic view of German operational plans from air raids to troop movements.

In the Battle of Britain the British Fighter Command could read, almost as quickly as the German Air Force commanders, the time and strength of incoming raids, the main bombing targets, the dispatch of reconnaissance planes. The Fighter Command was able to employ its slender resources with maximum efficiency.

Ultra played an even more crucial role in preparation for the invasion of the continent. Not only did the Western commanders have an intimate knowledge of the location, equipment, and movements of German air and land forces on the Western front before and on D-day, but Ultra intercepts were able to monitor the German reaction to the most fateful deception operation of the war.

A bogus Allied plan to land in the Calais area was passed to the Germans mainly through a variety of misleading reports from German agents in Great Britain who had been captured and "turned" by British intelligence. The measure of German gullibility in swallowing this false information came not only from their replies to the reports from these agents, but from the internal Abwehr counterintelligence. Ultra assured the Allies that Hitler and his generals had been gulled.

When D-day came, the Allies not only knew the exact disposition of the German forces that would confront them, but they also knew the Germans thought that the landings would take place in the Calais area. For days after the invasion the Germans considered the landings in Normandy a diversionary prelude to the main landings at Calais.

Hitler had been double-crossed by the XX committee in London playing back his own agents, and Ultra read his thoughts all the way.

Without Ultra the war in the West would have been longer and bloodier.

On the Eastern front there was no Ultra. The British could not supply their Soviet allies with Ultra intelligence without imperiling the security of its greatest weapon against Hitler. Soviet success in the defense of Moscow and the counteroffensive at Stalingrad hinged partly, if not substantially, on reports radioed to Moscow from two agents on the ground—one in Tokyo, one in Paris.

The work of both men was narrated in detail in the captured

documents I was reading, and the respect of the German and Japanese security officers for their quarry showed through the bureaucratic prose of their investigations and interrogations. Both men made a deep impression on me as well, for here was our first insight into Soviet intelligence agents at their best. Both men affected the outcome of the war. Each, in his own way, was a brilliant man. Their careers are classics in intelligence circles.

Richard Sorge, Ph.D., a prominent German journalist, worked in China and Japan. Léopold Trepper, a Galician Jew, college dropout, and refugee, operated in Western Europe. Trepper and his network (baptized the Red Orchestra by the Germans) plagued Hitler and Himmler personally for several years. He received ten years in the Lubianka and prison camp for his pains. Sorge, whose last report gave the date of the Pearl Harbor attack, was caught and executed by the Japanese. His exploits are commemorated on a Soviet postage stamp.

Both Sorge and Trepper were agents, not of the KGB,† or Committee of State Security, but of Soviet military intelligence, the GRU, or Main Intelligence Administration of the Red Army. The GRU, devoted mainly but not exclusively to military espionage, carried out most of Moscow's espionage operations in Europe and Asia just before and during the war.

The Nazi Journalist

Sorge's road to Moscow started in postwar Hamburg. Born in the Caucasus in 1895, the son of a patriotic Geman oil-driller and a Russian mother, he moved to Berlin with his family to attend school and, at the age of nineteen, became a private in the Kaiser's army. Wounded three times, he ended the war like many of his contemporaries—disillusioned, and in desperate straits. Like many of them, he read Karl Marx. An excellent student, he earned his Ph.D. in political science and on the day of his graduation joined the Hamburg section of the German Communist

---

† The genealogy of the KGB (Komitet Gosudarstvennoy Bezopasnosti), or Committee of State Security, rivals those of the Old Testament. The Cheka (1917–22) begat the GPU, the GPU (1922–23) begat the OGPU, the OGPU (1923–34) begat the NKVD, the NKVD (1934–41) begat the NKGB, the NKGB (most of 1941–46) begat the MGB (or Ministry of State Security), the MGB (1946–53) begat the KBG, which has persisted since March 13, 1954.

With a few exceptions I have used the designation KGB for the present organization and its various ancestors.

Party. An activist in propaganda work and street-fighting, he was spotted as a bright, educated militant by his Party superiors and was tapped for political intelligence assignments by the underground apparatus of the Third Communist International, or Comintern. For the next five years he was engaged in secret work: in the classroom in Moscow and on Comintern assignments in Europe, California (to write up the Hollywood film industry), and England (where British security paid him a visit). He operated under his own cover: as Dr. Richard Sorge, a German businessman with an office in Berlin traveling on overseas business. No forged papers, no fabricated life history, Dr. Sorge would ostensibly remain an open book for the rest of his career.

Always on the lookout for useful operators tested in the Comintern, the chief of the GRU, General Ian Berzin, secured Sorge's transfer in 1929 and gave him a demanding assignment: to consolidate and expand the GRU's scattered network in a China torn by civil war. His targets were the military strength and equipment of the warring armies, their political support among the population, and Japan's intentions in China. For four years, from 1929 to 1933, Sorge helped build the China network from bases in Shanghai and in Harbin, where he quartered his radio operator as a paying guest in the home of the American vice-consul.

By 1933 Moscow had become concerned not only with Hitler's threat in the West, but with Japanese intentions in the East. It recalled Sorge from China and reassigned him to Tokyo. For the next nine years the threat of a Japanese invasion of Siberia from its Manchurian base became the primary concern of the GRU in Asia.

General Berzin's decision to send Sorge to Tokyo was his most successful gamble. He was not at all certain that a white agent could operate effectively in an oriental metropolis under a tight military dictatorship with an alert security service. He sent out Sorge to test the water.

From the time Sorge reached Tokyo in 1934 until his arrest in 1941, the Sorge net produced the highest level strategic intelligence of any operation in this century, for it sat astride the communications and policy decisions of the Soviet Union's two principal enemies, the Germans and the Japanese.

During his stay in Moscow Sorge had handpicked his Tokyo team: two men from his China net and two fresh recruits plucked out of Paris and Los Angeles.

The two old China hands were Max Klausen, the GRU's top radio operator-technician whose cover was sales representative for a German export firm, and Ozaki Hozumi, the Shanghai correspondent for a Japanese newspaper, whom Sorge had recruited in China through an American communist writer reporting on the China scene.

Ozaki was the crux of the Tokyo operation. The scion of a wealthy Japanese family, with excellent connections at the top of the Japanese government and social hierarchy, Ozaki had become a devoted Marxist in his youth, but he had never joined the Party and his record in Tokyo was clean.

Sorge's file search in Moscow led him to the last two members of his team: Branko de Voukelitch, a Yugoslav exile active for the GRU in Paris under journalist cover, and a young Japanese artist, Miyagi Yotoko, domiciled in California, and a member of the Los Angeles branch of the Communist Party.

Before he left for Tokyo, Sorge made the most brilliant, if dangerous, move of his career. He went to Germany and joined the Nazi Party. His sponsors gave him excellent and legitimate recommendations, he was accepted into the Party, and he secured an assignment as the Tokyo correspondent of the influential *Frankfurter Zeitung,* which placed him in the highest rank of his cover profession. He consolidated his reputation by cultivating the highest Party and propaganda circles in Berlin: Goebbels himself attended his farewell dinner. If the Gestapo had properly checked out his membership application, his Communist Party record in Hamburg would have put him in jail.

One by one, the five men arrived in Tokyo and settled in. They could meet each other openly in the natural course of their social and professional lives. They became active participants in Tokyo's social and diplomatic life: three professional journalistic colleagues, a German businessman, and a talented young Japanese artist. All were acceptable members of Tokyo's smart international set.

The three journalists, the core of the operation, divided up their intelligence targets into three sectors: the German Embassy for the esteemed Dr. Sorge, the Japanese cabinet and military high command for the China specialist Ozaki, and the Western embassies for the old Parisian hand, Voukelitch.

The three journalists transacted much of their spy business under open social cover: at two- or three-man breakfasts and lunches and at cocktail and dinner parties. They occasionally

staged drunken brawls with their Japanese friends, and when the party was over, stayed behind to do their private business. There was no skulking even for Klausen when he visited one of his friends' apartments where his radio transmitter was housed.

Sorge's rigid rules of operation kept the three men clean for eight years.

The first, and simplest, rule was to avoid any association with Japanese communists, or communist suspects, and with any members of the sizable White Russian colony.

A second rule cut across the grain of conventional Soviet intelligence practice: never recruit an agent. The three men would alone collect secret information from sources who remained unwitting of its final destination. If they did not recruit anyone else to get information, no one in Tokyo would know they were intelligence agents.

The third rule was the most sophisticated of all: never ask questions. And, conversely, always have answers.

Journalists come by good cover naturally. It is their normal job to make the best contacts in town. In addition, they themselves are cultivated as knowledgeable sources by foreign offices and embassies who want information from them.

The singular quality of the Sorge net was its reliance on his maxim: "A successful agent is one who is a source of information himself." Sorge, Ozaki, and Voukelitch were bright and informed journalists whose broad knowledge and expert judgment made them valuable to precisely those officials who had access to the classified information they wanted. In no other operation I know of have Soviet agents been as useful to the sources they milked.

Sorge's impeccable Nazi credentials gave him entrée to German diplomatic and business circles (in 1938 he was offered the job of mini-Fuehrer to the Tokyo Nazi colony, but turned it down pleading lack of time). He concentrated on a German officer, Major Ott, who soon became the embassy's military attaché, and eventually ambassador. Ott, from the beginning, had no reservations about briefing a good Nazi journalist whose help gave Ott's reports to Berlin a quality of content far beyond Ott's capacity. When Ott became ambassador, Sorge had breakfast with him each morning, briefing him on the previous day's events. Sorge wrote the draft of the ambassador's regular situation reports to Berlin.

On one occasion Ott asked Sorge to act as official embassy courier to Manila and Hong Kong. Sorge's own valise (under diplomatic seal as well) contained almost a hundred cartridges of

film which he passed to an official Soviet courier in Manila, while
another Soviet courier supplied him with GRU funds during his
Hong Kong stop. Only rarely has Soviet intelligence been able to
operate under German diplomatic immunity.

Ozaki's China expertise put him in the same give-and-take situation with the highest Japanese government officials, including
the Premier, Prince Konoye. He became a member of Konoye's
informal brain-trust of young advisers, a full-time special adviser
to the Cabinet subcommittee on Sino-Japanese relations, and in
1938 principal secretary to the Cabinet. When Ozaki lost his
Cabinet job, he became intelligence officer in the Tokyo office
of the Southern Manchurian Railway, a post where he would be
the first, next to the Army command, to learn of troop movements
in the Manchurian sector so vital to Moscow.

Voukelitch made progress as well. His expert reporting to the
French and Yugoslav newspapers brought him an assignment as
special correspondent for the official French news agency, Havas,
and a semiofficial berth in the French Embassy. He became a
treasured contact of the British and American embassies, supplying them (within limits) with what Sorge and Ozaki learned from
their German and Japanese contacts, and securing in return confidential information on British and American policies in the Far
East.

Together with the sources developed by Klausen, mainly on
Japanese trade, and by Miyagi's low-level agents in the Army and
Navy, they provided thousands of documents and situation reports to Moscow. For eight long years, hundreds of urgent messages went by cable and courier. It was a density of coverage un-
matched from any other capital of a major power.

Yet it is not the quantity of material that counts in any espionage operation, but the vital reports that help shape major government decisions. Sorge had more than his share of coups even
before the vital take of 1941.

At the end of 1935 Ozaki (then a member of a China study
group) was allowed to peruse for some hours a top-secret forecast of Japanese political and economic aims for the next year.
The copy he photographed reassured Moscow that Japan had no
hostile intentions toward the Soviet Union, but in fact was actually considering a treaty with Moscow to clear the way for Japanese efforts in China.

Sorge forecast several weeks ahead of time the mutiny of the

Japanese military in February 1936 ("the February incident"), analyzing its roots and correctly predicting its failure.

He again forecast the Japanese invasion of China on July 7, 1937, and again reassured Moscow that the troop movements involved in "the China incident" were directed to the south and not against Siberia.

When the Germans made their first secret proposal for a political and military alliance with Japan, Moscow got details of the anti-Comintern pact even before the Japanese Cabinet and the German High Command learned about it—and a month before its public announcement.

As Hitler placed greater pressure on Tokyo in July 1939 to join in a military alliance directed against Great Britain and the Soviet Union, Sorge followed the moves in Tokyo with great care and reported its rejection by the Japanese Cabinet. He added, however, his own judgment that Hitler would continue to keep up the pressure and that eventually Tokyo might succumb.

A message from Moscow to Sorge implied that his reporting on the Japanese "threat" had exerted some influence on Stalin's decision to sign the Soviet-German nonaggression pact the following month.

The issue of a Japanese attack on Siberia came to a head in May 1941.

On May 1 Hitler informed the Japanese of his intention to invade the Soviet Union on June 22 and demanded Japanese military action against the Soviet Union in the East.

The German attack plan was reviewed by the Japanese Cabinet, and a memorandum based on their discussion was circulated to, among others, Ozaki in his official capacity at the South Manchurian Railway. Confirmed personally by Prince Konoye to Ozaki and by Ambassador Ott to Sorge, the latter sent a message to Moscow on May 12: "One hundred twenty divisions on Soviet border will attack along whole frontier June twentieth. . . ." He was only two days off. The attack came on June 22.

Japanese military intentions remained an open question that summer and fall: would they strike north or south?

On October 3 a Cabinet memorandum was circulated at the highest levels (including Ozaki) giving the final decision: Japanese military forces would move south against Southeast Asia and the Pacific. Japanese forces in Manchuria would be depleted to supply reserves for the southern advance.

Moscow went into high gear. Siberian divisions began rapidly moving to the West. They reinforced the Soviet units defending Moscow, and the battle for Moscow was lost by the Germans.

Siberian divisions reinforced the armies around Stalingrad, helping to throw back the Germans in the greatest counteroffensive of the war.

If the battle is the payoff, Sorge's net was worth a number of divisions.

The end of Sorge's net came only a few days after his crucial October cable. Two women played a role.

The first was the wife of a Japanese communist, Ito Ritsu, one of the subagents of Miyagi, the young artist from Los Angeles. Sorge's ban on recruiting agents and on Party contacts did not apply to Miyagi. Ritsu was suspected by the police of underground party work. The police interrogated his wife, who confirmed their suspicions. Arrested and interrogated, Ritsu led to Miyagi, and Miyagi to his friend Sorge.

With the arrest of Miyagi, Sorge was prepared to close down his operation, but his infatuation for a Japanese dancing girl kept him in town for a few fatal days. He did not know that the girl was an agent of the Japanese police.

Japanese security had detected Klausen's illegal radio transmissions some years before, but even with the importation of more advanced direction-finding equipment from Germany in 1939, it had not been able to locate the radio more precisely than the Tokyo area. After a Japanese security investigation abroad had detected leaks that could come only from high-level sources in Tokyo, Colonel Osaki, the head of Japanese counterintelligence, narrowed down a long list of persons with access to highly classified reports to a handful that included Sorge (for his German Embassy contacts), as well as Ozaki and Voukelitch. The colonel, with his eye on Sorge, introduced him to a dancer at the Fuji Club who was instructed to play hard-to-get.

One night in the club the dancer saw a man pass Sorge's table and slip him a piece of paper. She rode with Sorge to his suburban waterside chalet (his radio was hidden on a boat) and saw him tear up the crumpled paper and throw it on the roadside. The colonel, alerted later by her telephone call, retrieved it, his first piece of hard evidence, and arrested Sorge the next day.

The scrap of paper contained the last message Sorge planned to send before his escape. It read: "Japanese carrier air force attacking United States Navy at Pearl Harbor probably dawn November six . . . ."

At his trial in the spring of 1942, Sorge felt certain that Klausen had sent the message. Klausen said he did not. In any event, there is no evidence that Stalin got it or relayed it to President Roosevelt.

The first official information on Sorge's early days as a communist in Hamburg came to the Germany Embassy in Tokyo after his arrest.

Sorge belonged to that rare breed of action-oriented intellectuals, men such as Lenin, Ho Chi Minh, and the Italian Togliatti, who were more common in the first generation of Communist leaders than they are today. Like them he combined the urge to study and write with a capacity to plan, organize, and act in the demanding world of secret work. No simple collector of raw reports—not, in his own words, "a letterbox for information collected by others"—he was a research-analyst in his own right, both as journalist and intelligence officer. His considered estimates of the course of events, both in China and Japan, built up Moscow's trust, not simply the documents his net produced.

He had, again in his own words from prison, a "strong will to study." He immersed himself with academic thoroughness in the language, culture, and history of his target areas, and spent much of his time talking to Ozaki and Miyagi, not about business, but Japanese art and history. When he was arrested, his library contained almost a thousand books, mostly on Japan. "It was not skill nor the examinations that I had to pass at the Moscow Intelligence School but my basic study and knowledge of Japanese problems that counted most."

Sorge's brilliant mind was combined with a forceful personality and pronounced human impulses. A bachelor, with a bohemian life-style, he enjoyed to the full both women and drink. His talent with the bottle earned him high marks with the Japanese military brass who, like the Russians, loved to compete in drinking contests: they usually passed out with Sorge still more or less on his feet. He liked women, from his first American mistress in Tokyo to the dancer who brought him low.

Sorge's intellect gave him cover and access; his active personal life, freedom from suspicion.

Leopold Trepper, Sorge's colleague operating in Western Europe, was by contrast an intelligence technician, an astute and courageous operator working in the far more dangerous environment of German-occupied Europe. Both were men of supreme self-confidence and enormous energy.

Their paths crossed only once. It was in Brussels in 1938 when they reminisced about their common boss, GRU General Berzin, who was killed during Stalin's military purge. Trepper fitted Berzin's prescription for a good GRU agent: "a cool head, a warm heart, and nerves of steel."

The Belgian Industrialist

Trepper's road to Moscow started in a small village in the Polish Ukraine and ran through Palestine and France. The son of a poor Jewish salesman, he was both a Zionist and a communist militant in his teens ("I am a communist because I am a Jew"). Blacklisted by the Polish authorities, he emigrated to Palestine at the age of twenty, joined the Party, and led the clandestine life of a Party activist until he was arrested by the British in 1928. Deported, he began his second exile in Marseilles with a letter of recommendation to the French Party. In Paris he became a militant in the Jewish immigrant labor section and edited a Yiddish language newspaper until his application for training in Moscow was finally approved in the summer of 1932.

After completing his college education at a Comintern university for national minorities, Trepper, like Sorge, did Comintern work in Europe until he was recruited by General Berzin for the GRU in 1936. He joined the GRU to fight Hitler.

In the fall of 1938 he was dispatched to Belgium with a forged passport as Adam Mikler, a Canadian industrialist with $10,000 to invest—and the mission of setting up secure commercial cover for an espionage net in France and the Lowlands.

Unlike Sorge, Trepper had to start from scratch. He first recruited Leo Grossvogel, a respected Jewish businessman and ardent communist whom he had met in Palestine. They formed "The Foreign Excellent Raincoat Company" (Grossvogel was known as the raincoat king of Belgium), an export firm with branch offices in major European seaports. After a visit from the Belgian police, who suspected him of being a German, Trepper became Jean Gilbert, a Belgian industrialist born in Antwerp. With the fall of France in May 1940, he shifted his headquarters to Paris and established a new commercial cover: Simexco in Brussels, and Simex in Paris. Both firms prospered by selling black-market goods to the Germans. The profits from Simex paid for the network's expenses.

Trepper's main job outside his cover work these first months was to establish the mechanics of his network—safe houses, couriers, letter drops, meeting places—and to recruit agents. Most of his agents were Jews more than willing to work without pay against Hitler. Trepper, mainly with Grossvogel's help, shone as a technician, elaborating a complex and productive network of active agents working day-in, day-out in an extraordinarily hostile milieu. He recruited scores of agents who had to be, and with rare exception were, reliable. He faced communications problems, as we shall see, that defy description.

It was a highly productive network in, for the most part, the routine collection of military and industrial secrets in German-occupied Europe. It yielded information on troop locations and movements, industrial production and availability of raw materials, new German tank designs and airplane production, etc. Without direct access to the highest German installations in Berlin—or to high-level German communications such as Sorge had in Tokyo—Trepper was nonetheless able to contribute vital intelligence on German intentions and capabilities in the crucial period before Stalingrad.

Trepper himself mixed in the highest German circles in Paris. Like Sorge, he was his own best agent. Masquerading successfully as a Belgian businessman, he gave and attended elegant dinner parties, and reported on the morale and attitudes of the German senior officer corps as well as their often classified table-talk concerning Army troop movements in the West and future operational plans in the East. Simex contacts with its biggest customer, the Todt Organization, the construction firm for Hitler's "Atlantic Wall," not only gave him access to full details on German military fortifications and the disposition and movement of German troops, but supplied some of his agents with German passes that allowed them free movement almost anywhere in German-occupied territory. On one occasion a Todt pass saved his own skin.

There were countless other agents in Trepper's net—most of them unpaid. Jews, anti-Nazi French and Belgian businessmen and officers, and communists created a rich reservoir of men and women dedicated to fighting the Germans.

Through his liaison man with the French Communist Party, Trepper gained access to the classical source of military information: railwaymen who reported on German troop movements, logistics, bottlenecks. The French railroad workers were a mainstay of tactical intelligence for Trepper (and for the French resistance). Easily available reports from immigrant workers supplied the basis for compiling industrial production figures.

Anti-Nazi Frenchmen helped Trepper monitor the telephone lines out of the Abwehr headquarters in the Hotel Lutetia in Paris: Moscow could read the conversations between the Berlin and Paris offices of German counterespionage.

One Frenchman working in the Central Billeting Office supplied through his records of Germans on leave in Paris a microscopic view of German troop locations and transfers. Other Frenchmen and French women played the routine game of sex and alcohol: prostitutes in Paris nightclubs, "tourist guides" who steered German soldiers and officers to bars where they got drunk and talked freely to barfly agents—about morale, the location of their units, casualties.

Meanwhile the Simex units in Brussels and Vichy procured their share of German secrets. Trepper's man in Vichy, a hotbed of intrigue at the time, kept track not only of French diplomatic activities, but of the German order of battle within occupied France. Since Vichy had agreed to pay the cost of the military occupation, the monthly accounts of Vichy's expenditures that Trepper's agent procured provided a record of all German troop movements within France.

One of his most useful sources was a White Russian émigré, Baron Vasily de Maximovich, who had been recommended to him in 1940 as a man who wanted to work for his old fatherland. A man of breeding and talent, he was sprung from an internment camp by a German who recommended him as an obvious anti-communist to some officers in the Paris military headquarters in the Hotel Majestic, where he moved freely in and out.

The baron's value escalated when a German secretary fell in love with him. When she became secretary to Hitler's political representative in Paris, Otto Abetz, his files and dispatches began to flow in volume to Moscow.

And the baron had a sister ("six feet tall and built like a lumberjack," according to Trepper), a psychiatrist who ran a clinic near Paris, among whose patients was another German secretary, who worked for the head of the Sauckel organization in charge of manpower for the Third Reich. Thanks to her generous delivery of documents, Moscow could keep track of the state of the German economy through an insight into the labor requirements of the entire German industrial machine—and Trepper got blank forms and certificates of employment to protect the privileged status of his own agents as employees of the Third Reich.

Though the value in an extended war of systematic current reporting on routine matters of military interest cannot be underrated, it is always the notable coups that stand out in the performance of any net.

Trepper shared in the global coverage of Hitler's December 18, 1940, directive ordering preparations for the invasion of the Soviet Union. No top-secret German memorandum of such strategic significance has ever been shared by so many Allied services. A copy was handed over to an American consul in Berlin by an unidentified anti-Nazi in January. Apparently the British got it first through Ultra. Sorge got onto it through the Germans in Tokyo.

Trepper's warning of the impending attack was based on more distant and lower-level sources: a German engineer who had worked on the fortifications in Poland, French railwaymen reporting troop movements, a party of German officers on the eve of transfer to Poland. Trepper not only supplied the proposed date of the invasion, but identified some of the divisions being transferred from France and Belgium to the East. He had already reported Hitler's decision to abandon the invasion of Britain from his Todt and other sources along the entire Atlantic coast.

Trepper's second coup came a year later. On November 12, 1941, with the German armies close to the Moscow suburbs, Trepper's radio in Brussels reported on Hitler's Operation Blue, the thrust to the Caucasus. "Plan III, directed against the Caucasus and originally scheduled for November, will be carried out in spring 1942. All troops to be in position May 1. Whole logistic effort directed to this purpose begins February 1. . . . Details following." Moscow had nine months' warning of the offensive that would be stopped at Stalingrad. By the time the offensive started, the "details following" set out the entire operational plan, the divisions involved, and a statistical rundown on their equipment. Trepper helped at Stalingrad as Sorge helped in the defense of Moscow.

Throughout its short life—less than three years—communications were the plague of Trepper's net.

The only direct evidence the Germans had of Trepper's handiwork came from their monitoring of illegal radio transmissions.

Once spotted on the air, and the approximate source located, the Germans would go to work with their close-in direction finders, which were far more effective than the Japanese equipment. Once the room or house was identified, the Germans had the choice of surveilling the premises to identify other agents or to arrest the operator, capture his radio and codes, and get him to talk and possibly to cooperate in continuing the transmissions under German control. It was naturally a strict rule for Soviet radio operators to stay on the air the shortest possible time to elude the DF-ing vans.

With the German attack on Russia the Soviet radios began playing in full voice—from Brussels, Paris, Berlin, and Switzerland.‡ Their music came as a shock to the Germans who were convinced that Stalin had not up to then violated his alliance by sending agents into the Third Reich.

Trepper's first transmitter, in Brussels, was rolled up in December 1941. From then on operator after operator was located and arrested: again in Brussels, in Berlin, and in France. At one time Trepper was forced to use the French Communist Party link to the Comintern after wasting two months of transmission time before he could make the proper arrangements. There were no quick pouches to Moscow from Paris after the withdrawal of the Soviet mission.

The chorus of illegal transmissions—the music that led the Germans to name these networks the Red Orchestra—caused anger and frustration in Berlin. A special task force, the Red Orchestra Commando, set up in early 1942 at Hitler's personal order, began the chase: its men came from the Gestapo, Army counterintelligence, and the Nazi Party's security services.

It lasted ten months before they caught the "Big Chief." Scores of his agents were arrested and some talked, but the Commando had only three leads to Trepper: his photograph, one alias (Gilbert), and the fact that he lived in Paris.

The commando set trap after trap for the elusive M. Gilbert in Paris. They waited for him to appear for a renewal of his Ausweis, or residence permit. Overeager, his Todt contact called to

‡ The Red Orchestra also included two GRU nets independent of Trepper: the Schulze-Boysen group in Berlin and the *Rote Drei,* or Red Trio, in Switzerland.

The most thorough treatment of all GRU nets in Western Europe is Gilles Perrault's *The Red Orchestra* (New York, 1969). Trepper tells his own story in *The Great Game* (New York, 1977).

remind him. Trepper smelled a rat, and failed to appear. Two Gestapo officers, posing as German businessmen interested in buying industrial diamonds, sought to make contact. Trepper sent a substitute to sign the contract. The Gestapo offered even more tempting bait: the Todt contact offered to accept a "loan" for his cooperation. The bribe was delivered, but not by Trepper.

Trepper was ready to run and close down his operation. He had devised a perfect hideout for himself: in the other world. He planned to have a death certificate signed by a doctor he had met earlier, and a gravestone chiseled for M. Gilbert that the Gestapo could find. But, like Sorge, he stayed in town one day too long.

The wife of the director of Simex, who knew nothing about Trepper's unofficial work, recalled under Gestapo interrogation that her husband had given Trepper the name of the family dentist some six months earlier. He had arranged a final appointment to get his teeth in shape before he disappeared. He was caught as he entered the dentist's office on November 24, 1942, when the tide in the East had already turned against the German armies.

Part of the Trepper drama comes from the spectacle of a single man, a "despised Jew," eluding the combined might of the Nazi security forces. That elusiveness, in turn, reflected Trepper's technical competence in insulating his agents from one another and from him.

After his arrest Trepper gave his captors a textbook course on his operating techniques: the rigorous use of cover names, the limited number of agents any one handler or courier could identify, the separation of radio operators from the active agents, etc. He listed some of his rules for agents to follow: to live in the suburbs (for ease of countersurveillance), to carry no firearms, not to use a car, to send postcards rather than letters to each other, to arrange meetings on Sundays or holidays (fewer police), to meet only at busy places, etc.

In forwarding its report to headquarters, the Abwehr paid its respect to Trepper's professional competence—and its own ignorance of, even then, conventional espionage practice. "All previous experience acquired in the West was valueless to us. It soon transpired that the Russians had been working with great professional expertise. This is why it was necessary for the Abwehr to learn the theories governing the training and planting of Soviet agents, *theories hitherto unknown to its officers.*" (Italics mine.)

The Great Game

Moscow's coverage of the Germans in the West did not stop with Trepper's arrest.

The Commando had already begun to "play back" some of Trepper's captured radio operators, composing their messages and replying to Moscow Center's requests as though nothing had happened. The Germans now proposed to Trepper that he cooperate in this masquerade on the grounds that the German High Command wanted to maintain a channel of communication to Moscow (otherwise inaccessible) that could be used for negotiating an eventual peace treaty with Russia.

Trepper was quick to see through the German plot. He knew that Hitler would never make an accommodation with Stalin, and that the Germans' purpose was to dupe Stalin by concealing their real intention: to undermine the Allied alliance by creating suspicion in the West of a secret Soviet-German deal.

Trepper agreed to participate in order to protect Moscow Center from being duped. Now a special and useful prisoner, he gradually developed a close personal rapport with his captors that gave him enough freedom to move around Paris under escort. He managed on his own to compose and transmit via his French Communist Party contact a full report on what had happened to his net and on the true German purpose in the playback. The Center now turned the game around. It began asking for more and more precise military information which the Germans were forced to supply in order to keep Moscow's confidence. It also used the channel for passing the Germans such deceptive information as exaggerated statistics on the German casualties at Stalingrad.

On September 13, 1943, Trepper was allowed to enter a drugstore without his escort and escaped out of a side door.

The game, for both Moscow and Berlin, was over. Panicked by his escape, for it spelled the end of the "great game," the Commando kept it secret from Himmler.

Trepper, with new documents, went into hiding and finally ended up in November in a safe apartment in Paris, where he stayed quietly until he left for Moscow in January 1945 in the first Soviet airplane that landed in Paris after its liberation. He was an angry man, angered at Moscow Center for the colossal mistakes they had made: forcing his Brussels operator to stay on the air for four-hour stretches at a time, combining the true names and the addresses of the three top Berlin men in a single telegram, and refusing to believe his reports that the Germans were controlling the playback.

It was the KGB's job to investigate the security of its own and of GRU operations. The KGB investigators clearly had their own charges. Trepper was a protégé of General Berzin, who had been purged as a counterrevolutionary in the late thirties. He had collaborated with the Germans after his arrest and given them the names of some of his associates. He was a man from the West, in itself a form of contamination in Stalin's eyes.

What weight these or other factors played cannot be assessed, but the upshot for Trepper was ten years in prison. Freed after Stalin's death, Trepper returned to his native Poland still fated to another exile—this time to England in November 1973. He was a communist because he was a Jew, and it was as a Jew persecuted by the Polish authorities that he had first left his homeland.

Sorge, the intellectual loner; Trepper, the master technician: the stories of these two men became the staple of the lectures on "Soviet Intelligence" I was called upon to give for the next three years inside and outside the CIA. They were dramatic and instructive stories, yielding insight into communications, cover, security—the craft of operations. Yet it was the two men who shaped the operations that made the greatest impact on me and my audiences. Had General Berzin not had the perception to select the right man for the job, had lesser men than Sorge and Trepper been given their assignments, the crucial intelligence Moscow needed would not have been procured. It is an obvious lesson, not always heeded, that the key operational decision any service makes is the assignment of a field man precisely suited to the job he is asked to perform.

Both these men shared an underlying human trait: they were, like other key agents we will come across in this book, men of boundless energy, men with emphatic personalities that made a deep impression on the people they met.

They were also men of many parts. Both intelligent and good conversationalists, Trepper was somewhat more sociable than Sorge. Both were attractive rather than handsome; both womanizers and sturdy drinkers. In the capacity to hold liquor, Sorge comes out ahead. As we have seen, he simply drank his Japanese general friends under the table. Trepper, less confident perhaps, prepared for his drinking bouts by first lacing his stomach with oil to retard the flow of alcohol into his bloodstream.

Alcohol, I would find, played a key role in the lives of many other top Soviet agents after the war. Whether drinking beyond the normal measure is, like intense sexuality, a natural impulse of the powerful, high-strung man or a narcotic designed to relieve the anxiety common to spies, I must leave an open question.

Our study of the Sorge and Trepper cases was more than academic. Most members of Sorge's net were dead or in prison by 1945, but many of Trepper's innumerable agents and contacts were still alive: Where were they now? Under what name? Doing what?

No service loses track of the men who have served it well. The survivors of the wartime European nets were veterans of secret work tested in a Gestapo-run Europe. They were valuable assets to Moscow. We were convinced they would be used again.

During these early years the dossiers of Trepper's agents were filled in from the Gestapo files and the reminiscences of cooperative former members. The American and European services compared notes and spent countless hours chasing down leads. So far as I know, with a minor exception, none of the veterans of the Red Orchestra was ever located playing a new role in postwar Europe.

ON STALIN'S BLOODY BLINDSPOTS

Sorge stayed in a Japanese prison for almost two years before he was executed. Both Sorge and others at the time anticipated that he would be exchanged for Japanese spies in Soviet prisons. According to Trepper, who quoted a Japanese security officer imprisoned with him, the Japanese made three offers to exchange Sorge. Nothing happened.

These are facts.

Why did Stalin leave Sorge to his fate?

What follows is speculation.

From the time in 1936–37 when Stalin's "golden bridge" to Hitler was first conceived, it appears that NKVD chief Beria and the head of the KGB (then part of the NKVD) were the prime supporters of a temporary rapprochement with Germany. After the Nazi-Soviet pact was signed, the KGB apparently supported Stalin in his conviction that Hitler would not move against the

Soviet Union before he had won his war against the British. The KGB had no agents inside the top new *political* leadership and had no concept of the options open to Hitler.

Until Hitler's attack on June 22, 1941, it was the best judgment of Stalin and his intelligence chiefs (and of many in the West) that Hitler's troops on the Soviet border were there to back up an ultimatum that Hitler would soon deliver—a bluff to force further Soviet concessions, or to protect Hitler's eastern flank during his attack on Britain. What factors played the main role in Stalin's thinking are not clear, but one thing is clear: in the face of mounting evidence from the GRU's best agents in the enemy camp, he did not waver from his own conviction that Hitler would not move in 1941.

A man from Moscow visiting Trepper the day after the invasion relayed Stalin's reaction to his invasion report: "The big boss is amazed that a man like Trepper, an old militant and an intelligence man, has allowed himself to be intoxicated by English propaganda. You can tell him again that the big boss is completely convinced that the war with Germany will not start before 1944. . . ."

Here was Stalin's second blindspot: the British. For almost thirty years Stalin had nourished a paranoid faith in British duplicity. For him reports of a German invasion were rumors spread by the British to create bad blood between *their* two enemies, Hitler and Stalin, in the hope of bringing them to blows and taking Hitler off their back. It is ironic that Trepper was originally dispatched to Belgium in the fall of 1938 to set up a network along the Channel ports to penetrate the United Kingdom.

Stalin was blinded to the end. On June 10, twelve days before the offensive, Soviet Ambassador Maisky was briefed in London on the steadily accumulating evidence the British had received on the invasion. Four days later Moscow broadcast a communiqué that referred to "clumsily cooked-up propaganda" on the German threat.

When the attack came, Stalin ordered his commanders in the West not to shoot back at the invading Germans. Khrushchev interprets "this strange command" as based on the notion that the opening artillery fire was a provocation by a local German commander disobeying Hitler's orders. "Stalin was so afraid of war," he goes on, "that even when the Germans tried to take us by surprise . . . Stalin convinced himself that Hitler would keep his word and wouldn't really attack us." An underlying factor in

Stalin's mind, according to Khrushchev, was his mortal fear of Hitler: "I'd seen him when he had been paralyzed by his fear of Hitler, like a rabbit in front of a boa constrictor."*

Even if all this is correct, how could Stalin reject the evidence of his own agents?

They were both GRU agents.

Khrushchev has remarked on Stalin's dependence on the Cheka (his word for the KGB), not only for political but for military intelligence. Khrushchev found these Chekists "a fairly despicable lot," but Stalin, he insists, "considered [them] beyond reproach and believed anything they told him." Given the KGB's commitment to the German alliance, the KGB chief may even have been honest in persuading Stalin to disregard these uncomfortable reports. The KGB fortified Stalin's blindness.

The German attack induced in Stalin what appears to have been a virtual mental breakdown. It was some time before he got a grip on himself and became the heroic leader of the Patriotic War.

Once out of his funk, Stalin realized what his stupidity had cost the nation. How could he protect himself? By eliminating the direct witnesses of his stupidity, just as in the thirties he covered up his own crimes against the Party by purging the purgers who had framed his old comrades.

There were at least half a dozen such witnesses in Moscow and Berlin: the chiefs of the KGB and the GRU, the Soviet ambassador and the KGB and GRU residents in Berlin. Most of these men, all part of Stalin's "Georgia mafia," were no longer visible on the Moscow scene in 1946. What happened to them we do not know.

There were, of course, two other witnesses, the two men who had sent in the crucial reports on the coming attack.

Trepper was put in jail after he returned from Paris.

Sorge was in the hands of the Japanese police. Why bring him back alive to Moscow to bear witness to Stalin's fatal error?

Sorge, it appears, was a victim of Stalin's cover-up.

Long after the death of both men, Sorge became a Hero of the Soviet Union and the leading figure in a film entitled *Who are you, Richard Sorge?* He was lauded by *Pravda* as "the symbol of courage and devotion."

* For these and Stalin's following remarks, see *Khrushchev Remembers* (Boston, 1970), pp. 170–71.

II

FRONT-PAGE
SPIES

While we were reconstructing the wartime Soviet nets in the classified corridors of Que Building, live Soviet agents were suddenly making the headlines outside. They had been operating under our noses in Ottawa, New York, and Washington.

In March 1946 word was already out among the few interested intelligence officers that the Prime Minister of Canada had visited Washington the previous October to inform President Truman of a Soviet spy net uncovered in Ottawa that reached into the Allied atomic bomb program. In June a Royal Commission report narrated in enormous detail the espionage activities of the Soviet military attaché in Ottawa, Colonel Nicolai Zabotin.

The inside story of Zabotin's GRU network came from his own files.

When Igor Gouzenko, Zabotin's code clerk, a GRU lieutenant masquerading as a civilian, received his reassignment orders to Moscow, he decided not to return. He was, he later said, shocked that the Soviet regime was working against its Canadian ally. He also clearly preferred life in the West for himself, his wife, and child.

Gouzenko made excellent preparations for his defection. He

ruled supreme in Room 12 of the Soviet legation in Ottawa, a room barred by two steel doors, its windows protected by iron bars and steel shutters. It was broken up into several offices with steel filing cabinets for documents, an incinerator, and Gouzenko's own cryptographic materials. He was alone most of the time.

In the days preceding his escape he dog-eared individual documents and cables and built up a cache of scraps of paper he had been given to burn. When he left Room 12 for the last time on the evening of September 5, he had with him batches of cables to and from Moscow, agent index cards with cover names and brief notations ("takes money"; "Jew"; "he works well"; "he is afraid"), and pages out of Zabotin's case-officer notebooks listing meetings, money paid out, and intelligence reports delivered.

After a hair-raising thirty-six hours in which he was turned down by a newspaper office and the Ministry of Justice, he escaped the Soviet search team sent to his apartment, and found himself under the protection of the Royal Canadian Mounted Police.

The Canadian agents, easily identified from the Gouzenko material, included over a score of well-placed government officials, scientists, and research technicians. Dr. Raymond Boyer, a chemist with an international reputation, became a member of the National Research Council in July 1940 and supplied information on advanced research on a high explosive (RDX). His material gave Moscow the ability to build RDX plants. A source in the Department of Munitions and Supply passed to the Russians production figures on aircraft and ships and secret correspondence with the British Ministry of Supply. Other sources provided a steady stream of information, often detailed, on top-secret research on radar, fuses, aerial photography, high explosives for depth bombs, and other ordnance.

Zabotin had heard from Dr. Boyer about American experiments with uranium in their work on the atomic bomb, and he knew that British atomic research had been, for safety reasons, transferred to laboratories in Montreal and an experimental plant at Chalk River in Ontario. In the summer of 1945 he pulled off his major coup.

Dr. Allan Nunn May, a British physicist, had been working since April 1942 on atomic energy matters in England, where he had been recruited as a Soviet agent. He was later transferred to Canada. He not only knew about his own theoretical work and what was going on at the Chalk River plant, but had visited the Argonne Laboratory in the United States three times in 1944.

On August 9, three days after the bombing of Hiroshima and shortly before he was to be transferred back to England, May gave his Soviet contact a long report on the New Mexico tests and the bombs dropped on Japan—and two samples of uranium: an enriched specimen of U-235 in a glass vial and a thin deposit of U-233 on a piece of platinum foil. The two samples were at once flown to Moscow by a GRU officer.

Zabotin's nets ranged far beyond military-technical matters. He had a source working in the classified registry of the British High Commission, a major in the Ministry of Defense, a clerk in the Department of External Affairs, and a score of other government employees who produced thousands of classified documents of at least marginal interest in Moscow.

Zabotin's remarkable success (he had been operating for less than three years) was almost entirely due to the cooperation of the Canadian Communist Party, then known as the Labor Progressive Party. Two men played key roles.

Fred Rose (born Rosenberg in Poland, of Russian parents), the Party's organizer for Quebec, had been elected a member of Parliament and was able to supply information from secret parliamentary sessions and talks with senior government officials. He also played the conventional Party support role, recommending useful agent-candidates to Zabotin, mostly Party sympathizers in good positions to supply classified information. These men were then approached independently by Zabotin's case officers without their being aware of Rose's behind-the-scenes role.

Sam Carr (born Kogan in the Russian Ukraine) had been the Party's organizing secretary since 1937 and was running a Party net before Zabotin took over in June 1943.

Carr went much further than Rose: he handled agents directly for Zabotin, whose notebook listed him under "Second Group (Ottawa-Toronto) . . . Jew. Organizer. Studied with us in 1924–26 in the Soviet Party School. Speaks Russian. . . ." His registration card in GRU files added: "Financially secure, but takes money. It is necessary occasionally to help."

Carr literally was an "organizer." He not only spotted potential recruits for the net, but himself recruited some of them as agents and handled them under Zabotin's direction—men such as Professor Boyer. When the deputy chief from Moscow Center visited

North America (under suitable guise) on an inspection trip, Carr alone of the Canadians had a meeting with him.

With Carr playing the role he did, the Canadian Communist Party became an integral part of Soviet intelligence.

The New York–Washington Nets

Later in 1946 I made my first contact with the Soviet intelligence unit in the Federal Bureau of Investigation: three men in a room stacked with folders. The unit was going through the same process as ours of retrieving anything "Russian" from central files bulging with Japanese and Nazi cases. At the same time the Bureau's operating sections and field offices were already knee-deep in ongoing Soviet spy cases in the Washington and New York areas.

In October 1945 Elizabeth Bentley had informed the FBI that she had been operating for seven years as a courier to a Soviet spy ring in Washington. She was placed under surveillance during meetings with her Soviet contact, "Al," who turned out to be Anatol Gromov, first secretary in the Soviet Embassy. FBI Director Hoover bombarded the White House and Justice Department with her detailed accusations against a score of Washington government officials, but President Truman refused to take action on her uncorroborated charges. It was not until July 31, 1948, that she made the headlines as a witness before the House Un-American Affairs Committee.

A second Soviet courier had to wait even longer before his charges were brought into the open. Whittaker Chambers, a courier for six years to a group of high-level government employees in Washington, broke with the Communist Party in 1938, and, several days after the signing of the Soviet-Nazi pact, recounted his spying career to an assistant secretary of state, A. A. Berle. Berle filed the memorandum of his conversation. Chambers did not speak out in public until he appeared before the House Committee on August 3, 1948.

Although the Canadian case had caused ripples in the American press, the testimony of "the Red Queen" (Bentley) and "the Mystery Witness" (Chambers) brought the high drama of espionage and sex into the rapidly evolving red scare.

When our focus in Que Building shifted from Sorge, Trepper, and Zabotin to the Washington nets exposed by Bentley and

Chambers, we were clearly dropping from the professional to the amateur level of espionage. The Washington nets were, by almost any standard of "secret work," casually if not sloppily managed. Their communications were clumsy, their "clandestine" meetings laughably insecure, their intelligence targets amorphous. They would not have survived a month under the alert scrutiny the Japanese gave Sorge or the routine investigative work of the Gestapo.

Both the Bentley and Chambers nets followed the same structural pattern: an American Communist Party official in charge, a secret Party member as courier, and secret communist cells in the Washington bureaucracy as sources.

The Peters-Chambers net is the best documented and most revealing specimen of the Party's underground work.

Whittaker Chambers joined the Party in 1925 out of a sense of personal desperation ("I am an outcast"). As an undergraduate at Columbia University, though not Jewish himself, he became part of a group of radical Jewish intellectuals who introduced him to the Marxist critique of the capitalist system and the search for social justice. A first-class writer, Chambers worked on the staff of the *Daily Worker* until 1929, drifted away from the Party but rejoined it in 1931, and became editor of *The New Masses*.

In late 1932 or early 1933, Chambers began his career in secret work. He "dropped out," divorcing himself from all open Party activities and breaking off all Party contacts.

He was assigned to a man known as J. Peters, a man of a dozen aliases who carried out both open Party activities (Chambers first met him in 1929 in the offices of the *Daily Worker*) and also managed at least part of its confidential or underground operations. A resident alien who was never naturalized, trained in the Lenin School in Moscow, a frequent traveler in and out of the United States during the late twenties and thirties, Peters played the role of Comintern representative in the United States and also of the Party's front-office liaison with Soviet intelligence. Peters in effect filled three roles: he was a normal American Party functionary, a guide and adviser from Comintern headquarters, and the Party link with Soviet intelligence.

Peters assigned Chambers, among other tasks, a job as his liaison with a Washington cell of secret Party members originally formed in 1934 by a Party labor activist, Harold Ware, son of Mother Bloor, the grand old dame of the Party's early days.

The Ware cell, or group, was secret in order to protect its

members from any discrimination or hostility that open Party membership might inflict on their careers. Other secret cells existed among journalists and school teachers as well as government officials.

Though they did not carry cards, members of the Ware group were under Party discipline, paid Party dues, and attended regular cell meetings just as in any open cell. They were useful to the Party for two reasons: they gave the Party influence in the government ("infiltration") and provided inside information of interest of the Party ("gathering information" for the Party is technically not "espionage"). They were not "agents" in any proper sense, and certainly not "Soviet agents."

The Ware cell met as a group in a member's apartment or a studio owned by a sympathizer, and Peters occasionally came down from New York to attend their meetings. Chambers collected their dues and brought them to Peters.

At this stage the group devoted itself mainly to Party business and operated as well as an amateur consortium passing documents to the Party. When, according to Chambers, two of its leading members were isolated from the group and handled separately by Chambers on Peters' behalf, the two men were not being isolated from the others as "spies," but as elite Party members with the most promising future in their government careers.

Although Chambers had been introduced to several of Peters' Soviet contacts in New York when he went into secret work ("Herbert," "Ewald," "Ulrich," "Bill"), the Washington cell did not come under Soviet guidance until 1936.

Previous Soviet intelligence efforts in the United States had been casual and sporadic. For Moscow, America was still an undiscovered country in the twenties and early thirties. Its principal intelligence targets were naturally Great Britain and Germany, and what happened in Washington or New York was politically and militarily almost irrelevant to the Soviet national interest. The inferior quality of Soviet intelligence officers assigned to the United States in the thirties reflected its appraisal of the importance of the job to be done.

In early 1936 Peters offered to sell the documents coming out of the Washington cell to the GRU (only in 1934 did Chambers discover that he was in touch with GRU, and not NKVD, officers), and to use the proceeds for Party business. He proposed the idea to "Bill," who did not like it, but agreed to look at some samples. After an inspection of the take, he rejected the offer. Then in mid-1936 a new officer appeared on the scene, a Colonel Boris Bykov, and Peters made his deal.

When Bykov accepted the gift of the Ware group, he insisted on meeting several of its members personally and tried to pressure Chambers into putting them on the GRU payroll. Chambers objected, pointing out that they supplied documents out of political principle, and Bykov compromised by making a gift of Bokhara rugs "woven in Russia" to four of his new agents.

Even though information collected by the Party can be easily passed on to a KGB or GRU contact, it is the *direct* use of Communist Party members by Soviet case officers that demanded, as we shall see, a crucial policy decision for Moscow both before and after World War II. Only when Colonel Bykov arrived on the scene and met personally with *his* new agents, did the Party net become a Soviet espionage "ring." Chambers, the old Party courier, now transmitted instructions and intelligence reports from and to Moscow.

With Bykov in charge, the random conveyance of documents by his new agents in Washington ("anything of interest") became more selective. Moscow, in contrast to the Party, had no serious interest in the American target *per se,* but only in American policy and actions that affected the immediate threat of German and Japanese military and industrial power. Bykov ran the net, both directly and through Peters, for two years until it collapsed with Chambers' defection in 1938.

That same year, Elizabeth Bentley dropped out of her open membership in the Party and became part of another net run by the Party. The Golos-Bentley net operated as a straight Party affair from 1938 until Golos' death in 1943.

Elizabeth Bentley, an unemployed Vassar graduate, returned in 1934 from a year in Italy and moved into the Party by way of the American League Against War and Fascism. A hard-working activist for several years, she got into secret work by offering to supply the Party with publications and correspondence from the Italian Library of Information in New York, where she was working as a secretary. She was turned over to "Timmy," who introduced her to underground work, instructing her to drop out of the Party and out of "progressive circles" and pose as a political conservative.

"Timmy" was Jacob Golos (born Rasin in Russia), an old Party hand well known for his years of work as an organizer and editor. A Ukrainian Jew, imprisoned and exiled under the czar, he escaped via China to Japan to join his family in the United States. He went to Columbia Medical School and returned for a time to the Soviet Union in the twenties to work for the Revolution, both as foreman of a coal mine in Siberia and, on the evidence, for the domestic security service.

Golos, then working as the head of a communist firm, World Tourists, played a triple role in New York: as a member of the Party's Central Control Commission, as head of the Party's secret work, and as liaison with the KGB.

Golos quickly transformed Bentley into a right hand for his secret operations. She helped him entertain Party visitors from Canada (including the luckless Sam Carr), and penetrated the McClure Newspaper Syndicate on his behalf, smuggling out correspondence and file documents—both straight Party business. She also became a cut-out or intermediary, to several of Golos' intelligence agents: a chemical engineer who collected industrial blueprints; Walter Lippmann's secretary in Washington, in whose files the Party had an interest; and the organizer of a secret cell within the Institute of Pacific Relations (otherwise staffed by many prominent innocent, or unwitting, persons). All these activities were purely Party business, though information of any value was transmitted as well to Golos' KGB contact.

After the German attack on the Soviet Union in June 1941, the KGB interest in American policy toward the Soviet Union heightened, and Golos was instructed to develop inside sources in Washington. In July Golos made contact through Party headquarters with the leader of a secret Party cell in Washington, which included Party members and sympathizers in sensitive government jobs. This was Bentley's main net, and she, like Chambers, played a double role on her biweekly trips to Washington: to collect Party dues and deliver literature, and to transmit to Golos the intelligence the net had collected.

By the summer of 1943 about forty rolls of microfilm were going up to New York in Bentley's knitting bag every two weeks, both from this group and from such solo agents as Bentley's "infant prodigy," an air corps statistician, and several agents in the Office of Strategic Services.

In March 1944 Bentley took over a second group headed by a War Production Board statistician, and the intelligence take increased.

The KGB had been putting pressure on Golos to allow them to

take over direct management of his Washington sources, but Golos steadfastly refused. After Golos died in 1943, one leader of the cell was turned over to a Soviet handler. Bentley met the new man from Moscow assigned to "straighten" out the net: he planned to fire the marginal sources and handle each useful agent with a separate KGB case officer. Bentley's defection in late 1945 appears to have been sparked mainly by this imposed turnover.

The new man, "Al" (Anatol Gromov), gave Bentley the KGB's rationale: "The set-up is too full of holes and therefore too dangerous," he told her, and her close connection with Golos endangered the whole operation.

Thus, somewhat belatedly, the KGB tried to "modernize" the Washington net. It had very little time to do the job, for Bentley walked into the New Haven office of the FBI in August and testified to a grand jury before the end of the year.

How closely Gromov or his predecessors guided Golos' work cannot be known, but the essential fact is clear: for five of her seven years as courier, Bentley worked in an operation set up and controlled by the Party, not the KGB.

What caused the greatest furor as Bentley and Chambers testified was not the nature of the secrets that had been "sold" to the Russians, but the stature of the Washington officials who supplied them.

From Chambers came such names as Alger Hiss, a member of the Ware group, who in 1936–38 worked in the State Department and later became a senior official in the negotiations for the United Nations; Harry Dexter White, an assistant secretary of the Treasury and from 1946 director of the International Monetary Fund; and Julian Wadleigh, who worked in the Trade Agreements Section of the State Department.

Bentley not only named White again, but Lauchlin Currie, an assistant to President Roosevelt, and a score of other officials.

The controversy over Alger Hiss's relationship with Whittaker Chambers is still alive. Was he guilty of espionage?

For a counterintelligence officer, whose task is not to make final judgments but to weigh the available facts about a suspect spy, I would have to say that the evidence presented against Hiss at both his trials, in Whittaker Chambers' *Witness,* and in FBI files recently released leaves little room for doubt that Alger Hiss was a member of a secret Party cell in Washington and that he supplied classified documents for the use of the Party and, most likely, for transmittal to a Soviet case officer.

To avoid these conclusions demands a flight from common sense.

The weight of the evidence of Hiss's complicity in espionage can be dismissed or lightened only by assuming that Whittaker Chambers was a brilliant and inventive liar, that the typewriter on which State Department documents were copied was a fake duplicate of Hiss's typewriter, that the microfilms were forged, and that the documents themselves were stolen from Hiss's desk in the State Department—in short, that Alger Hiss was framed. Of the countless conspiracy theories advanced during thirty years in defense of Hiss's innocence—conspiracy by, among others, the FBI, the OSS, the CIA, the KGB, domestic right-wingers—none holds up to even casual inspection.*

The number and variety of agents listed by both Chambers and Bentley—communists, secret communists, sympathizers—served to heighten the impression that in the late thirties and during the war Washington was riddled with Soviet spies working against the American interest—an impression assiduously cultivated for its political value by Republicans, conservatives, and professional anti-communists.

What was the value of all these secret documents to Moscow?

If the samples of the take we do have fairly represent the overall production of the two nets, it is safe to say that the value of the Chambers net during 1936–38 was virtually nil; of the Bentley wartime sources, at best, minimal.

Moscow's concern in 1936–38 was with the military intentions of the Germans and Japanese. In Bykov's words, "We want everything that bears on the preparations the Germans and Japanese are making for war against us." There is nothing in the "Hiss documents" on record that adds anything to Sorge's on-the-spot coverage in Tokyo. There is little in the economic intelligence supplied by White and Wadleigh from Treasury and the Trade Agreements section of State that could have clarified Moscow's estimates on either the industrial potential or intentions of Germany and Japan.

The value of Bentley's wartime sources must have been distinctly greater. Once at war, Moscow's requirements grew, including not only basic military data on U.S. forces (troop strength and allocations, production figures, etc.), but such political matters as official American attitudes toward the Soviet Union, for-

* For the most recent, and most careful, weighing of the evidence against Hiss, see Allen Weinstein, *Perjury* (New York, 1978).

eign wars, and secret negotiations with Great Britain and the East European governments-in-exile. Here again, however, measured against the production of several high-level Soviet agents operating during this same period—a British Embassy official in Washington, a British intelligence officer in London—Bentley's was of little value.

Probably of greater intelligence benefit to Moscow than the government documents was the hard technical data supplied by lesser figures at the Aberdeen Proving Ground in Maryland and the Bureau of Naval Ordnance on radar, proximity fuses, and bomb sites.

In any event, whatever their real value, these reports were obtained on the cheap: the Party did the work, and only a few hours of Soviet case-officer time was required.

In describing both these nets I have made a point of distinguishing "Soviet" from "Communist" espionage operations.

The distinction is more than a quibble. The issue for us in Que was not whether the information collected by the Party eventually ended up in Moscow, or whether the GRU or KGB determined what intelligence was to be collected, but how the nets were run. However experienced Party workers are in "secret work," the mechanics of secret operations that are the same for all practitioners were usually applied more sloppily and with less self-discipline by the relatively untrained Party worker. Both nets broke most of the rules of cover and "compartmentation" so assiduously taught in secret service schools.

Chambers' cover was broken from the start of his "secret" career. His former Party associates knew what he was up to, and he kept up his earlier friendships with non-Party members, some of whom knew he was in "highly secretive work." At one time he announced that he was "engaged in counterespionage for the Soviets against the Japanese." During his stay in Moscow in 1933, ostensibly for a GRU training course (something he never admitted), he sent postcards to his friends.

Nor did he maintain even elementary secrecy in his relationships with some of his "agents." By his own report he had a public lunch with one of his Washington contacts to talk about art and music. Above all, if he is to be believed, he handled his ace agent, Alger Hiss, like an old family friend. Other "agents" in the net visited each other, went to art exhibits, and played Ping-Pong.

Bentley's work was even less secure, for she treated her Washington sources as friends, a kind of family she had to take care of. In her last meeting with one leader of one cell she lamented "the end of the good old days—the days when we worked together as comrades."

Though younger and less well known in the Party than Chambers, she broke her cover from the start by having an affair with her well-known Party boss, Golos. She handled agents on a personalized basis that violated the simple KGB rule against becoming emotionally engaged with an agent (Golos broke the rule as well). She met her American contacts in their own houses and apartments, and her Soviet contacts for dinner at Longchamps in New York or at a waterfront restaurant in Washington. There was each year a wholesale distribution of Christmas presents.

I recall most vividly the scene in a kitchen with Bentley and several of her agents sitting around the table. Bentley paws through a batch of microfilm and copied documents, sorting them out, takes shorthand notes and shoves the take into her knitting bag before she leaves for New York.

The most fateful lapse, of course, was the total lack of compartmentation, of insulating each agent from all the others. Here was one woman who could, like Chambers, identify more than a score of agents.

In both nets the mechanics of copying purloined documents could hardly have been clumsier. Again, on the evidence, State Department documents allegedly supplied by Hiss were painstakingly retyped by Mrs. Hiss on the famous and incriminating Woodstock typewriter. Years later Elizabeth Bentley sat down one night with Walter Lippmann's secretary and her two Party roommates, and all four spent the night retyping the files she had brought home from his office. Some of Bentley's agents did make use of a Minox camera—one had a photographic laboratory in his basement—but it was not until 1943 that documents brought out overnight were routinely photographed on film, often of poor quality, supplied by the KGB.

Why, then, did both operations survive until they were blown by Chambers and Bentley?

The West was extremely naïve in coping with Soviet espionage. Neither communists nor Soviet spies were a matter of investigative concern in Ottawa or Washington before the mid-1940s. The wholesale transmittal to the Institute for Pacific Relations of thousands of classified documents reflects the easygoing attitude, by giver and receiver alike, toward the handling of "official secrets." The casual rejection by Assistant Secretary Berle of Chambers' first exposure of "Soviet agents" in 1939 was not a cover-up, but reflected a genuine disbelief that "one of us" could be a Soviet spy. Neither Canadian journalists nor the police were ready to recognize Gouzenko as a Soviet defector in 1945.

The wife of a GRU official working in New York in the early thirties said later in Moscow: "If you wore a sign saying 'I am a spy,' you might still not get arrested in America when we were there."

The Secret of the A-bomb

It was the mere *fact* of spying, not its invasion of meaningful American secrets, that caused the public hullabaloo in 1948. Just two years later, when Julius and Ethel Rosenberg were arrested and tried on a charge of conspiracy to commit espionage, it was not the crime or the criminals but the secrets transmitted that produced the most dramatic headlines.

Julius and Ethel Rosenberg were arrested on July 16, 1950, and their trial on a charge of conspiracy to commit espionage opened in New York on March 6, 1951.

The Cold War had started in earnest with the Soviet takeover of Czechoslovakia and the Berlin Blockade in 1948. The war scare was on, the communist witch-hunt had reached hurricane force on the East Coast, and "red" had become etched in moral and emotional accents. The Washington nets now seemed minor skirmishes, for the Rosenbergs were accused of passing atomic bomb secrets to a Soviet intelligence official in wartime. Soviet espionage became a brutal political fact of life in an America normally more concerned with domestic than foreign conspiracies.

In late 1943 Julius Rosenberg, a long-term open Party member, "dropped out" of the Party and became an agent for Soviet intelligence. The evidence indicates that he became a full-time agent for a KGB case officer, Yakovlev, under official cover in the Soviet Consulate in New York City. There were no Party intermediaries, no secret cell mettings, no Party connections. As a solo agent, Rosenberg carried out such operational chores as he was assigned: picking up reports (probably in dead drops) and recruiting people he knew. Yakovlev was far more competent and professional than the ham-handed Bykov, but he made one fatal mistake that blew his operation.

The basic charge at the trial was that the Rosenbergs recruited Ethel's brother, David Greenglass, to secure classified information on the atomic research and development program at Los Alamos, where he worked as a machinist. Greenglass was accused of passing the information ("sketches and description of the very bomb itself") both to his brother-in-law in New York and to Harry Gold, a professional Soviet intelligence courier. The evidence for the Rosenbergs' participation in the Soviet net was furnished mainly by David Greenglass and his wife, by the confession of Harry Gold (who was already serving a thirty-year sentence for espionage), and by several of the men who worked for or with Rosenberg.

Rosenberg was not simply an agent or a courier, but a "principal agent," a man who handles and recruits other agents for his case officer. He handled, on Yakovlev's behalf, sources at General Electric in Schenectady, New York, and at the turret-lathe plant in Cleveland. His work as a recruiter was literally a family affair: he recruited, or tried to recruit, relatives or friends. Whether or not he recruited her, he enlisted the cooperation of his wife, recruited her brother Greenglass at Yakovlev's instructions, employed his sister-in-law to convey his request for information to Greenglass, recruited one college classmate and tried to recruit another.

How not to recruit an agent is the lesson of Rosenberg's approach to a former classmate. In Washington in 1944 he called on his former classmate, whom he had not seen for years, and bluntly enlisted his cooperation in getting secret reports from the Navy Bureau of Ordnance on anti-aircraft and missile-firing control devices. Rosenberg told him that his apartment-mate and fellow worker was already passing him information for the Russians. Later his former classmate *talked* about espionage, but never came through.

Rosenberg's crucial operation was literally a family affair.

In 1943 his brother-in-law, David Greenglass, was assigned as a machinist to the Manhattan Project at Oak Ridge, Tennessee, and in August 1944 reassigned to Los Alamos, New Mexico, where he worked in a section concerned with high explosives.

According to Greenglass, Rosenberg sent a message to him in November by Greenglass' wife, Ruth, asking him to supply information on the Los Alamos project for the Russians. He justified the request with a simple rationale: if both the United States and the Soviet Union have the atomic bomb, the balance of power will bring a lasting peace. Ruth memorized the recruitment pitch and delivered it to her husband—who, after sleeping on it, agreed.

Greenglass came to New York on leave on New Year's Day, 1945, and gave Rosenberg the famous sketch of the "lens mold," a key device for detonating an atomic bomb. He was also introduced by Rosenberg to a woman, Ann Sidorovich, who he said would probably meet him in nearby Albuquerque to pick up further reports. In case Ann did not herself come for the meeting, Rosenberg gave Greenglass a jaggedly cut half of a Jell-O box that would match the other half brought by an alternate courier.

In June 1945 Yakovlev switched couriers. Not Ann but Harry Gold was assigned to make the meeting in Albuquerque.

Harry Gold was the one outsider at the Rosenberg trial. Gold was an old hand at espionage. The son of Russian parents named Golodnitsky, born in Switzerland, he came to the United States at the age of three, became a chemist, and worked for the Russians as an industrial spy and a courier from the mid-thirties. He supplied Moscow with "secret" industrial formulas from the firms he worked for, and also serviced other industrial agents: a research chemist for Eastman Kodak, a steel company employee, and others. He was a simple, understandable man. Not a communist, he simply liked spying, and over the years had become a competent professional. It was through no fault of his that he had ended up in jail.

Gold first met Yakovlev ("John") in March 1944 and acted as his courier for the next two years. His principal assignment was to contact Dr. Klaus Fuchs.

A German-born refugee from Nazism, the son of a Lutheran pastor, Klaus Fuchs had taken a degree in mathematics and physics at a British university, and after a brief internment in Canada as an enemy alien returned to England and worked on classified atomic research. He volunteered to work for the Russians and provided regular reports on his own work in the British atomic research program for some eighteen months before he left for the United States in December 1943. His handling was turned over to Yakovlev.

Gold had various meetings with Fuchs from June 1944 on: in Brooklyn, in Manhattan, in Cambridge, Massachusetts. At the Cambridge meeting in early 1945, Fuchs informed him that he was to be assigned to the Los Alamos project. Yakovlev arranged a rendezvous for Gold to meet Fuchs at Santa Fe, New Mexico, on the first Saturday in June.

When Yakovlev directed Gold to make a second stop in New Mexico to meet Greenglass in Albuquerque, Gold protested vigorously. Fuchs, as an important scientist, was probably under constant surveillance, and a second meeting in the area would be dangerous, if not insane. Yakovlev insisted, and gave him the other half of the Jell-O box and contact instructions.

Gold was right, but not in his fear that the Greenglass contact would imperil the Fuchs operation: it was Fuchs who destroyed the Rosenberg operation.

Fuchs's exposure after he returned to England was triggered by an indiscreet reference by a Soviet atomic energy specialist to an item of information that suggested a leak from Los Alamos. Investigation narrowed down the suspects to Fuchs, who readily admitted his complicity when faced by the British authorities. After some confusion he identified Harry Gold as his KGB contact stateside. With Gold's arrest in Philadelphia, the link between Fuchs and the Rosenbergs tightened: if Gold talked, he could expose Greenglass. If Greenglass talked, he could expose Rosenberg. Both talked.

The fatal error was made by Yakovlev, perhaps out of haste to get a timely report of value to Moscow Center. Strict compartmentation permits no exceptions: any link is a weak link.

Was Rosenberg guilty as charged?

Again, as in the case of Alger Hiss, the evidence against Julius Rosenberg is, for a counterintelligence officer, convincing if not incontrovertible. To dismiss that evidence requires the assumption of an even more elaborate conspiracy than in the Hiss case: a conspiracy against the Rosenbergs by a professional Soviet intelligence officer (Gold), their close relatives (the Greenglasses), and several former associates. Their statements, and the tangible evidence presented at the trial, leave little room for innocence.

How important Greenglass' reports were to Moscow no one can say.

Judge Kaufman at the trial contended that the Rosenbergs had given Moscow *the* secret of the bomb. Yet the bomb had been a high priority target for both the KGB and the GRU from 1943 on. Two qualified scientists, Dr. Fuchs and Dr. Allen Nunn May in Zabotin's net, had been reporting from inside the Allied atomic program for some years. Other American Communist Party operations had developed sources in the University of California Radiation Laboratory, the Metallurgical Laboratory in Chicago, and the Oak Ridge atomic plant.

Precisely what each man contributed is known only in Moscow. How their intelligence fitted in or added to what Soviet scientists had already discovered or learned from captured German scientists cannot be assessed. What we can be sure of is that Stalin was not surprised when President Truman told him at Potsdam that the Americans had a new and powerful secret weapon.

ON COMMUNISTS AS SPIES

What impressed me personally in reading through the wartime records and the transcripts of the postwar trials was the total devotion of many of the men and women who had dedicated their lives to the communist cause.

In America, as in Europe, the heyday of the communist appeal came in the early thirties with the depression and the rise of Hitler. The political appeal of revolutionary Marxism was reinforced by the Soviet leadership of the anti-fascist crusade, and many young Americans, Party and non-Party, joined the International Brigade fighting Franco in Spain. Countless Europeans gave their lives as underground communists fighting Hitler in prewar and wartime Europe.

I had been as remote from these currents of political life as a committed campus-bound academic can be. At Union College until 1931 and for the next four years at Harvard, I was an unthinking New Deal Democrat. I had never met a "socialist," much less a "communist." Even a year in Hitler's Hamburg in 1935–36 did not extend my political convictions beyond a deep faith in the Sermon on the Mount and the Bill of Rights. During my two months on the island of Majorca, which I left a month before the Spanish Civil War broke out, reading and writing on nonpolitical matters occupied my mind to the exclusion of European events.

When I found myself lecturing to Army Air Force recruits at the beginning of the war on "why you are here," I followed the instructions of the officer in charge: because the Japanese had attacked us and Hitler had declared war on us. The answer of many recruits was even simpler: "I wuz drafted."

For my totally apolitical mind the world of real communists, of impassioned believers willing to lay down their lives for the "cause," came as an emotional and intellectual shock. My own cool temperament made such intense commitment almost incomprehensible, but as I read their interrogations and confessions, and began to study seriously the basic Marxist and Leninist texts that had converted them, I understood them better, and even managed to explain to my military audience why some of the best men in Europe had become communists. I voiced my respect for their personal qualities, for the many Sorges and Treppers among them, a notion harder for Americans to accept as the Cold War got hotter.

These men and women found faith in Marxist doctrine, and through it became members of the Communist Party and agents of Soviet intelligence. Their faith, like all faith, was irrational, but once committed, the true believer became dedicated to the "cause," often at enormous personal sacrifice. Those who question the depth or sincerity of their convictions need only read the biographies of a few communists who worked underground in Hitler's Europe. The American communists who paraded before the House Un-American Affairs Committee in the late forties are not fair specimens of the breed at its best.

The convinced Party member was the ideal recruit for Soviet intelligence. He was already above "false" patriotism. He was ready to work for the Russians out of obedience to Party discipline or from a desire to serve the fatherland of socialism. His own self-esteem was often enhanced by being one of the few to be selected for special assignment. He did not need to be recruited—he was simply asked to do a job.

The progress from Party work to espionage is a simple enough transition, even for those who never worked in a secret cell. Even an open Party works in a conspiratorial atmosphere: secret meetings; secret letters; secret plans, say, for setting up a front organization or penetrating a labor union. Members of secret cells are even more aware of the need for caution, living as they do in fear of exposure and the loss of their jobs. Anonymity, careful contacts, having and keeping secrets, are already an indoctrination into secret agent work.

The transition from Party worker to Soviet agent was made even easier by the habit of members to "gather information" for the Party. Whether from a factory or a government office, whether useful or not, any information supplied by a member gives him practice in transmitting "intelligence." "Passing it on" can become an easy habit whatever its final destination—Party headquarters or KGB/Moscow.

III

OLD HANDS AT THE SECRET GAME

In 1947, when the remnants of the wartime Office of Strategic Services became the nucleus of America's first peacetime intelligence service, the KGB celebrated its thirtieth anniversary.

In that same year Soviet intelligence already had several top-drawer agents in the democracies. One was operating in the heart of our atomic energy program. Another sat in the British Embassy in Washington. A third man, a senior official of the British Intelligence Service, headed its anti-Soviet operations section in London. Within a few years a Soviet agent would be working in the front office of the German Intelligence Service, and another in the French military establishment, where he would survive for almost twenty years.

In Europe and the Far East the KGB was ready to go at the end of the war. KGB/Moscow sent hundreds of hastily recruited agents into the Allied occupation zones of Germany—German POWs and civilians released from the East on their promise to cooperate with the Russians after their return. KGB main headquarters in East Germany in the Berlin suburb of Karlshorst grew rapidly and dispatched hundreds more of German and Polish agents through the Berlin gateway. West Berlin was already riddled with Soviet agents aimed at the recruitment of American soldiers and German civilians working in military and intelligence installations. Here were the beginnings of the most extensive peacetime espionage programs ever launched by a modern secret service.

Of even greater strategic value in the long run was the KGB's quick integration of the East European intelligence services into its own system. By 1947 all but the Czech services had become appendages of the KGB. The KGB contingents that came along with the Soviet troops at the end of World War II reorganized and restaffed both the security and foreign intelligence services of the satellite countries, set up their files and training programs, established their targets, and for some years ran them with KGB officers in the direct chain of command. Even when the KGB generals and colonels became "advisers," the KGB maintained its hold through the agents it recruited within the ranks of the satellite services.

Only in Yugoslavia, the one "ally" not under Soviet military control, did the KGB come to grief. With no physical border and no Soviet hand in the establishment of the government or the security services, Moscow was forced to use covert means to ensure its control of Tito's regime. The KGB attempt to penetrate the Belgrade regime and to subvert its security service was a fiasco, and played a role in intensifying Tito's hostility to Stalin's takeover attempt.

Thirty years' experience gave the KGB many of the advantages that come from bureaucratic age: experienced case officers, tested operational methods, a firm organizational structure, etc. One that cannot be discounted is the vast experience it had gained during the interwar years in observing and countering the work of those intelligence services that the American service would rely on after the war. Soviet intelligence had grappled with the British, French, and Polish services in countless operations. Moscow knew their leading personnel, how they thought and worked, and their communications systems. All had at one time or another been penetrated. They were familiar enemies.

Yet agents come and go, as we have seen, and the KGB's headstart gave it far more substantial advantages than agents-in-place, operating bases, and friendly fellow services.

The Index

The guts of a service are its files, the data bank on all the persons it has come across over the years or decades. The Index includes not only millions of "notes" or "cards" on people, but photographs, tape recordings, telephone taps, surveillance reports, and domestic mail intercepts. Without an extensive central file at home on the people he must work with or against, an officer in the field is moving in the dark. He can waste his time developing a useless recruit or be fooled into recruiting the wrong man.

In 1947, and even more so today, the KGB stood head and shoulders above any other service in the range of personality information it possessed on foreigners. The extent of the KGB's central index boggles the mind: twelve to fifteen million foreigners, dead and alive, on file in Moscow.

The core of the index is full biographical detail on every man or woman who has been a member of any Communist Party for the past sixty years (their friends, relatives, employers, etc.); the name and identifying data of anyone who has ever been a member of a communist-front organization, from the World Federation of Trade Unions to the Soviet-American Friendship Society, and every subscriber to a Soviet or Communist Party publication; the name of every applicant for a visa to the Soviet Union, of everyone with whom Moscow has done business, of invitees to Soviet film showings, embassy receptions, National Day celebrations.

And this is only the core.

From 1917 on, Moscow had had a mania for "Who's Who" information on *anyone* in the outside world. Today, as before, all Soviet officials and visitors abroad who meet anyone officially or socially write a squib for the file giving name, job, appearance, relatives, anything that can be elicited in the course of a normal conversation. These are all the product of the global communist enterprise and the vast reach of Soviet diplomatic, military, and trade representatives on all continents.

The routine goes even further: the systematic collection of biographical data from the increasing number of "Who's Who" books in the industrial countries, lists of attendants at scientific

conferences, government and corporate directories, foreign diplomatic and university faculty lists, military directories, telephone
books; officers of political parties and labor unions, newspaper
and magazine mastheads, right-wing associations.

The information on selected groups reaches even deeper: a full
dossier on any agent who has worked for the KGB (or the GRU)
and *anyone* he has ever been in contact with; the name, address,
and relatives of any Soviet citizen who has emigrated from the
Soviet Union; the identity of "secret workers" for the Comintern
or any Communist Party illegal apparat; local communist penetrations of the police or security services; the names (and informants if available) of every intelligence and security service officer,
clerk, and cleaning woman.

The most valuable and thorough biographical listings naturally
come from the professional observations by KGB and GRU
officers of people whom they have either met casually or spotted
as potential recruits. The GRU instructions sent to Colonel Zabotin to collect data on his contacts in the Canadian military will
give some notion of what Moscow wants on a man before even
considering his recruitment:

1. *To clarify the basic data:*
   (a) Present position, where did he work previously;
   (b) Prospects of remaining in the service . . . and where;
   (c) From what year in the service; does he like it?
   (d) His relations with his immediate superiors.
2. *To elucidate biographical data:*
   (a) Age, parents, family conditions;
   (b) Education, principal speciality, special technical or
        other knowledge;
   (c) Attitude toward politics; party affiliation . . .
   (d) Financial conditions: inclination toward establishing
        material security for his family (for instance,
        intentions to engage in business, to own a motor car,
        to have a home of his own); and what hinders the
        fulfilment of such plans;
   (e) Attitude toward our country (the Soviet
        Union) and our politics;
   (f) Wherein does he see the prosperity of his country
        (for instance, in friendship with America, or
        retaining British influence in the world).

3. *Personal positive and negative characteristics:*
   - (a) Inclination to drink, women friends—or good family man;
   - (b) Lover of good things—or inclination to solitude and quietness;
   - (c) Influence of his wife on his actions—or independence in making his own decisions;
   - (d) Circle of acquaintances and brief character sketches of them.

When a KGB officer in the field requests a trace from Moscow on someone he has met, the odds are very high that he will get an informed response on the desirability of continuing the relationship. In the end, of course, he cannot recruit an agent without Moscow's approval, which will be at least partly based on their file check.

The value of this data-retrieval system is not vitiated by time, as we shall see later in scores of cases. To cite only one early example: David Greenglass joined the Young Communist League when he was sixteen; assigned years later to the Manhattan Project (reported by a fellow worker), the Central Index showed him as the brother-in-law of a man already doing espionage work. Rosenberg was then instructed to use him.

The Clandestine Mentality

Though its files give the KGB an outstanding advantage over Western services, there is a more intangible quality of Soviet intelligence that is perhaps its greatest strength. It is the natural product of the origins and character of Soviet society, what I choose to call the clandestine mentality, the psychological tendency and ability to think and act in secret.

Not only did the new Soviet regime inherit a conspiratorial tradition that gave the KGB a unique position among its executive agencies, but the conditions of Soviet life, especially under Stalin, promoted a kind of mentality that intensified the Russian capacity for "secret work." It is precisely opposite to the open mentality of men brought up in a free society.

The Bolsheviks owed their success in the October Revolution

to twenty years of conspiratorial action, both inside Russia against the czarist secret police, the Okhrana, and outside Russia through secret communications with its secret cells inside. Secret work—secret couriers, secret meetings, secret presses, bank robberies, safe houses, forged passports, escape lines—laid the basis for the assumption of Soviet power in 1917, the most successful covert political action operation in this century.

Within a short time Lenin applied the process in reverse: secret work against the opponents of his regime both at home and abroad. The Cheka and the KGB today are the natural heirs of the Okhrana.

The clandestine mentality is rooted in a conspiratorial view of the world: the world is an unsafe place, for someone out there is plotting against me. Under Lenin the plotters were the counter-revolutionary elements—the monarchists, the czarist officers, the land owners, and merchants. Under Stalin the enemy was everywhere, from the Politburo down to the local NKVD office. Under both, the capitalist world around them was a constant threat—hostile, intervening, plotting.

Since the world is a threatening place, only secret counteraction can guarantee survival.

No one can draw up a profile of the Soviet psyche, much less of the uniquely qualified KGB officer at home or abroad, but a penchant for working in secret against secret "enemies," a basic distrust of other people, above all foreigners (even foreign communists), and the need to be alert, to act very carefully, are surely among its components.

Nowhere is this conspiratorial tradition more clearly exemplified than in the basic structure of Soviet intelligence operations abroad.

In making our first studies on Soviet intelligence we were mainly concerned with the mechanisms through which it operated. From the captured records, from the Canadian and Washington nets, from the testimony of prewar Soviet intelligence defectors, the picture became reasonably clear: two parallel apparats were functioning, rigidly insulated one from the other.

Each of the Soviet services (GRU and KGB) depended on one set of case officers under official cover in Soviet embassies and other official installations (men such as Zabotin, Yakovlev, and Gromov)—these were the "legals"—and a second parallel apparat of professional Soviet intelligence officers under unofficial, or private, cover (men such as Sorge and Trepper)—the "illegals."

The Legals

The legal residencies are the backbone of every contemporary foreign intelligence service. The KGB residency is housed within the Soviet Embassy or other diplomatic installation, its chief and case officers live and work under the cover of an official job, and most of them enjoy diplomatic immunity. They can range in size from a few men to hundreds.

We learned little about the GRU and KGB residencies in New York and Washington from the operations of the Communist Party nets in the forties, but Gouzenko's documents from Ottawa and, later, the KGB resident's defection in Australia gave us an intimate view of their internal functioning.

The core of the residency is its communication and file room, a central, well-guarded repository of codes, code machines, cable traffic, and operational memoranda and correspondence with Moscow. It is immune to outside search. It is insulated from the resident and his case officers.

The diplomatic staff is similarly immune to arrest and imprisonment. When mistakes are made and a case officer is caught red-handed, he is sent back home to cool off for a while in a headquarters job. This reduces the anxiety level of the officers who enjoy diplomatic immunity.

Other bureaucratic advantages are obvious. Each officer works under the supervision of his chief. Young officers on their first assignment work in a secure training ground. Communications with headquarters are efficient and sacrosanct. The diplomatic pouch is always available for bulky reports or objects. The ambassador is there to protect them. Nonintelligence employees can be used to carry out useful chores.

What became clear to Moscow Center, after Gouzenko walked out, was that the residency kept too much information in its files: the records of active agents (each with his little index card) and the brief notations in the case officer's operational notebook of meetings held, intelligence passed, money paid out. It was this information, astutely selected by Gouzenko, that blew all the Canadian agents—and that simple fact became a lesson to Moscow:

keep the barest minimum of sensitive information in the foreign residencies.

Today there are strict limits placed on the amount and kind of information that can be retained in legal residency files. The current KGB and GRU handling of bureaucratic paper in the field puts to shame the most rigorous practices of high-security agencies in the United States or Europe.

All communications from and to Moscow are now handled in microfilm: each residency has its own photography shop. All written communications must be destroyed in the field except for the barest essentials. Each document retained is numbered, and each page in it. These are kept in the code/file room, and are checked in and out in the course of a workday. The contents of the code-room safes are systematically checked each day down to page numbers. Regular inspectors from Moscow monitor compliance with the rules, and violators are disciplined.

This rigid system not only minimizes the sensitive information on active agents that a defector or a break-in can procure, but places the residency in a position where it must constantly rely on Moscow to get the background (past meetings, past performance, old name checks) on its current operations. It has no case file, and only the Center can fill in the background or carry out a security review of a case. With this system no residency can take action without the Center's knowledge or implicit approval.

The crucial function of a residency—to recruit new agents—is not hampered by this central control: it simply guarantees that Moscow's judgment will be brought to bear on the proposed action it recommends. It can be taken for granted today that even stupid or short-sighted approaches in the field have the Center's approval, e.g., the three U.N. employees' "recruitment" of a U. S. Navy lieutenant commander in New Jersey in 1977, or the parallel approach to a Royal Canadian Mounted Police officer in Canada.

Though the KGB case officer under diplomatic cover leads a reasonably safe life, his immunity sometimes fails to guard his personal health. Some local services have been known to pounce on a KGB officer at a secret rendezvous with a native agent and rough him up, sometimes severely, before he has a chance to identify himself as a diplomat.

An extreme case occurred in Africa. Two KGB officers were returning to their African post from a trip abroad with $100,000 in their pockets. They traveled by car and entered their country of assignment by a ferry crossing. As the car ferry reached the dock, they were seized by the local police, their tires slashed, and their bodies stripped. They were left standing in the hot sun until the police were able to check their credentials with headquarters. Communications were slow.

A KGB officer making a meet with an agent outside a staked-out soccer stadium is suddenly surrounded by police. He tries to escape to hide his identity, but he is caught and severely clubbed before he can cry "diplomat."

For the most part, however, the KGB case officer in the West now goes home from his daily stint at the office unscarred and unscared to talk with his wife and look at TV.

The supreme operational advantage of working abroad under official cover is the ease and security with which an intelligence officer can meet people.

The main task of a KGB officer in the field is to spot likely candidates and study them as potential recruits. The wider the circle of his official and personal acquaintants, the more successful he will be at his task. His cover gives him a natural circle of contacts: a political officer in touch with Foreign Office officials, a Tass representative looking for a worthwhile native journalist, a commercial attaché lining up leading businessmen or bankers.

Other normal diplomatic activities can widen the circle: people one meets at diplomatic receptions, National Day celebrations, Soviet film showings. A KGB man plays tennis or chess, joins a club, goes on shooting expeditions. His wife can give language lessons. A Soviet family finds a native family congenial for picnics. In these and a myriad other ways, the KGB gets to know people well enough to size them up as prospects for a sales pitch.

All in all, the KGB officer assigned to a Soviet installation in the West can look forward to an active gregarious life in comfortable bourgeois surroundings. Meeting people is not a crime.

Yet he labors under one serious disadvantage. The member of a legal residency has a fixed place of work and a permanent abode. He is always locatable and, with a little effort by the local security service, identifiable. In many cases he is known to be an intelligence officer even before his arrival from his behavior on previous foreign assignments. The legal becomes a fixed target for security services: photography, surveillance, telephone taps, etc.

There is a still greater disadvantage: if diplomatic relations are broken, with or without war, the entire residency disappears overnight.

Herein lies the real pressure for the KGB's building up a parallel net of illegal residents in the major capitalist countries.

The Illegals

The illegals, professional intelligence officers under cover of ordinary citizens, form the KGB's parallel system. These men, almost always totally insulated from official Soviet installations, are able to continue operating even with the rupture of diplomatic relations or in the event of war. Since they are buried, in the United States, Canada, or West Germany, as properly documented citizens or resident aliens, they are impossible to locate unless they make a mistake.

In peacetime a fully staffed illegal residency consists of a senior officer, the resident himself, with one or two assistants, and a radio operator. Each member has a different cover job in separate physical locations, but they are linked by clandestine arrangements for meeting secretly and for passing messages, money, or intelligence to each other through dead drops. The residency, however small, is supplied with the money and paraphernalia required for secret operations. It is a self-sufficient espionage center in miniature buried in a metropolitan or suburban neighborhood.

The preparation of an illegal demands an extraordinary investment on the part of the KGB. The careful selection of a bogus identity, a life history, or legend, to provide a legitimate background, and the preparation of documents to support the legend require the greatest skill and range of knowledge to avoid any inconsistency that might draw the attention of immigration officials, police, business associates, or neighbors.

The training of illegals, most of them Soviet intelligence officers, can take as much as six or seven years of language and area studies, communications training, and building a false identity.

The first postwar illegal caught in the United States was the famous Colonel Rudolf Abel, who operated under the name of Emil R. Goldfus as the owner of an art-photography studio in Brooklyn, New York, from 1948 to 1957.

Colonel Abel was an experienced intelligence officer who had served in Germany during World War II. Born William Fischer in England to Russian émigré parents, he lived in England from 1903 to 1921, when his father went back to the Soviet Union to help the Revolution. With a fluent command of English, Russian, and German, he was a natural candidate for an illegal assignment.

Shortly after the war he was given a new identity, entered a camp for displaced persons in Germany, and immigrated to Canada with thousands of other East Europeans. He entered the United States as a legal immigrant in 1948 and for nine years led a quiet, inconspicuous life in Brooklyn with many friends on the bohemian edge of the local art world. As an independent businessman, his frequent absences (for trips in the United States and occasional visits to Moscow) caught no one's attention. Most of the people who knew him liked him.

After several years Moscow decided to expand the residency by assigning him an assistant, Reino Hayhanen, a Soviet intelligence officer born in Finland who had been given the identity of Eugene Maki, a first-generation Finnish American born in Idaho whose family had emigrated back to Finland. The KGB simply got a copy of Eugene Maki's birth certificate from Idaho (the original Maki had died in Finland), and with it obtained a legitimate American passport from the American Embassy in Helsinki.

Hayhanen was a poor choice. Lazy, undisciplined (he secretly married a Finnish woman), an alcoholic, he did nothing during his years with Abel until he was ordered back to Moscow for "consultations" in 1957. Afraid of what his reception might be, he turned himself in to the American Embassy in Paris and told the story that led to Abel's exposure.

When he was arrested, Abel's studio was found to contain a radio receiver and a short-wave transmitter (with an improvised aerial to a neighboring roof), a schedule for coded broadcasts from Moscow, over $20,000 in American bank notes and a bankbook with reserve funds, photographic equipment (naturally), but microdot equipment as well, and a well-stocked larder of concealment devices (hollowed-out bolts, batteries, and coins).

In his briefcase were two photographs marked Shirley and Morris with $5,000 in bills attached by a rubber band.

It turned out only later that these were the pictures of Morris and Helen Cohen, who were associated in some way with the Yakovlev-Rosenberg net right after the war. Morris, the American-born son of Russian immigrants, fought in Spain in the Abraham Lincoln Brigade, and on his return married the communist daughter of Polish immigrants, got a job in Amtorg in New York City, and later became a cook in the Army. Both disappeared from New York after Harry Gold's arrest in 1950.

The Cohens emerged years later as key members of an illegal residency in England that was wiped out in the so-called Naval Secrets case. By then the Cohens turned up as the Krogers after an international journey that brought them from New York to London via New Zealand, Japan, Austria, Paris, and other stops.

Peter John Kroger and his wife, Helen Joyce, assumed the cover of antiquarian booksellers and worked as assistants to the illegal resident, Gordon Lonsdale, who ran a legitimate business selling pinball machines to pubs and nightclubs. Lonsdale, born Conon Molody, the son of a Soviet scientist, had been sent to California by his mother to get an American education. He lived there from the age of eleven to fifteen, and was well qualified to take on the identity of a Canadian businessman, his cover in England. The real Lonsdale had emigrated to the Soviet Union from Canada and died there. Molody was born again with his documents.

All three were exposed when a British agent Lonsdale was handling was identified by a defector as a man on the staff of the British Naval Attaché in Warsaw who had been recruited by Polish intelligence and turned over to the KGB. After a brief tour in Warsaw, the recruited agent, Henry Houghton, had been assigned to the Portland Naval Base in England, where he had access to classified information on underwater research, a subject of perennial interest to Moscow. The surveillance of Houghton led directly to the exposure of Lonsdale and the Krogers.

The Krogers' house in a London suburb was even more richly equipped than Colonel Abel's studio. A short-wave radio for listening to Moscow on high-frequency bands, a high-speed transmitter powerful enough to reach Moscow, a microdot reader in a box of face powder, microfilm inside a Bible, flashlights and a cigarette lighter as concealment devices, cipher pads, and call signs and schedules for broadcasts to Moscow, cameras and chemicals, seven passports, and thousands of pounds, dollars, and travelers checks.

Lonsdale's illegal network was able to operate on its own with no support from the KGB legal residency in London. What agents other than Houghton the net handled is not known, for all three illegals refused to talk.

Two sidelights on the hazards of illegals emerged after their arrest.

Since the case achieved some notoriety, pictures of Lonsdale and the Krogers appeared in *Life* magazine and were seen by a retired high-school athletic coach in the Bronx. When he saw Kroger's picture, he is reported to have said: "Kroger, my eye. I remember this guy. His name is Morris Cohen. How could I forget him? He was only a half-pint but he wanted to try out for the football team."

In checking out Lonsdale's identity in the Canadian town he claimed for his birthplace, a sharp-eyed Canadian investigator noted from the medical record that the infant Gordon Lonsdale had been circumcised. The Lonsdale in London had not.

The lot of an illegal is not a happy one. If he is a married man, and must leave his wife and family behind in Moscow, he can be a lonely man and can at best see them every two or three years when a secret vacation is arranged for him to return to the Soviet Union. He can become bored, scared, or neurotic with no one close by to hold his hand. If he is caught, he can end up with a long term in prison.

How many illegals were trained and dispatched in the early and mid-fifties is unknown, but the KGB apparently did not get down to the illegals as a serious business until 1952. In June of that year the KGB sent out a circular to its legal residencies abroad instructing them to give priority to the construction of illegal residencies in preparation for a pending outbreak of war. One of the Moscow letters sent to the legal residency in Australia reads in part:

> The aggravation of the international situation and the pressing necessity for the timely exposure and prevention of cunning designs of the enemy, call imperatively for a radical reorganization of all our intelligence work and the urgent operation of an illegal apparatus in Australia which could function uninterruptedly and effectively under any conditions.

The instruction then specifies the kind of information required for the preparation of illegals: the systematic collection of information of immigration procedures, blank passports, possible sponsors for immigrants, how to set up a small business, etc.

It can be assumed that similar notices were sent to KGB residencies all over the world.

How many Soviet illegals are operating in the West now?

Even after many years of experience with captured illegals, Western security services remain puzzled by the extent of this parallel system. In the late sixties, estimates based on the testimony of defectors, the size of illegal training classes in Moscow, and the confessions of arrested illegals ranged from several hundred to a thousand dispatched to the West. Since illegals do not operate forever, a more realistic guess would place their total at sixty or seventy. Are they in place mainly as "sleepers" to be activated in time of war or a break in diplomatic relations? Are some, or most, of them actively handling agents? Is there a KGB yardstick for determining what Soviet agent will be handled by an illegal rather than a KGB man under official cover?

What we can be reasonably sure of is that the KGB will continue its system of illegals for the indefinite future. They are not only useful, if not essential, to its current operations, but they are in the long run indispensable. Only they, in time of war or the cut-off of diplomatic relations, can take over some of the legal nets and continue to operate as spies on enemy terrain. Had the Soviet invasion of Afghanistan brought a diplomatic break with the Western powers, illegals now in the United States would more than repay the KGB for its heavy investment in securing their services.

ON THE SPY WHO DID NOT SPY

What did Colonel Rudolf Abel do in Brooklyn to earn his reputation as a master spy?

Among all the evidence in the Abel case there is no indication that Abel transmitted one item of classified intelligence to Moscow.

The evidence is replete with all the rich abracadabra of secret communications—recognition signals, concealment devices, dead drops, secret meetings—between Abel and Hayhanen, and between Hayhanen and his local residency contact. Abel had a one-way radio for receiving Moscow broadcasts, but his transmitter was apparently never used. He sent microdots glued under the staples of *Better Homes and Gardens* to Paris.

What was the content of these secret communications? Microfilms of letters to and from his family in Moscow, instructions from Moscow on communications, including codes and ciphers.

The messages in the split nickel deciphered after Hayhanen's arrest had to do with sending money, a formula for soft film, a letter from Mother, a confirmation of packages delivered to his wife, greetings from the comrades. Not a single piece of intelligence.

Abel did not, so far as we know, handle a single agent. During his frequent absences from his studio, both in the States and in Moscow, he gave no instructions to his assistant, Hayhanen, to service a dead drop, much less pick up and transmit to Moscow any intelligence reports. If he had had any agents reporting anything of value, he would not have left them lying fallow for months at a time.

What, then, did he do during the years he had Hayhanen with him? Apparently only minor operational chores: locate a Swedish ship engineer near Boston, locate a Sergeant Rhodes who had been recruited in Moscow, take some photographs in the New York metropolitan area (for future meeting sites?), make a trip to Bear Mountain to bury some money for the wife of an arrested agent.

The mechanism was there for more serious work. Why was it never used? An illegal never tries to recruit an agent on his own, for he exposes himself in the act of approaching a potential recruit: one error and years of preparatory work go down the drain. What he is in place for is to accept a "referral," to make contact with a KGB agent already recruited and tested.

Apparently Moscow Center had nowhere recruited an American of sufficient quality to assign to Abel.

There was a more general ground for the Center to be cautious with its man in New York. Abel came to Canada shortly after Gouzenko's arrest and the eviction of the entire GRU apparat in Ottawa. His first years in Brooklyn were at the height of the spy-fever, and the early fifties were not much quieter. It made good sense for him to lie low.

Why was Abel sent in the first place?

Abel was a natural for an American assignment: born and reared in England, trained and proved in wartime intelligence work, he was ready for quick dispatch. America was a priority target. The American operations were in a shambles, why not send him there as an investment in the future?

Was Abel a "sleeper" who never got any real work to do? Most likely. Was Abel so clever an operator that he covered up the agents he handled even from the man who was sent out to help him? Most unlikely.

It cannot be proved that Abel never handled an agent, but there is no evidence that he did. Perhaps Hayhanen's statement to the FBI should also apply to his boss: "I did not engage in espionage activity and did not receive any espionage or secret information from anyone during my stay abroad. . . ."

Yet, the demurral might run, why would the Russians make so much over a spy who never spied? Khrushchev exchanged the U-2 pilot Francis Gary Powers for him in 1962. The Presidium granted him the Order of Lenin for his exploits. He has an established place in the roster of KGB heroes. Rumors of where he was and what he was doing cropped up for the next ten years in the Western press and intelligence services.

Moscow cannot be faulted for making the most out of the Abel image created in New York. His arrest, trial, and release made global headlines. He became the model of the super-spy, mild, composed, taciturn, efficient, a high-grade specimen of the brilliant array of KGB agents operating quietly in the West. The West, ironically, made Abel a celebrity, and Moscow would not be inclined to argue the case.

IV

THE MOSCOW TRIAD

The field structure of Soviet intelligence was naturally of the greatest practical concern to us in the early postwar years, for legal residencies were already operating against American forces in Berlin, Vienna, Pyongyang, and Tokyo. In many of the cases that came to our attention, we could not determine who was behind them: the GRU or the KGB. Many of the agents did not know either, for there are no tell-tale methods that distinguish the *modus operandi* of the one from the other. Even Whittaker Chambers was briefly under the impression that he was working for the KGB.

It was essential to round out the picture of the headquarters structure in Moscow. Even a fragmentary version would at least provide the basis for the interrogation of any Soviet intelligence personnel who had once worked in Moscow—and a few low-level defectors had become available in Europe.

The materials on Moscow were slim in 1946. There was a series of translations into English of German counterintelligence studies based on wartime interrogations of captured Soviet intelligence personnel, as well as a brief analysis of headquarters structure by the British service and a few outdated accounts of prewar

Soviet defectors. Out of these sparse items we composed a slim outline that was sent to our field stations.

The internal structure of any secret bureaucracy can best be determined from men who have worked inside it. Stalin's death in 1953 and the purge of "Beria's gang" by his successors sparked several defections from the KGB that enormously enhanced our picture of the inside workings of Soviet intelligence headquarters. Two officers defected in Tokyo, one in Vienna. Several Soviet agents in our employ during the mid-fifties had spent one or more tours at headquarters.

Later defectors who had worked in Moscow filled in and updated our knowledge of the organizational components, supplied the names and job titles of department and section heads, traced the shifting of functions, noted policy changes and reported on squabbles among the intelligence services. Oleg Penkovskiy, a Western agent in Moscow in the early sixties, had an unparalleled view of the workings of the GRU.

What we now know is infinitely greater than what we knew twenty years ago, but the Moscow picture can never be kept up-to-date without a steady flow of fresh defectors—or an occasional mole in the upper reaches of Soviet intelligence.

The story of Soviet intelligence abroad is the story of two, for a time three, competing secret services, each a prey to the bloody ups and downs of domestic Party politics under Stalin. The roster of KGB and GRU officers killed by their own regime must run into the thousands, if not the tens of thousands. Only after Stalin's death did an intelligence career become orderly and nonlethal.

It is also the story of how one service, the KGB, became bureaucratically and politically number 1.

The GRU

The Soviet military intelligence service is a straight-forward foreign intelligence service focused on, but not confined to, the procurement of secret military-technical information. The GRU (Glavnoye Razvedyvatelnoye Upravleniye), or Chief Intelligence Directorate of the Soviet General Staff, was and remains a completely self-sufficient operating service with its own files and separate communications, its own legal residents (until recently under military attaché cover), its own separate unit for dispatching and controlling illegals, and its own reporting channels to Moscow.

Operating primarily against military targets, it naturally bore the main burden of wartime espionage against Germany and Japan—it recruited and directed both Sorge and Trepper. It engineered the main nets aimed at the Allied atomic program from London and from Zabotin's residency in Ottawa. It also dabbled, as we have seen, in the American Communist Party's New York–Washington nets. It now operates in every Western capital and in most countries of the Third World.

During the twenties and early thirties the GRU was the premier Soviet service—aggressive, extensive, and innovative. It was not only predominant in the Moscow hierarchy, but its performance was far superior to that of the old Cheka hands in the KGB. It developed entirely new techniques for carrying out its operations abroad, notably the system of illegals, the use of secret radio transmitters, and the multinational cover corporation.

Much of the credit for these innovations must go to General Berzin, for whom both Trepper and Sorge had the highest regard. An old Cheka hand, Berzin became deputy chief of the GRU in 1920, then chief from 1924 to 1935. Known as "the old man" (*starik*), he was on all accounts a born leader who created genuine devotion and a spirit of group morale. Harsh on failures, he was respected for his talent, hard work, and high standards. He was another of the action-oriented intellectuals common in the early Bolshevik ranks.

It was Berzin who thought up and instituted the system of illegals as he saw the vulnerable Soviet official installations raided and ransacked in the twenties.

The GRU under Berzin's tenure placed great reliance on secret radio communications with its illegals abroad. Radio operators, like Sorge's Klausen in Shanghai and Tokyo, were highly trained not only as code clerks and radio operators, but could assemble transmitters from locally available components. When war came and speedy reporting became essential, as we saw in the Sorge and Trepper nets, Berzin's initiative paid off handsomely.

An equally creative mechanism for peacetime operations was Berzin's use of the multinational corporation, a single administrative complex that could provide cover for illegals in half a dozen countries. In the early twenties the GRU set up several global trading companies with "branches" from Western Europe to China. They eventually "blew," as all extensive commercial covers do, for the exposure of a single branch invites the attention of security services to all its other branches. By a curious coincidence one of the last branches to blow was a company selling raincoats. Trepper's cover was also a multinational corporation selling raincoats with branches in Belgium, Holland, and Paris.

A commercial company with foreign branches has two distinct advantages. It not only supplies cheap and inconspicuous cover for a whole series of illegals, but a built-in system of international communications via commercial telegrams and business correspondence with open codes or secret writing.

For one-man cover operations Berzin favored small, independent retail shops selling radios and small electric appliances, as in Shanghai, or, as in Abel's case, a small photographic studio.

All three of Berzin's innovations became part and parcel of KGB practice from the mid-thirties on. For his pains Berzin was framed in Stalin's purge trials and killed in 1938. He taught the KGB a great deal.

The GRU was to have its share of security and morale shocks in the postwar period as well. In 1958 a GRU lieutenant-colonel was arrested and revealed as a long-term Western agent in Europe, and only four years later Colonel Oleg Penkovskiy (a friend of, among others, KGB Chairman Serov) was found spying for the British and Americans. These events naturally reduced the confidence of the Party in the military intelligence arm.

The singular power of the KGB derives from its combining both the functions of internal security and secret foreign operations, as if the FBI and CIA in the United States or MI5 and MI6 in England were to operate under a single intelligence czar. Not only is the KGB the main bulwark of the Communist Party's power in the Soviet Union, as we shall see, but its dual authority makes for greater efficiency (national security knows no borders) and avoids the high-level policy infighting between domestic and foreign services common in Western capitals. When its chief sits on the Politburo, as KGB Chairman Yuri Andropov now does, there is even less room for jurisdictional battles.

The KGB Complex

The heavy KGB structure in Moscow is broken down into four Chief directorates and a series of separate directorates, most of them with internal breakdowns rivaling any of the organizational charts of Western government bureaucracies.

There are four Chief directorates:

—The First Chief Directorate is the foreign intelligence service *per se,* the KGB as we know it abroad operating its legal and illegal residencies.

—The Second Chief Directorate is, in effect, the domestic security service that runs the internal control system, which will be examined in Chapter V.

—The Fifth Chief Directorate is also purely domestic and concerns itself with specialized groups of dissidents among the Soviet citizenry (see Chapter XIV).

—The Chief Directorate of Border Guards seals off Soviet territory from illegal entry and unofficial exits.

Top dog among the remaining directorates is the Third, or Armed Forces Directorate, whose twelve major departments focus on the security control of the Soviet Armed Forces. It has officers assigned to all military units from the Ministry of Defense down to company level, to the militia, or police, and to the internal troops under the Ministry of Internal Affairs. Other directorates deal with surveillance, communications, technical devices, and personnel.

It is the combination of domestic and foreign responsibilities that gives the KGB a built-in superiority over the military intelligence arm of the General Staff. Its Armed Forces Directorate places it in direct security control of the GRU as well as the rest of the military hierarchy. The KGB makes the final security checks on new GRU recruits and must approve the dispatch of the GRU to the field for either permanent or temporary assignments.

It was the KGB that interrogated Trepper on his return to Moscow. It was the KGB that investigated the case of Oleg Penkovskiy in 1962. It is the KGB that now runs down any rumors or suspicions of GRU laxity or insecurity both at home and overseas.

The superior clout of the KGB extends far beyond the field of foreign espionage. It has been gradually converted in the past twenty years into an action arm of the Communist Party. It now works directly under the Politburo and the Central Committee.

After Khrushchev solidified his power in the late fifties, an all-Union conference of KGB workers convened in Moscow in

May 1959. They were instructed on the new line: henceforth the actions of the service would be geared to the overall political line and strategy of the Party, and its foreign actions closely integrated into the Party's foreign policy directed at the top by the Politburo. The Party chain of command was made clear in the appointment of KGB chief Andropov to full membership in the Politburo.

The work of the KGB abroad is now directly coordinated with the foreign activities of the International Department of the Central Committee. The International Department, with "instructors" for each major area of the world, normally maintains Moscow's relations with other Communist parties, but also carries out confidential diplomatic actions not entrusted to the Foreign Office. Its representatives have been detected on temporary assignments to the Soviet Embassy in Cairo in the sixties and in making contacts in Panama before the signing of the Panama Canal treaty with the United States.

What this means, in effect, is that the Party now has available the same kind of centralized instrument for political action abroad that Stalin enjoyed in his Moscow-run Comintern. And, as in the old Comintern days, the combined actions of the KGB and the International Department create a complex pattern of personalities, affiliations, and official trips bound to baffle Western security services.

The First Chief Directorate

The unique position of the KGB in the Soviet bureaucracy makes a career in the First Chief Directorate (FCD) one of the more attractive job opportunities in the Soviet Union. Secret work has its appeal in communist or capitalist societies, and in a police-run state it is generally safer to be in the police. In a party devoted to clandestine actions, it is a privilege to be part of its secret arm. But, more than this, the opportunity to work abroad is an even greater privilege in a country whose citizens are not free to travel. Living in the West for a time, enjoying generous import privileges, just "getting away" will appeal to many temperaments.

Membership in an elite service extolled in film and fiction reinforces self-esteem and provides opportunities to the ambitious: to become a chief of a residency, or even an ambassador, to climb the Moscow ladder to the front office, or even the Politburo. In an individualized service, a one-on-one profession, outstanding personal qualities and professional brilliance may be noted at the highest levels (the Order of Lenin has been bestowed on scores of case officers).

The FCD, of course, has all the attributes of bureaucracy, East or West: the emphasis on paper performance, the cover-up of errors and inadequacies, the equation of ends and means, bootlicking, the cardinal urge for promotions, infighting at higher levels.* Yet it would be shortsighted to assume from this that the KGB is constipated, that it throttles individual initiative, that it works by rote, that it runs scared. The quality of the agents recruited by the FCD in the past twenty years belies this common put-down.

The structure of the FCD in Moscow is known in some detail by Western services both because of the agents they have had in it and the officers from it who have defected while abroad.

The routine direction of legal residencies abroad is managed by a series of departments, or divisions, each responsible for a specific geographic area—the United States and Canada, Latin America, etc. These desks form a large-scale enterprise, directing with minute attention their residencies' conduct of active operations, planned recruitments, and coordination between residencies. They are busy receiving and answering cable and pouch traffic, making name checks in the central index, recommending likely agent-candidates, authorizing recruitment approaches.

A sub-directorate of the FCD handles the selection, training, dispatch, and control of illegals, and supervises the work of the illegals sections of the residencies which are instrumental in collecting the information required to document illegals and provide them with airtight legends.

Another sub-directorate, in charge of the technical collection system for all overseas operations, is the Scientific and Technical Directorate, which establishes intelligence requirements for all legals and illegals overseas, as well as for the procurement of openly available information. Here, in a kind of wholesale human data bank, sit hundreds of specialists, each an expert on a single sector of the modern industrial machine, from textile mills to computer hardware. Each specialist knows what Soviet industry

* It also now has a big headquarters building. It recently moved from downtown Moscow to a gigantic edifice in the suburbs near the Moscow Beltway. Its new mausoleum matches that of the CIA in Langley, Virginia, and of the J. Edgar Hoover Building in downtown Washington.

knows and what it does not know. Each specialist tries to find out what Western technology knows that he does not. Each directs the S&T collectors abroad on what to go after in his field of competence, evaluates what they produce, and sends follow-ups for amplifying data. The questionnaires I have seen are as precise and detailed as the specifications of an engineering contract or an advanced research and development contract.

The counterintelligence service has a double function: to protect the security of Soviet officials abroad (as well as the security of the entire Soviet colony) and to penetrate foreign security and intelligence services—a strictly counterespionage mission. Its successes in placing moles within the British and German intelligence services give it a high rank in the Soviet bureaucracy.

These four units are the guts of the FCD.

The liaison department handles relations with intelligence services in East Europe and Cuba through its "advisers" in those services. It forms the channel for siphoning off intelligence reports of value from its sister services and transmits to them information the KGB considers of interest to them. It also transmits operational requests to them, and can take over a Czech or Cuban agent the KGB itself wishes to handle.

Two other sections deal with more specialized operations abroad. A disinformation unit fabricates misleading or deceptive propaganda actions abroad that require covering up their source (see Chapter XII). A separate "executive action" department (Department V since 1969) specializes in "wet," or bloody, affairs. It had up to the early sixties the task of assassinating anti-Soviet émigrés and renegades from the Soviet intelligence services (see Chapter VI). It now apparently prepares sabotage plans for the Western industrial nations in the event of war.

The remainder of the FCD is largely administrative, the finance, logistic, technical, and communications personnel that, in Moscow as in Washington, smother the operators in paperwork and committee meetings.

The Comintern's Secret Operations

In their fieldwork the KGB and the GRU operate in the same way, and many foreign agents do not know which service they are working for. Since even Soviet legals operate anonymously under simple pseudonyms like Bill or Herman, their affiliation can be detected only by tracing them from a secret-agent meeting to their offices—and even then only their cover position can be identified. If an agent works for an illegal who is under, say, commercial cover, he is completely in the dark.

Confusion in the field—who is working for whom?—was even greater between the two world wars. Not only were there four official Soviet nets at work (legals and illegals for both the KGB and the GRU), but there was a fifth service, the secret operational arm of the Comintern.

Beneath the open facade of the Third Communist International founded by Lenin in March 1919 lay a vast conspiratorial apparatus dedicated to political action. It worked in public as the executive instrument for world revolution under an Executive Committee, held world congresses, put out a regular "newspaper" (*Imprecorr,* or International Press Correspondence), set up international fronts, and issued directives to its "national sections," the parties abroad. It was, in fact, the binding force behind the world's far-flung communist parties.

Much of the Comintern's routine work, however, demanded secrecy: passing Moscow's subsidies to local parties, smuggling fugitives from the police across frontiers, maintaining contact with underground parties.

Though concentrated in Europe, the Comintern's secret facilities covered the globe. Its courier lines formed a fine mesh, crisscrossing Europe from Hamburg to Berlin, Berlin to Moscow, Paris to Marseilles, from Hamburg and Le Havre to North and South America, from Marseilles to Singapore to the Dutch East Indies. In the twenties and thirties couriers carried leaflets and money for a coup in Java, dropped off cash payments to seamen's harbor units from Genoa to Shanghai, transported bundles of illegal literature to Tokyo on a roundabout route through American West Coast ports.

The Comintern had thousands of safe houses and contact addresses in every European country: private homes, bookstores, butchers, even a "Comintern hotel" here and there for secret travelers. Its "liaison agents" located in all European and some American cities provided contact points for traveling functionaries (political instructors, strike specialists, accountants) and safe addresses for bulky mail, passed subsidies to local Party leaders and organizations—as well as monitoring the local

Party's program, thus giving Moscow a double-check on the Party's routine progress reports (often inflated).

Couriers shuttled between Berlin and Moscow (the so-called Red Express carried Trepper to Moscow), and "relay points" were set up at every European frontier with a "guide" to hand on a courier or a man-on-the-run to a safe contact on the other side.

Crucial to its underground work were forged passports, and these were manufactured by the Comintern's West Bureau, located in Berlin until Hitler forced its transfer to Copenhagen in 1934. The German records (based on Gestapo interrogation of arrested communists) gave an impressive picture of this wholesale passport factory: its printing facilities, its laboratories for producing passports, concealment devices, and secret inks, its highly trained experts able to counterfeit any European currency.

The Comintern's secret work was almost inextricably mingled with the work of Soviet intelligence. Though under Soviet control from the start, the Comintern was a genuinely revolutionary action organization dedicated to a political purpose, and until 1934 its secret apparatus worked in parallel with the official Soviet services. When Moscow's line changed to the anti-fascist Popular Front and the parties were harnessed to the defense of the Soviet state, the Comintern's secret apparatus simply became an adjunct of Soviet intelligence.

The Comintern had much to offer Soviet intelligence. The foreign communist leaders in Moscow were among the most capable men of their generation: Georgi Dimitrov, Ho Chi Minh, Mao Tse-tung, Boleslav Rutkovski (later "Beirut"), each slated to become Party heads or presidents of Bulgaria, North Vietnam, China, and Poland, respectively. They were in a position to call upon the services of communists, socialists, and sympathizers in their own countries to staff the secret nets designed to forward the Revolution, nets for revolutionary action, sabotage, distribution of propaganda—and espionage. The men they chose were action agents, men schooled in secret political work—organizing underground presses and escape nets; harboring the hunted; infiltrating labor unions, newspapers, business enterprises, government offices, and the Gestapo itself.

They were men and women, sometimes teenagers, of high purpose, dedicated to the Revolution, self-disciplined and obedient Party members. Tested in the streets, in police jails, in Gestapo interrogations, the best and the brightest were chosen for secret work by their Party leaders or coopted by Soviet intelligence.

They were of another breed than the staff officers of the KGB or GRU who, however patriotic, were career bureaucrats in a shaky bureaucracy.

Comintern agents also, for the most part, operated in their own countries, at home in speech and culture, politically sophisticated, at a time when many Soviet officers were living abroad for the first time and were consequently uncouth in speech, dress, and manners.

For almost twenty years, then, Soviet intelligence was departmentalized in a triad of competing services: the KGB, the GRU, and the Comintern. In the jurisdictional squabbles that were inevitable with all three services working at such close quarters, the pecking order was simple: at the bottom the local Party worker in the police or in the Army, above him the "international worker" of the Comintern, and above him "the man from Moscow" who could take over an agent from the Party or the Comintern and demand his or her help when he needed it.

Both the KGB and the GRU used the Comintern's courier lines when it was convenient, borrowed young communists to carry out routine tasks like infiltrating White Russian émigré groups, and directed the apparats of the European parties working against the police and armed forces. In New York, Colonel Bykov took over the Chambers net at his pleasure. In Moscow the GRU took over such Comintern staff men as Sorge and Trepper at its pleasure.

The lines of secret work crisscrossed in every European capital and port city up to the mid-thirties.

The plural approach to overseas operations ended as the result of two steps taken by Stalin. In 1935 the Comintern was thoroughly integrated into the official Soviet intelligence services: both Party and Comintern nets were taken over, and top Comintern operators reassigned, for the most part to the GRU. In the case of Trepper's net, for example, Moscow Center not only supplied him with trained GRU case officers, but with several old Comintern hands: one of its best forgery experts by the name of Raichman and an experienced radio specialist, Wenzel, whom the Gestapo had been seeking for years. When Trepper lost his own radio communications, he passed his material for transmission to the French Party's Comintern transmitter.

The crunch on the American Party came, as we have seen, only in 1942, and in spite of the foot-dragging efforts of Earl Browder, Golos, and Bentley, the KGB took over the Washington nets.

The second and final stage of integration came with Stalin's decision to centralize the Soviet intelligence and security effort under the KGB. It was marked by the assignment of Stalin's man, Lavrenti Beria, first as deputy chief, then chief, of what was then the NKVD. A certain amount of cross-fertilization between the two services had already taken place—the head of the KGB's First Chief Directorate (then the Foreign Department) took over the GRU in 1933, and in 1937–38 when Yezhov was chief of both services, the KGB was able to cannibalize some of the GRU's best field agents into its own nets.

The Passing of the Comrades

During its first thirty years the recruitment of reliable agents in the West was child's play for the KGB.

All services prefer agents acting out of personal conviction, for moral or political beliefs tend to be a more enduring guarantee of loyalty than material or neurotic needs. Between the wars, and during World War II, Soviet intelligence relied almost exclusively on men and women who were predisposed to become "agents for a foreign power" out of political conviction: open card-carrying communists, secret Party members, Marxist intellectuals, Party sympathizers, and anti-fascists. Party members, open or secret, formed the main reservoir of "ideological" agents until the late forties.

Open or secret cells and Marxist study groups are made to order for assessing agent-candidates by a Party spotter working for a Soviet case officer. The spotter can unobtrusively collect full biographical information, build up a psychological profile through the eyes of other Party members, determine his specific job and access to classified information. The Soviet case officer, KGB or GRU, can take his pick for a direct meeting, and even if the prospect refuses to spy, he is unlikely to denounce his Soviet contact to the police.

Yet the use of Party activists or secret workers has one singular drawback: most of them already have dossiers in the police files. Even for a man who has never been arrested for his political activities, the odds are that his name, aliases, addresses, or friends are in those dossiers. A police swoop, a random document check, a marginal snitch might net him. A secret agent on file has lost some of his secrecy.

There is another, broader objection, first raised by Trotsky, against mixing straight Soviet government activities such as diplomacy and espionage with the political programs of foreign communist parties dedicated to the revolutionary seizure of power in their own countries.

Both Sorge and Trepper objected to mixing the Party's political work with Soviet espionage on very practical grounds. For Sorge, involving an intelligence operator in domestic Party matters abroad could only impede his main job of collecting information. Commenting in his prison memoirs on the trips he made for the Comintern, he recommended that

> any basic and comprehensive intelligence program should be kept apart from the internal quarrels controlling local parties; that . . . special envoys would have to be sent out to settle purely national and limited party problems, but that such men should be able to devote themselves . . . to basic intelligence activities. . . . This separation, I said, was also imperative because of the frequent need of the intelligence operative for secrecy. . . .

Trepper reports that after a public scandal in France in 1937—when the Popular Front policy would be affected by a direct display of the Soviet-Communist tie-up—"the heads of the Comintern decided that Soviet intelligence would no longer use communist militants. There would be a total separation between the secret service and the party—a decision that was overdue but justified."

The Comintern's "decision" was meaningless. The exigencies of wartime made any communists anywhere live candidates for the Soviet agent nets: for Trepper in Western Europe, for "Bill" and "Al" in New York and Washington. Only Sorge in Tokyo kept his net almost clean of Japanese communists.

The Canadian case finally forced Stalin to a decision on this politically sensitive issue.

When the activities of Colonel Zabotin, Sam Carr, and Fred Rose were blown in the fall of 1945 with Gouzenko's defection, there were repercussions in Canada and the United States. The publication of the Royal Commission's report in 1946 exposed the Canadian Communist Party as a Soviet instrument working against its own government. The political fallout affected parties around the world, underlining the equation of "Communist" and "Soviet" that had been created under the Comintern.

The reaction in Moscow was quick and emphatic. Stalin decided that from then on Soviet intelligence would not allow direct use of foreign communists as agents in its operations.

The political dangers were clearly foremost in Stalin's mind. The employment of native communists in Soviet espionage not only provides hard evidence for Soviet interference in the domestic political affairs of another country, but fortifies the image of the Party as the tool of a foreign power, an image not helpful in securing members or votes.

The value of this abstention has increased as the parties became more independent over the coming years and sought, from 1956 on, to become "mass parties." The political hazards of mixing Soviet intelligence with Party work are greatest today in the European parties, whose efforts to prove their distance from Moscow could be irretrievably blunted by a KGB taint. If even a mid-level official of the Italian Communist Party were to be put on trial as a Soviet intelligence agent, its effect on Italian (and French) attitudes toward the Party could be catastrophic—even without the help of anti-communist propaganda.

The ban on using Party members as working agents has not deprived the KGB of many other useful services the foreign parties can and do perform today. The Communist Party, American, French, or Italian, can pass on items of interest from its own collection of political or industrial "intelligence." Of even greater utility is the Party's help in spotting likely non-communist candidates for recruitment—in government offices, research laboratories, or defense plants. It can service KGB requests for information on a particular person.

These are (legally) innocuous actions. The Party stays clean, and the KGB is not contaminated by loose connections it cannot totally control.

The ban was neither absolute nor permanent. Dozens of espionage cases in West Germany and France in the postwar years featured many men and women with open or secret Party affiliation. Nor can the rule be considered inflexible even today—it is unlikely that Moscow would turn down a well-placed European bureaucrat because he has a Party connection.

ON THE HUMAN FACTOR

With the virtual elimination of foreign communists as easily recruitable agents, what the KGB faced after 1946 was the challenge faced by all Western services: to recruit as agents men and women with no built-in predisposition to work for them, people politically neutral or even "anti-Soviet," people who had never thought of spying for anyone, for whom a "spy" was a strange and remote creature outside the range of normal living.

The task of the KGB case officer in the field now became to meet people, to single out prospects, to determine the vulnerability of intellect and character, of needs and loyalties, that might lead him or her to accept a foreigner's invitation to commit a crime against his own country.

For the past thirty-five years the main rule of KGB work abroad has been to spot and study likely agent prospects.

If there is one phrase that defines KGB practice, it is "spot and study." Spot anyone who might be useful—a junior government official, a laboratory technician, a German or American businessman, a typist in the Pentagon or NATO. And then study him or her close up, directly or through an already recruited agent, to establish a profile of his character, personality, or ambitions, his needs and weaknesses, his income, to *understand* the man behind the face who will say yes or no to a carefully tailored proposal to work for the Russians.

"Spot and study" is the unending preoccupation of every KGB officer in the field, however many agents he may already be running.

Why men do what they do—marry, kill, or spy—is open only to surface explanation. A spy is, like any man, unique and complicated. He often does not know himself why (sometimes even how) he became a spy. And his mental and emotional life while he is a spy is a mystery even to his own handler.

None of our academic fraternity has yet done a thorough analysis of the psychology of secrecy or the psychology of spying, though the research material is voluminous: thousands of spy-trial transcripts, the self-serving confessions of former spies, the interrogations of spies in prison, psycho-biographies, etc. It would be a daunting task, and the courtroom antics of psychiatrists probing the criminal mind hold little promise for a successful conclusion.

The KGB case officer is a pragmatic psychologist. Though every agent prospect is unique, he is human and therefore vulnerable in simple, practical terms: rich and poor alike, educated or simple-minded, brown, black, or white.

The KGB has found by experience, by trial and error, what makes a more or less educated German or American willing to work for it. It starts with the premise of an ordinary human being brought up in a "bourgeois" society where the individual is mainly concerned with his own personal interests. For the KGB the "bourgeois psyche" is soft, self-centered, greedy, and ambitious. Many persons in a capitalist society—the outs, second-class citizens, ethnic minorities—are frustrated and neurotic beyond the common lot of men.

Most men, according to an old Comintern hand, have a hidden crack in their head, and it is the KGB's job to find that crack and widen it.

Among the countless frailties of human nature are greed, loneliness, ambition, and sexual desire. A weak ego with low self-esteem seeks reassurance. A strong ego demands gratification. Some men are deeply frustrated, some are natural rebels, "angry men" eager to vent their anger. Most men fear loss: the loss of their jobs, their status, or their wives. That fear is often stronger than the fear of jail. These are the cracks the KGB looks for.

A live KGB prospect can be forced to spy or he can be persuaded to spy, and in most cases no depth analysis is required for the KGB to select the right approach. All men in all walks of life are vulnerable to both coercion and persuasion.

The KGB has found by experience that a man's love for his family and sexual blackmail can be most usefully exploited in forcing him to become a spy. In the case of Western women the KGB's favorite formula is to enmesh them in love affairs to the point where coercion by blackmail is frequently not necessary. Passion itself is the persuader.

Money is the simplest form of persuasion, and the recipient need not have a low income to respond to its appeal.

The KGB does not rule out "ideological" recruits, but it now uses the term to cover a far broader spectrum of attitudes than Party affiliation or commitment to Marxist principles. *Any* friendly or uncritical attitude toward the Soviet Union is an invitation to study: sympathy with the Soviet people, political agreement with Soviet policy, even a distant attachment of ethnic origin. In this broad sense ideological sympathizers are of necessity "negative" in their attitudes toward the United States or other capitalist countries. They are preferred to those who work only out of material self-interest, a lower rung on the moral ladder.

The roster of known KGB agents recruited since World War II ranges across the full spectrum of Western society: countless members of the European and American establishments—legislators and politicians, generals and sergeants, diplomats and junior government clerks, businessmen and journalists, scientists and technicians—have been placed on the KGB payroll. Westerners working for the KGB range across the full spectrum of the human psyche: the honest and the grubby, the ambitious and the meek, the greedy, lonely, and desperate. Many are ordinary men and women of ordinary talent, inconspicuous in their appearance and habits. With few exceptions, they are not communists.

Each has been spotted, studied, and hooked—from a janitor at an American Embassy to a Jesuit in the Vatican, from a Frankfurt police inspector to a senior German intelligence official, from a sergeant in the Pentagon to a major general in NATO. Each had a crack in his head, and a KGB officer found it.

V

CITIZENS AND SPIES

Within a few years of the end of World War II Moscow faced the American threat on both the diplomatic and military fronts.

The aggressive intentions of Washington were clear in Moscow's prism. It was making a determined effort to create and lead a coalition of European powers in a global anti-Soviet crusade: "containment" for Moscow became the newest version of "capitalist encirclement." The retention of American troops in Europe and the Marshall Plan, it was assumed, were designed to stabilize American power on the European continent, to "imperialize" Europe by creating American satellite regimes in Germany, France, Italy, and the United Kingdom. American efforts to pare the power of the French and Italian Communist parties fitted the formula.

The United States, with its monopoly of the atomic bomb, its undestroyed industrial might, its growing ring of military and naval bases around the Soviet Union from Scandinavia to Japan, its virulent anti-Soviet propaganda, its illegal overflights of Soviet terrain, its parachuting of agents into the Soviet Union from the Ukraine to Vladivostok, became the Main Enemy (*Glavni Vrag*) or, in a more polite translation, Principal Adversary.

The priority of the American target was highlighted by a series of directives in succeeding years. A Moscow letter to the Australian residency in 1952 placed high priority on counterintelligence work against American operations aimed at the Soviet Union and the East European democracies. In December 1953 a special order by Premier Georgi Malenkov placed the United States Air Force at the top of the KGB target list—its personnel, production facilities, training, and technological research—as well as American work in atomic energy and bacteriological and chemical warfare. As late as 1959 the then head of the KGB, Alexandr Shelepin, reaffirmed at Khrushchev's personal order the priority of the American target to a conference of senior KGB officials in Moscow.

The highest level intelligence was required to expose the plans of the aggressive Americans and their allies, but even more urgent was the need to guard the security of the Soviet Union itself against capitalist intrusions.

The cardinal factor in Soviet defensive security was Stalin's determination to isolate the Soviet Union from the rest of the world during its postwar stabilization. I recall a conversation a senior official of the Agriculture Department had with Stalin in 1947. Its gist was simple: if we let in foreigners now when we are in such bad shape, they will only feed anti-Soviet propaganda abroad. If we let our own citizens see what life is like in the West, their dissatisfaction will only be greater. Put in these simple terms, it seemed to me at the time a sensible and realistic policy.

The solution was simple: to seal off the borders of the Soviet Union for entry or exit and to build a curtain between East and West Europe.

Within months of the end of the war, the Soviet frontiers were tightly sealed. The system had, and has, three components:

The physical control of the border itself maintained by Border Guards posts and patrols behind formidable physical obstacles: barbed wire, plowed strips, trip mines, and flares.

A dense network of informants in the area behind the frontiers to report on the presence of strangers and of Soviet citizens without proper papers or special resident stamps.

A forward reconnaissance area up to fifty miles beyond the frontier in which it sends or recruits agents. In frontier areas bordered on both sides by the same ethnic population, this is a relatively easy job: in the Azerbaijan area of Iran, in Afghanistan, and along the western sectors of the Chinese border.

With the borders sealed, the security control of the Soviet population became a purely domestic function, the charge of the KGB's Second Chief Directorate. From Lenin's day to this it has been the main guarantor of internal security. It was a vital element in the power struggles under and after Stalin. It is now the principal instrument for monitoring the political attitudes and behavior of the Soviet citizenry.

The directorate's officers blanket the Soviet Union. They are attached to every institution of Soviet society, some openly, some under cover. They are an integral part of the governmental machinery from Soviet and Republic bureaus down to the *raion,* or county, level. They form part of the staff of industrial enterprises, collective and state farms, schools and colleges, and research institutes. They are the Party's eyes and ears in every corner of Soviet society.

The broad task of the KGB is to monitor the daily lives of the Soviet citizenry and to detect and investigate any "anti-Soviet" actions or words. Its main function is that of a political police controlling the "political" actions, and guaranteeing the loyalty, of the Soviet citizenry. It is assisted in this task by the Party, the police, and government officials. It follows up on any tips, denunciations, or leads from these sources and enjoys their total cooperation in investigating particular cases.

The men of the Second Chief Directorate are a different breed from those of the First Directorate operating abroad.

Internal security workers carry out surveillance, bug or tap, write reports, check files, run informants, interrogate, and investigate. None of these is an art except interrogation, and top-level interrogators are at a premium among all police, security, and intelligence services.

The domestic security man operates on his own familiar terrain dealing with fellow citizens of the same cultural background and language. He is himself safe and secure, and has at his immediate command the resources not only of his own service and other government agencies, but of many elements in his community: party records, factory personnel officers, and the like. His work is at best routine, often mechanical. It is only one grade above the secret detection of crime by plainclothes policemen.

Several hundred thousand men like him keep the Party securely in power. They run the most effective control system of any modern industrial state. It was this system that we faced in the late forties and early fifties in our effort to dispatch agents into the Soviet Union in order to determine what military preparations were being made to attack Western Europe.

Documents and Informants

The Soviet control system rested then, as it does now, on the ability of control organs to identify and locate for his lifetime each and every Soviet citizen. Personal documents are its nub: each man or woman was required to carry a basic identity document, or internal passport, valid for five years. Each adult was also required to carry a labor book recording past and current employment (with all entries signed by factory personnel managers), a military status book, and, when appropriate, a party card or an officer's identity book. These documents were later consolidated into a fourteen-page internal passport equivalent to a detailed personal history of its bearer: ethnic origin, parents, education, previous jobs and salaries, places he has lived, etc. In the current issuance of new internal passports, which started in the late seventies, members of collective farms are included for the first time.

Each citizen is more than a number in a central record. He carries his own official file card in his pocket.

The basic control is registration by residence. In cities and towns, the apartment-house concierge reports to the local police on the comings and goings of tenants and maintains a register of overnight visitors. No citizen can travel without his internal passport, spend a night in a hotel, or visit another city for more than three days. If he moves from one locality to another, he must register with the police. He cannot move without permission, and the KGB can keep him in one place or prevent him from moving to an "undesirable" area. He cannot move from a town to a big city without police permission—he must have a job *and* a place to live.

The KGB is the brain and skeleton of the control apparatus. Its flesh is the unpaid informant. Each echelon of the security service has its own roster of informants from the top offices in Moscow down to the town or village level. This network of unpaid KGB informants provides the Party with the cheapest and most effective instrument for controlling the Soviet citizen. Good informants are often rewarded for their work.

It is hard for a citizen in either a closed or an open society to refuse to cooperate with its security organs in the protection of the state. In a closed society it is almost impossible.

The KGB officer meets with few turndowns in recruiting informants. Party members will cooperate without hesitation. For a non-Party member to refuse to assist the state in ferreting out disloyal citizens is evidence of his own disloyalty. For persons with a strong distaste for informing on their fellow workers or students, there are pressures brought to bear: demotion, losing a job or a scholarship, getting a permanent black mark in a police dossier.

Once he agrees, however reluctantly, to cooperate, the informant has to play ball for his own protection. He can promise himself not to report on his friends or colleagues, but he faces two problems. He is under pressure by his handler to come up with "useful" information. When his failure to report is itself a cause for suspicion, he is bound to find something to report. And when he does hear someone say something he knows he should report, he is faced with a serious dilemma. He knows he will be tested. Did citizen X criticize the Party, or even the Leader, out of a spontaneous impulse—or was he following the instruction of *his* KGB handler? A climate of provocation robs any man of his self-assurance.

How many informants the KGB ran in the late forties or early fifties cannot be estimated, but their number must have been formidable considering the challenges faced by the Party in restoring the controls broken up during the war, especially in the western regions. At one period in the thirties, it was reasonably estimated, the KGB ran more than five million informants, a network of eyes and ears that blanketed the Soviet Union from the Ukraine to the Pacific.

A control system becomes even more effective when it enjoys the cooperation of *all* its citizens in monitoring each other. In the postwar atmosphere of the forties Stalin transmitted his own fears and suspicions to the entire population. The campaign against "enemies of the state" was promoted by Party propagandists and by the Soviet press and radio. A high degree of "vigilance" became a patriotic duty.

The cardinal virtue of an informant system is not its size or extent, but the belief of the citizenry in its existence. Once a citizen is convinced that he is surrounded by informants, it does not much matter whether or not he is. If *any* wall has ears, perhaps it is this one. An occasional notice in the press of a local denunciation, or the rumor of an informant in the citizen's factory or apartment house, will keep him on his toes.

The effect on the ordinary man is to heighten his own sense of vulnerability. If he denounces someone else, he proves his "revolutionary vigilance" to the authorities. His may be an honest denunciation, but meaner motives also operate: to get back at a mean boss, a disagreeable neighbor, a rival suitor. And then there are in every society the simply nasty or sadistic types, the writers of poison-pen letters, the slightly insane who flourish in an atmosphere equating the snitch with the patriot.

It is in times of stress that the control system attains its ultimate goal: the atomized citizen. Robbed of trust in others, the individual becomes isolated from his neighbors, his friends, even his family. It is the end of small talk, the main occupation of mankind, and can make allegiance—to the Party, the Army, the trade union—a surface gesture only. A Me-generation can be born in different climates. In the Soviet Union under Stalin it was Me against the enemy, and the only recipe was to play ball with the regime.

It was into this system of (almost) total control that American intelligence attempted to insert resident agents in the late forties and early fifties. In 1949 the White House authorized the dispatch of agents into the Soviet Union to report signs of any impending military action. From 1949 to 1952 in Washington, and during the next year in Munich, Germany, our main dispatch base, I was assigned the task of developing communications with the existing resistance groups in the Baltic and the Ukraine and of establishing resident agents at select airfields and rail junctions within the Soviet Union. We knew, and the Pentagon knew, that the control system confronted our agents with almost insuperable odds against survival, but war threatened, and the White House demanded early warning. With the outbreak of the Korean War, seen by some in Washington as a diversionary action for an attack on Europe, the pressures for early warning increased.

Since the borders were effectively sealed (especially to a man carrying a radio), our agents were dispatched by air into sparsely inhabited areas with access to a not-too-distant railway station. They were supplied with forged documents and a legend, or false life history, that would stand up to a cursory inspection by the railway guards or a random check by the militia—not to a professional KGB interrogation. Their task was to "legalize" themselves as quickly as possible in their target area.*

Here the cracks in the control system worked to our advantage. Even totalitarian control is never total. Under Stalin (and more so under Brezhnev) there were uncontrolled elements of Soviet society. There were people who lived without registration papers: escapees from labor areas, men without jobs or official residents who lived back in the cities, uprooted citizens from the war areas of the west. Black marketeers and buyers of foreign currency flourished then as they do now.

Forged papers could be bought—though they were expensive. Men without papers could find lodging without registering, or get a job—especially with foremen of construction projects who needed more workers to fulfill their quota.

The casualties in those operations were high. Some agents were captured in or near the drop zone. Several fell victim to the routine check on documents while they were enroute to their destination by rail. Others, we could only guess, were turned in by suspicious neighbors or traveling companions—voluntary one-time informants.

Some of our agents did integrate themselves into the Soviet system. One eventually became an employee of the Moscow sanitation department.

Radio Playbacks

Of the captured agents several were immediately publicized, but the KGB decided to play back several others by securing their cooperation in sending back radio messages composed by the KGB. The Germans had played back Trepper's radios into the KGB. It was now the KGB's turn to play back American radios into the CIA.

Radio playbacks can play a significant role in wartime, but their value in peacetime is much more limited. In both cases it is a difficult game to play, and the KGB got little profit out of their playback efforts in the early fifties.

In World War II, for the first time, agents equipped with radio sets were parachuted or infiltrated into the enemy's territory by

* These operations are described in Chapter 2 of my book, *The CIA's Secret Operations* (New York, 1977).

both the Germans and the Allies. Capturing radio operators and turning them against their distant dispatchers became a practical and, in some cases, valuable endeavor.

For the most brilliant use of doubled enemy radio agents credit must be given to the British. In the now well-documented Double-Cross operation, the British captured a series of German agents infiltrated into Britain and secured their cooperation. They continued their work under control of the British, whose deftness left the Germans convinced that their agents were operating freely. By the careful use of correct information and of bogus information that could nonetheless be verified by visual observation (acts of sabotage, mock military installations, etc.), German confidence in the reliability of their agents was built up step-by-step.

The most immediate profit from Double-Cross was to confine the infiltration of German agents to a minimum, for German intelligence hardly needed more agents when those on the ground were performing so well. The greatest profit came from the use of these channels into German intelligence to pass misleading information, most importantly the location of the planned D-day invasion.

The requirements for success were demanding. *Every* German agent in the British Isles had to be brought under control, for a single free agent could expose the game by reporting facts that would puncture German faith in the reliability of the controlled agents. This was achievable only in a limited geographic area—like the British Isles. The notional performance of each German agent and the coordination of their separate streams of reporting also demanded a finely tuned central control that could not permit a single false note or discrepancy that might trigger German suspicions.

The Germans were deceived throughout by Double-Cross—and the British by a German playback in Holland.

Though German wartime intelligence was notorious for its bureaucratic infighting at headquarters and for inefficiency and bungling in the field, it has one bloody radio playback to its credit: Operation Nordpol. For eighteen months German counterintelligence controlled the British covert action to support the Dutch underground. Several Dutch agents dispatched by air from Britain were captured and agreed to collaborate with the Germans in maintaining their radio contact with London under German control. Agent after agent was sent into Holland only to fall into the hands of the Germans who captured the new agents being parachuted in and seized the arms and ammunition dropped to the mythical underground.

Again, the absence of any independent Allied source of information in the target area made it impossible to check the encouraging reports coming in over the German-controlled radios.

The Germans also, as we have seen, tried to play back Trepper's captured radio operators to establish a trusted channel to Moscow and, for a brief period, succeeded.

The two counters employed to detect a playback are the danger signal(s) given to the agent before his dispatch and the analysis of his "fist," or touch, on the telegraph key. The latter became important only when the KGB substituted another operator to handle the agent's set. In the several cases of playback in our operations at this time the KGB had persuaded our agent to handle the key himself.

The danger signal in such cases became the crucial indicator. It can be negative (omitting or changing an element in the normal procedure of sending a message) or positive (including an inconspicuous phrase). Since any service is aware of this practice, the operators were given two indicators—one to give up to their interrogators.

The indicator is not foolproof, especially if the fool is on the receiving end at headquarters. It is reliably reported that a British case officer, receiving a message from his agent on the Continent without an all-clear signal, reminded him in his next message to include that signal in the future.

The KGB effort to play back the radios of parachuted Western agents in the early fifties followed the Nordpol pattern: to invite in other agents or to trace Western agents already operating in the Soviet Union.

Moscow clearly had an exaggerated notion of how many "imperialist" spies were operating on Soviet terrain: the handful of agents they did catch were, for them, the tip of the iceberg, and were exploited for the simple purpose of uncovering other agents in the imperialist net.

The most persistent KGB attempt to play an agent back in order to uncover other American agents on Soviet terrain was made in their handling of a singleton agent dropped in the Far East.

Ilya, we will call him, came on the air within two days of his landing and gave no danger signal. He was not heard from for over six weeks. Then he resumed contact—giving the danger signal.

To cover up his six weeks' silence the KGB concocted a fairly reasonable story: Ilya had cached his radio set, went into town looking for a job, and got taken on by a traveling circus. He lost his job. Penniless and still with his original forged documents, he went back to his cache and asked for help.

For the next dozen messages the KGB emphasized Ilya's helplessness and his urgent need for money to get himself out of an area he considered dangerous. The implication throughout was that another agent be sent to help him.

Finally, a packet of rubles was sent to the address Ilya had given. It was not delivered by another agent, but simply mailed to him out of the central Moscow post office.

Our concern, of course, was to keep Ilya alive as long as possible by playing ball with his KGB handler. After some months the KGB had clearly decided that the operation was not worth the effort and broke off communications.

Another playback, this time by secret writing correspondence, displayed a marked degree of ineptness by the KGB. Boris had been infiltrated across the border north of Leningrad with instructions to communicate by sending back secret-writing messages in normal correspondence to various cover addresses in Europe. The KGB arrested him and wrote his messages for him for almost a year. A handwriting analysis showed that the secret-ink messages had been written by seven different persons.

Playbacks by secret writing were clearly not the KGB's strong point.

Resident Spies

Agents sent into the Soviet Union from outside presented the KGB with its most dramatic, if intermittent, challenge. That challenge continues to the present day, though the regime's repeated call for vigilance against foreign spies—even during the thaw and the later détente—has been a propaganda rather than a serious security measure.

What is of greater, and more continuing, concern to the KGB is the potential for espionage of the foreign officials assigned to Moscow. These diplomats, above all the capitalist diplomats who can speak Russian, are a constant threat, for the KGB assumes that their primary mission, like that of KGB residents in capitalist countries, is to recruit Soviet citizens to spy on their government.

The work against foreign residents in the Soviet Union is carried out by six departments of the Second Chief Directorate, each with its target nationalities: the United States and Latin America; Germany, Austria, Scandinavia, etc. Other departments concentrate on tourists, foreign students, and journalists.

The American department, like the others, has a double function. It closely watches American Embassy personnel to prevent American officials from carrying out espionage activities, carefully monitoring any American contacts with Soviet citizens, and it also works on recruiting American diplomats or journalists for whatever classified information they may be able to provide from the American Embassy. These recruits, proved and tested on the spot, are then available for transfer to KGB officers in the United States.

The concern with Americans in Moscow displays the paranoid Soviet focus on foreigners at its height. Since the war hundreds, if not thousands, of microphones have been concealed inside American installations, including several dozen in the Great Seal of the United States, which hangs in the ambassador's office. Monitoring American telephones has, naturally, been incessant. Thousands of surveillants and informants have been employed on the American target. Dozens of American diplomats have been framed.

For over sixty years the entire foreign colony in Moscow has been blanketed by a control apparatus designed, ideally, to monitor every contact of every diplomat with any Soviet citizen. The apparatus takes the form of an *agentura,* a network of informers, agents, and surveillance squads that keeps a round-the-clock eye on all the foreign diplomats, journalists, and businessmen in the capital.

The KGB virtually owns Moscow. It controls the NPDK, the personnel bureau through which resident foreigners must hire the Soviet personnel that are indispensable to the life of the foreign colony: chambermaids, chauffeurs, utility repairmen, translators, and interpreters. It has thousands of cooperative informers: hotel registration clerks, restaurant managers, taxi drivers, (most) Intourist guides, and, of course, the police, or militiamen, who guard the embassies and private residences.

When called upon, the KGB employs its own special facilities: special surveillance units, telephone taps, movie and TV cameras, hidden microphones. Their bugs in Western embassies have become notorious.

The KGB also enjoys the support services of East European and Cuban diplomats, who report on their contacts with their Western colleagues. Its most useful informants, those closest to the targets, are the Soviet journalists, artists, writers, *and* government officials who mix in Western circles.

The *agentura* is a two-way facility. It not only monitors any improper contacts by the foreign residents, but it assesses their potential use as Soviet agents—not only in delivering the secrets of their embassies, but for their long-term use in future assignments. The Second Chief Directorate plays offense and defense with the same team.

The conditions for entrapment are ideal in Moscow. A clerk is inveigled into exchanging hard currency for rubles on the black market. A Western ambassador is recruited because he has a collector's passion for Russian ikons: a Soviet friend volunteers to find some for him, and he is hooked because exporting ikons is illegal. An American woman succumbs because she is threatened with official refusal to issue her an exit visa. A journalist is lured into making a private meeting with "someone you will find interesting." As late as 1977 an American U.N. employee born in the Ukraine attended a UNESCO conference in Tbilisi, Georgia, and was threatened with exposure of his cooperation with the Germans during World War II. In each case the KGB has a handle on the culprit, or thinks it has. Enough cooperate to make the campaign worthwhile.

The KGB also stands ready to frame a foreign official or journalist when the government needs some local exhibits to express its displeasure with the arrest of a Soviet agent abroad or to build up a spy bank for future spy exchanges. A simple frame-up can also provide a warning to a local embassy that appears to be overzealous in mixing with Soviet citizens.

The full facts are, of course, hidden, but it is highly probable that every Western embassy in Moscow has been penetrated, for a time at least, by one of its employees, diplomat or clerk, working for the KGB. Penetrations of the American, British, French, German, and Norwegian embassies are on record.

The main handle has been sexual entrapment. As far back as the early twenties the London *Times* ran an article on sex traps for the unwary diplomat in Moscow. In the seventies both diplomats and journalists found themselves in the wrong bed with an attractive Muscovite. During these years the KGB's exploitation of the sexual impulse has involved as many practices as sex itself: plain man-woman encounters through pimps or prostitutes, or casual weekend adventures; woman-man affairs that lead to passionate love; man-man sex with or without love; kinky sex for exotic tastes. Only the techniques of getting "evidence" have changed with the advancement of audiovisual technology.

There is no call-girl racket in Moscow—perhaps because of the relative paucity of telephones—but there are willing women and men who can be called on short notice by the KGB.

Some approaches are crude and abrupt. An apparently amateur prostitute tries to solicit an obvious foreigner on Gorky Street. A visiting businessman returns to his hotel one night and finds in his bed a naked well-built brunette. An attractive member of the young set makes a pick-up at a discotheque.

These are shots in the dark.

The KGB has elaborate facilities in Moscow for constructing more effective scenarios: attractive women and men under suitable cover (say, ballet dancer or artist) and hotel rooms and well-furnished "private" apartments supplied with microphones, peepholes, and TV cameras.

The classic approach is simple and almost foolproof.

One of the first Americans recruited in Moscow after the war was a sergeant in charge of the Moscow Embassy motor pool, the same Master Sergeant Roy Rhodes who appeared at the trial of Colonel Abel. In 1951 the lonely Rhodes (his wife and two-year-old daughter were in the States) went on a drunken party with some Russians and found himself in bed with a girl the next morning. Six weeks later the girl asked him for another date, announced she was pregnant, and confronted Rhodes with her "brother." Under his pressure Rhodes agreed to cooperate, and made more than a dozen secret meetings in the next two years and signed receipts for a total of $3,000 paid him for his (modest) services.

Before his departure from Moscow he was instructed to write "special letters" to the Soviet Embassy in Washington as a signal for a meeting with a Soviet case officer in Mexico City. Moscow's interest in Rhodes was his possible assignment to an Army Communications school for training as a mechanic on code machines. Since Rhodes did not make the contact, Abel was instructed to run down his location and given his background: "He was recruited to our service in January 1952 in our country which he left in June 1953. Recruited on the basis of compromising materials but he is tied up to us with receipts and information he had given in his own handwriting."

The dirty picture gambit is even more impressive.

In the late fifties a young Indian clerk, whose wife and two children were at home in India, was singled out for attention. He met a young, well-dressed English-speaking Russian girl. After a few dates in public she invited him to her apartment and to her bed: the bug and camera recorded the scene. The KGB now went one step further: adultery, after all, is only a minor offense in many societies. The Russian girl arranged a double-date with a second couple, and the four had a mild alcoholic orgy. The Indian clerk, drugged, found himself in bed with the other man. The camera clicked.

A few days later a KGB officer confronted the clerk in the rigged apartment with glossy prints of his adulterous and homosexual escapades. The photographs would be sent to the Ministry of External Affairs in Delhi and to his wife and parents if he did not cooperate. He (understandably) agreed: both family and career were at stake. He was not asked to filch secrets out of the Indian Embassy: the KGB had higher purposes. He was given instructions for a meeting upon his return to New Delhi after the end of his tour, when he would become a direct penetration of Foreign Office communications.

The scenario has been repeated scores of times in Moscow. We know only those occasions when the "target" refused the invitation, accepted and confessed, or was caught in his subsequent career. We can only guess at the number of recruitments we have not heard about. What we can be sure of is that the KGB would not invest substantial resources in a program that fails to return a steady profit.

Most recently, on February 16, 1981, the media reported that the KGB, presumably by sexual entrapment, tried to frame and recruit the U. S. Assistant Military Attaché in Moscow, Lt. Col. Holbrook, who was allegedly to be reassigned as military adviser to the staff of Vice-President Bush. Holbrook reported the incident and the KGB was exposed at its oldest game.

The gay gambit need not involve entrapment when the mark is a practicing homosexual. In Moscow, as in every capital, there are gay men who seek each other out for their private pleasures. The visiting gay can be wooed and won for espionage without much pressure if he falls in love with the KGB plant.

In the mid-fifties, before the British Foreign Office began weeding out its homosexuals with the same rigor the American State Department practiced in the late forties, several young Englishmen were caught in this velvet mousetrap. In 1952 a twenty-four-year-old radio operator, William Marshall, was convicted and sentenced for violating the Official Secrets Act: he had been caught in the gay trap during his Moscow assignment. Ten years later another case broke into public view: the celebrated Vassall affair.

William Vassall, a clerk in the Admiralty, worked in the office of the naval attaché in the British Embassy from March 1954 to July 1956. The son of a cleric, of good but poor middle-class background, Vassall showed no particular competence as a clerk, but had advanced in his civil service career by his likable gregarious personality. He was a talented amateur actor and religiously inclined.

Vassall was also a homosexual, and had been an active practitioner in London, Egypt, Mexico—and Moscow.

He obviously did not have to be trapped. Yet his story at his trial in 1962, followed the classic scenario: a drunken party, homosexual acrobatics, photographs, threats of exposure. There was more to it than that.

There worked in the British Embassy at the time an interpreter and administrative assistant, Sigmund Mikhailsy, a Pole who did not like Russians. Half "gopher," half pimp, he helped the staff get theater tickets and special items of food. He also helped the junior clerks improve their social life, among them Vassall (with whom he reportedly had a brief affair). For the duration of his tour, Vassall enjoyed the peculiar fleshpots Moscow had to offer.

Within six months of his arrival in Moscow Vassall began supplying embassy documents, and for the next seven years—in Moscow and in London—he microfilmed documents from the Naval Intelligence Division and the Secretariat of the Naval Staff. He played his spy role with energy and zest. He was well paid, almost doubling his salary, and lived it up in London nightclubs and on fancy holidays. It is hard to picture him as a reluctant recruit.

The most notorious case of sexual entrapment in Moscow involved a patient and elaborate effort to secure the cooperation of the French Ambassador, Maurice Dejean. It was a high-level operation, reportedly laid on by Khrushchev himself, and was played out in the high-level Moscow society of elegant apartments and dachas, fine dinners, and talented writers, actresses, and senior Party officials.

The KGB had studied the ambassador and his wife, Marie-Claire, before their arrival in Moscow in December 1955, and kept close watch on them for some months afterward: by surveillance, through his chauffeur and her maid, and from informants in the diplomatic colony. The fifty-six-year-old Dejean's true Gallic taste for attractive women was the nub of the action.

Parallel plots unfolded in the next two years.

A KGB lieutenant posing as a young diplomat met Mme. Dejean at a Black Sea resort and saw her several times in Moscow at diplomatic functions. He invited her to a picnic outing and introduced his friend Krotkov, a writer and artist.

Mme. Dejean invited her picnic hosts to the Bastille Day reception at the embassy (Khrushchev was the guest of honor), and Krotkov arranged another picnic to include Mme. Dejean.

Mme. Dejean and Krotkov become good friends—but no more.

Then the second plot unfolded.

Enter the heavy, the director himself, as lead: Lieutenant General Gribanov, head of the Second Chief Directorate—the J. Edgar Hoover of the Soviet Union. Under the name of Gorbunov, a senior official, he had equipped himself with a *pro tem* wife, a French-speaking KGB major, Vera.

Vera was introduced to the Dejeans at a diplomatic reception and invited them to dinner to meet her "husband." The four developed a close social relationship. At their Moscow apartment and their dacha outside Moscow (supplied by then KGB chief Ivan Serov), the Dejeans met the cream of Moscow's intellectuals and artists.

Dejean and Gribanov-Gorbunov become good friends.

The first plot is resumed, now with the ambassador as the mark.

A special film exhibition was arranged for the Dejeans to meet the film colony, and Krotkov placed Lydia, a fluent French speaker, next to Dejean at dinner. She supposedly was a divorcée. After a series of restaurant and French Embassy parties attended by Lydia, Dejean visited an old Georgian artist, a lover of things French, with Lydia acting as his interpreter. He offered to drive her home.

Dejean and Lydia became lovers.

Abruptly the script is rewritten, for it now demands, not a divorcée, but a married woman. Lydia was taken off the stage and replaced by Lora, an actress whose "husband" was a geologist on frequent trips to Siberia.

Dejean and Lora became lovers.

One day the two came back from a suburban picnic to her apartment and started making love. A rough-looking bully-boy equipped with cleated shoes and knapsack entered and acted the part of the outraged husband. He beat up the ambassador and threatened to go to the authorities and have him expelled.

The two plots now merged: Dejean and Gribanov, Dejean and Lora.

That same night Dejean had been invited to dinner at Gribanov-Gorbunov's dacha. He recounted the afternoon episode and asked his friend for help in avoiding a public scandal.

A few days later Gribanov-Gorbunov assured him that he had arranged to keep the outraged husband quiet. Their friendship deepened.

End of play, for the last act was never played out.

Gribanov not only knew Dejean's secret, but he had created a personal obligation that Dejean would someday be called upon to repay. The KGB planned to use its handle after Dejean returned to a high post in Paris. The defection of a member of the cast on a trip abroad blew the operation to French intelligence in good time.

Many of these cases of sexual entrapment in Moscow make pathetic reading, above all that of Ambassador Dejean's military attaché. Snared by the routine sex gambit, he committed suicide.

There is, of course, a way out.

A Western correspondent was treated to the classic approach while his wife and children were on vacation in the States. He met a young woman student at the University of Moscow, dated her, visited her in a *six*-bedroom apartment, and finally slept with her. Confronted with the photographs, he reported the event to his embassy and transferred to his home base.

The rejection of blackmail can also be carried out with flair. A French military attaché in Prague got the full treatment. Confronted with the film of his escapade, he asked for a copy to send back to his wife as proof of his continuing virility.

KGB officers who have run these operations successfully in Moscow have secured honors and career advantages. No scorecard can be filled in, but it is a logical deduction from the investment the KGB has made in the sex routine that at least a handful of young diplomats and clerks now operate as agents in Western chanceries.

ON TERROR

An informant-ridden society creates caution in its members. Mass terror, as practiced by Stalin in the thirties, creates an obsessive fear: Am I next?

Terror can be measured by its scale, its methods, and its rationality.

Stalin's terror during the 1930s is beyond cold statistics: millions executed or imprisoned in labor camps. Add the suffering of millions more: the wife left alone, an uncle gone, old school chums vanished. Add the fears of the "innocent," the 2 A.M. knock on the door reverberating through the apartment house; the empty desk in the office, the institute staff disappearing one by one, the Party cell or the county office shrunken overnight, a new face in the editor's chair.

Its methods were more brutal than any regime's except Hitler's extermination of the Jews. They included mass executions, mass deportations, "class" round-ups on the one hand, physical and mental torture of arrested prisoners on the other.

Above all, it *appeared* totally irrational. No one knew *why* X had been arrested. Stalin's purposes were clear only to himself. Even his closest colleagues did not believe he would simply destroy all the old Bolsheviks who had made the Revolution—and surely not his devoted followers who had never opposed his will. When no one was guilty (of what?) and no one was innocent (of what?), anyone can be arrested. Why, why, why, was the tragic query of those in and out of prison.

Terror is most effective if capricious: no lists by category, no recognizable grounds for *that* list, no motive for placing *that* name on the list. No one could *understand* whom else Stalin might seek out. There was therefore no rational means of avoiding the list: "Anyone" may be "guilty." No one is "innocent."

Stalin's purges were a vast operation of preventive surgery: the isolation from society of those who (in his mind) *might* infect the healthy.

Stalin set the categories, the KGB supplied the lists. Anti-Party elements? The lists include former Mensheviks, Social Revolutionaries, and their relatives. Churchgoers? The lists of Orthodox,

Baptists, Jehovah's Witnesses are readily collated. Anyone with foreign contacts? List them all—stamp collectors, Esperanto enthusiasts, relatives abroad. And the broadest category of them all: anti-Soviet elements. Who are they? Anyone.

Any purge, even within the Communist Party, any public trials of so-called political subversives or foreign saboteurs, have an effect far beyond their victims. They are both an instrument for the education of the citizenry and an outlet for their accumulated tensions.

Everyone participates. There are national propaganda campaigns in the press, letters to the editor, mass meetings, vigilance campaigns. All are designed to enlist the emotional support of the "masses," be it against a foreign enemy (Germans or Americans) or the enemy within—inefficient Party bureaucrats and factory managers, local scapegoats like Party officials or minority spokesmen, national scapegoats like Army generals or top officials. The ordinary citizen is whipped up into feelings of hate. He attends mass meetings and parades, shouts appropriate slogans ("Shoot the mad fascist dogs" or "Stamp out the snakes," à la Peking). The confessions of his renegade leaders, Politburo member or local magistrate, confirm as they focus his hate.

The final step is the mass hunt. The people join in the search for victims, denounce both friend and enemy, denounce the boss, even turn in their relatives. They become the engineers of their own repression.

Wild rumors circulate, gossip is rampant, facts are garbled. Some sit tight. Others cooperate by denouncing someone as a proof of their own virtue. In either case personal security is shattered.

Purges and spy campaigns, any kind of witch-hunt, have a stimulating effect on a security service. The men of the KGB were, after all, the main instrument for finding and exterminating these criminal threats to the Party. They must do their work with loyalty and enthusiasm. They investigate, make arrests, hold administrative trials with the same feverish enthusiasm. After all, they must produce, show "achievements." The Party says there are enemies: there must be enemies. Confessions are forced, plots are concocted. As they do their work with the denunciations passed to them by the Party, the repression gathers momentum. The head count rises.

Even Stalin was forced to slow the momentum to avoid a totally exhausted society. The simple expedient was to purge the purgers.

VI

ÉMIGRÉS AND ASSASSINS

The Second Chief Directorate of the KGB has the task of capturing enemy agents once they reach the Soviet Union. The First Chief Directorate seeks to identify them before they are dispatched.

By the spring of 1952 Western-occupied Germany had become an arena for the most concentrated and wholesale KGB operations the First Chief Directorate had ever been called upon to perform in peacetime. Their intelligence targets were clear and close at hand—the Allied occupation forces and the nascent German institutions they were nurturing.

Their counterintelligence targets were equally accessible. West Germany had become the principal American base for both open and secret operations against the Soviet Union and East Europe. American-sponsored radios were broadcasting their anti-Soviet messages from Berlin and Munich. American-manufactured leaflets were being smuggled in by the hundreds of thousands across the Iron Curtain by line-crossers and balloons. American intelligence agents were crossing the Curtain to reconnoiter Soviet barracks and airfields, and to recruit spies in the Communist Party and government offices in Warsaw, Prague, and Budapest. Large quantities of money and matériel were being sent in to support the major resistance movement in Poland and the Ukrainian partisans still holed up in the Carpathians.

Above all, American agents were being air-dropped on Soviet terrain.

The principal base for American operations into the Soviet Union from 1949 to 1953 was the Munich area in southern Germany. After organizing the Soviet Division at headquarters and getting Soviet case officers into the field in Berlin, Vienna, Istanbul, Teheran, and Tokyo, I finally received my own field assignment to Munich in May 1952. Our headquarters base was located on the fourth floor of an old German casern, and my office under the eaves was only slightly less dismal than 2242 Que. The main work of the base—recruiting and training agents for dispatch— was done outside: in a series of safe houses near Munich, where the agents were trained, and in Displaced Persons camps in the American Zone, where most of the agents were recruited.

The main headquarters for KGB operations in Occupied Germany was located in Karlshorst, a suburb of East Berlin. It was the largest operations base of the First Chief Directorate outside of Moscow.

KGB/Karlshorst was a compound within a compound. The headquarters for the Soviet High Command, the Soviet Control Commission, and other Soviet administrations was an extensive area of the Karlshorst suburb that had been taken over just after the war by the Soviet occupying authorities and formed into a strictly Soviet settlement surrounded by an iron fence in front and barbed wire around the rest of the perimeter. It was patrolled on the outside by German police and trained police dogs. Soviet sentries controlled the main entrance.

On the eastern end of this guarded area sat the KGB headquarters, a former hospital, three stories in height, surrounded by a solid wooden fence. It was dotted with sentries who carefully checked all documents: at the gate at the fence, at the entrances to the hospital, and in the corridors.

KGB officers could call on a large motor pool and a series of once elegant one-family houses used for meetings with agents and couriers, for interrogation, and for housing illegals in training or transit to the West. Only KGB officers could leave the "settlement" at any time of day or night and bring anyone in or out.

Among the wide variety of operations the Karlshorst residency directed against the West, those of most immediate interest to our Munich base were its wide-ranging and persistent efforts to penetrate the anti-Soviet émigré organizations in the American Zone.

Trust

For thirty years Moscow had been obsessed with the threat posed by its former citizens who had emigrated and survived in the capitalist world. It saw these people as a double threat: to Soviet security and as a political danger to the Soviet regime. The security concern is understandable: émigrés were a reservoir of potential agents the West could use to penetrate the Soviet Union. The political threat resolved itself into the correct Soviet conviction that only its émigrés would be capable of setting up a provisional government of Russia and, under the right circumstances, becoming a successor to the Communist Party regime.

No one else could run Russia. Lenin had operated out of Geneva and Zurich, Trotsky out of London: the pattern had already been set.

This intense obsession of Lenin, Stalin, and Khrushchev with the Soviet emigration is hard to grasp except against the backdrop of Soviet experience between the wars.

The Trust operation of the twenties was directed against the million-strong anti-Soviet emigration that settled in Paris, London, and the Balkans after their defeat in the Russian Civil War. Well organized, supported by the British and the French, they were a powerful second Russia of the dispossessed readily available for another military intervention.

The Cheka was given the task of neutralizing the threat. It mounted the most brilliant and ingenious wrecking operation in KGB history. The KGB remained proud enough of this operation to sponsor a semifictional account of Trust just before its fiftieth anniversary in 1967. It was given wide distribution as another example of its brilliant defense of the fatherland.

Trust was the code name for the Monarchist Union of Central Russia (MUCR), ostensibly a powerful anti-Soviet organization within the Soviet Union. The operation began when an underground leader came out to the West in 1921 to establish liaison with the Whites outside. He told them what they wanted to hear: that the MUCR was a strong, well-organized resistance movement, that unrest was growing, and that the Bolshevik regime was on the verge of collapse.

The Whites—and the British and French—were sucked in. First-rate up-to-date intelligence came out of Russia in a steady stream. Trust messages passed from Berlin and Paris to Moscow and back in a week. The Trust provided border crossing points for agents sent in from the West, and more and more émigré operations were channeled through Trust facilities. The game went on for several years.

Two events aroused suspicion in the West.

The notorious anti-czarist and anti-Bolshevik terrorist, Boris Savinkov—a man for whom Winston Churchill had great respect —was urgently invited by his top agent inside to come back to Russia in early 1924 to lead a revolt in Georgia against the Red regime that had been badly shaken by Lenin's death in January. He returned on a forged Italian passport along a Trust safe route via Berlin and Warsaw. He was trapped in a safe house near Minsk.

Another irreconcilable foe of Bolshevism, Captain Sydney George Reilly, met the same fate. Reilly was an extraordinary figure. Born Rosenblum in eastern Poland, he emigrated to England, married the daughter of a British naval officer, and worked for British intelligence. His daring exploits against the Bolsheviks during and after the Revolution gained the admiration of Soviet intelligence ("be like Reilly" was the parting admonition of one KGB chief to a resident assigned abroad years later).

Reilly was enticed to return to Russia by a tested and reliable woman courier, Maria Schulz, who held out to him the prospect of making contact with leading figures in the anti-Bolshevik opposition. He was caught as he crossed the border at another "safe" Trust crossing.

The tragic game finally ended in 1926 as Western scepticism about the reliability of Trust's military intelligence began to mount. The disappearance of a top White general in Paris (with a forged suicide note) confirmed their doubts.

To crown their coup, Soviet intelligence sent out the top case officer for the Trust operation, Edward Opperput, to "defect" in Finland. He told the real story of Trust. From 1921 on the Russians brought under their own control the key Trust agents Inside and penetrated the Outside emigration at a high level, thereby controlling both ends of the Trust communication lines. By writing all the messages that went out from the Inside, and reading those sent in by the Outside, they had not only managed to run almost all White cross-border operations into the Soviet Union but to monitor and, for the most part, control all significant developments within the principal anti-Soviet émigré groups in Europe. By providing Western intelligence with their most valuable political and military "intelligence," Moscow removed the need for them to launch additional intelligence operations. The subsidies provided by the British and French to their Trust contacts Inside were used by the OGPU to pay for the operational expenses incurred in this lengthy operation.

The principal Soviet purpose in the Trust game was to convince the West that the Soviet state was crumbling and that further armed action was not required to unseat the Bolshevik regime. At the same time they deterred independent actions by the émigrés Outside under the pretense that terrorist acts Inside could only impede the progress of the internal opposition.

In dissolving Trust and publishing its history to the world, the Soviet service finished it off before the West could denounce it, thereby gaining maximum publicity for the exposé and bringing confusion into the ranks of the duped émigrés. It was a "sting" of the first order.

The Postwar Émigrés

After World War II Moscow's obsession with its former citizens did not weaken.

The overall concern of the KGB over Allied use of émigrés as agents for work inside the Soviet Union was reflected most clearly in a Moscow letter sent to the Australian residency in June 1952.

There live in Australia a series of displaced persons and traitors of our native land, who conduct suspicious correspondence with their relatives and friends in the Soviet [sic].

In their letters they show an interest in the fate of their relatives, and in the material situation of Russian people and their participation in the political life of the country; they check the correctness of their relatives' addresses, express hope of a swift meeting with them,

and ask that correspondence should be maintained in secret. . . .

We presume that this correspondence is being conducted not without the knowledge of intelligence organizations. It is also possible that these people are being
specially prepared for transmission to Russia.

At the end of the war in Europe, Stalin made a determined and
successful effort to repatriate Soviet citizens left behind in occupied Germany: several million prisoners of war, forced laborers,
troops who had fought for the Germans, and Balts and Ukrainians who had fled the advancing Soviet armies in the last phases
of the war. The Western allies had formally agreed to a postwar
exchange of citizens on both sides and forced the repatriation of
Soviet soldiers and citizens in the face of wholesale resistance—an
action later hailed as a crime against humanity, for these repa-
triates were automatically considered traitors by Stalin and
treated as such on their return.

After the forced repatriation there still remained in Allied-oc-
cupied Germany thousands of émigrés from all parts of the Soviet
Union—from the Ukraine, Byelorussia, the Baltic states, Georgia, Armenia, Uzbekistan. They were organized into their own
national groups: benevolent self-help associations, national coun-
cils, provisional governments. They wrote anti-Soviet propaganda
leaflets and magazines, staffed Radio Liberation (later Liberty),
and supplied agent-candidates for CIA operations.

The agents we had been sending into the Soviet Union since
1949 were, for the most part, recent Soviet émigrés, and the
KGB knew broadly where they were being recruited and trained.
It was the aim of both Moscow and Karlshorst to penetrate
émigré circles in the American Zone and insert Soviet-controlled
agents into our Munich operation.

Any emigration is an easy target for the security service of the
home country: the Chinese in Southeast Asia, the Cubans in
Miami, the Palestinians outside Israel. A common language and
cultural outlook, relatives at home, a nostalgia for the old country ease a recruitment approach.

The anti-Soviet emigration in Germany was particularly vulnerable. Most émigré groups were loosely organized, often filled with
political rivalries, and competing for support from the occupation
authorities. In an atmosphere of personal jealousies, professional
gossip, and the fight for physical and political survival, it was

relatively easy for the KGB to hire routine informants, recruit useful agents, or introduce new émigrés under its control.

The work was carried on both out of Moscow and Karlshorst. Moscow specialized in sending out bogus defectors for direct penetration of the American effort.

In one case the Center went to great pains to offer an attractive agent-candidate on a silver platter: a Soviet captain in the role of a legitimate deserter. It invested an entire year in briefing and training him for his mission, including a trip across Russia to places of interest to American intelligence. During his interrogation at the Defector Reception Center near Frankfurt, in supplying the build-up material he had been given, he included, not too awkwardly, suggestions for three safe-drop areas for future American air operations. Neither he nor his suggestions were accepted as legitimate.

Moscow Center's particular concern with the Ukrainian resistance groups was mirrored in the dispatch of another Army officer, a major, purportedly from the Kharkov headquarters. His cover story, detailed and persuasive, as an emissary from an active resistance group in the Ukraine, was designed to have him enlisted by CIA as a link, or at least as a consultant, in its Ukrainian operations. Since our own direct links had given us a reliable view of the situation inside, his story did not hold up.

KGB/Karlshorst had a much simpler job: to recruit émigrés already on the spot. Many of these people were highly vulnerable to Soviet pressure or enticement through their families still in the Soviet Union: some had parents, wives, or even children left behind.

The mechanism itself was an easy and economical routine. A courier from Karlshorst—an émigré on their payroll, an East German, occasionally a Soviet civilian—arrived at an émigré's house or flat and handed him a letter from home; from his mother in Kiev, a sister in Latvia, an old father in a village outside Moscow.

The letter, and the courier's words, carried the same message: if you will work for us against the enemies of the motherland, both you and your family will be rewarded for your cooperation.

Some approaches were more elaborate.

A member of a Soviet athletic team visiting West Germany telephoned a well-known émigré journalist and brought him greetings from his brother in the Soviet Union. He was invited to visit Berlin and had lengthy discussions with KGB officers in the

Karlshorst compound. He was recruited, trained in microdots and photography, and given three assignments: to report on the activities of his émigré friends, to spot and cultivate likely agent-candidates for the KGB, and to penetrate the CIA's operations into the Soviet Union.

His mission (under CIA control throughout) lasted for several years, with personal meetings in Karlshorst three times a year. Since he had the full confidence of his KGB case officer, he was able to identify more than a dozen KGB case officers and give the location of several of their safe houses, as well as feeding them misleading information on the CIA's relations with various émigré groups.

He also, following his instructions, recommended several agent-candidates to the KGB who actually worked for the CIA; to open up another small window on Karlshorst's activities.

Another Karlshorst operation fell into the same trap. A Georgian working for Radio Liberty, one of the KGB's prime targets, agreed to work for the KGB under CIA control, and was regularly visited by an East German courier. Now apparently trusted, he was asked to recommend another Georgian on the radio's staff. The second Georgian was recruited several weeks later and reported back what we wanted Karlshorst to know about the Georgian emigration.

For those who agreed (honestly or with reservations) to help out, the KGB went to great lengths to assure their loyalty. One Ukrainian invited to Karlshorst (with false papers supplied by the courier) to meet his KGB case officer was given the privilege of calling his sister in Kharkov from the telephone in the main conference room of military headquarters. Another prospect was given a conducted tour to visit his relatives in the Soviet Union and to see for himself how much had changed for the better since he had left. Some were flattered on their visits to Karlshorst by the personal attention of impressively senior Soviet officers who underlined the theme of atonement: all will be forgotten if you help us now.

Yet, even in the most pleasant of these confrontations there floated the notion that his family would be punished for a man's refusal to cooperate. In the more obdurate cases the threat was made explicit: no job or food for your family.

Karlshorst's most productive operation reached high up in the NTS (Narodny Trudovoy Soyuz), the People's Labor League, a group of ethnic Russians devoted to the destruction of the Soviet regime by building secret cells within the Soviet Union itself. The NTS was particularly troublesome because of its efforts to contact and recruit Soviet soldiers stationed in East Germany and Soviet officials stationed abroad. It is still active today.

In November 1949 a Soviet Army officer deserted from the Soviet forces in East Germany for love of a German woman and assumed a new German identity. Tracked down by Karlshorst, he was pressured into becoming an agent, for he had a wife and two children in the Soviet Union. He was assigned, among other tasks, to join the NTS. A bright, competent man, he soon became an instructor at an NTS espionage school and a "consultant" to American Army intelligence. He recruited a variety of subagents and passed on his reports to Karlshorst by a German contact, who had been assigned to him.

The KGB's first public blow against the NTS came in May 1953 when the Moscow radio announced that four NTS men who parachuted into the Ukraine a month earlier had been captured and executed. The subsequent security investigation led to the Soviet officer's exposure and arrest.

Both the NTS and the Ukrainian emigration posed the greatest political threat to the Soviet leadership. The most powerful ethnic minority in the Soviet Union, Ukrainian nationalism was deeply rooted in a cultural and linguistic elite. As a border state, the Ukraine was critical to Soviet security, and the devastating impact of the German occupation coupled with large-scale collaboration with the Germans had made it the shakiest area within the Soviet Union. More than forty thousand Ukrainian resistance fighters were still, in the late forties, fighting in the Carpathian Mountains.

Penetrating these two emigrations was clearly not enough for Moscow. The KGB was given the task of killing their leaders.

The Liquidation of Political Opponents

Political murder was a common practice in prerevolutionary Russia for opposition groups other than the Bolsheviks. A terrorist like Boris Savinkov, who was killed in the Trust operation, had at least a dozen assassinations to his credit. Hundreds of czarist officials met their deaths at the hands of terrorists before and after the 1905 Revolution.

Indiscriminate killing of anti-Soviet elements within the Soviet

Union during the Civil War and the wholesale liquidation of anti-Stalinist elements during the thirties were a bloody feature of Soviet rule in the interwar years, but these murders were carried out by the Communist Party and the security services officially and "legally" against their own citizens within the confines of Soviet jurisdiction. The assassination of individual persons living abroad posed the challenge of executing a delicate and demanding secret action operation that would not be traceable to its perpetrators in Moscow.

Moscow's policy of foreign assassinations was highly selective. The only targets, with rare exceptions, were former Soviet citizens. There is no evidence on the record that the KGB has ever been instructed, under Stalin or Khrushchev, to kill a foreign government leader or native politician. No attempt was ever made on Hitler's life, perhaps regrettably, though one cannot say whether this abstention was a matter of principle or simply the inability to find an opportunity.

These former Soviet citizens fall into two categories: activist leaders of the Soviet emigration, and renegades from the official, mainly intelligence, services.

Since the assassination of anyone in a foreign country poses a sensitive political issue for any regime, a separate "Administration of Special Tasks" was established in December 1936 operating directly under the then NKVD chief, Nikolai Yezhov, for obvious security reasons. The efficient functioning of this unit required special equipment and special training for actions not normal to the intelligence mission: sabotage and assassination. The run-of-the-mill intelligence officer does not make a good hit man.

The KGB's liquidation of the regime's enemies abroad has ranged from the brutal to the subtle, from gun and ax murders to the use of exotic poisons. Its most notorious assassination of an émigré leader, that of Leon Trotsky, is one of the least subtle on its record.

Expelled from the Soviet Union in 1929, Trotsky had lived in exile in Turkey, France, and Norway until he found political asylum in Mexico in January 1937. Throughout his exile the KGB had kept close track of his movements, associations, writings, lecture tours, organizing efforts. Its dossier on him filled three floors in Moscow. Its main effort was directed at penetrating Trotsky's entourage.

Jack Soble, a Soviet agent (arrested in New York in 1957),

had become a member of Trotsky's circle in 1931–32 and supplied some of the evidence employed to fabricate a Trotsky plot to assassinate Stalin on May Day, 1936, in the purge trials. Another KGB agent, Mark Zborowski, became a close confidant of Trotsky's son, Lev Sedov, and played a role not only in stealing Trotsky's archives in Paris, but acting as a finger-man for the murder of Trotsky's secretary in Spain, of the secretary of the Fourth International in 1939, and finally of Lev Sedov, who died under suspicious circumstances in a Paris hospital in 1938.

After an attempt on his life in Mexico in January 1938, Trotsky had heavy security provided by his own guards and the Mexican police.

The task of killing him was assigned to a senior KGB official, Leonid Eitingon, an old hand at terrorist work. He had been deputy chief of the KGB in Spain and had worked during World War II with Colonel Abel on "special operations" in Poland and the Baltic states.

The first attempt by Eitingon (under the name of Leonov in Mexico) employed the services of a Mexican communist painter, Siqueiros, in a straight terrorist attack.

On May 23, 1940, Siqueiros, disguised as a Mexican Army major, raided Trotsky's villa with a goon squad of twenty men equipped with submachine guns, incendiaries, and a dynamite bomb. They cut the telephone lines, subdued the Mexican police guards and an American on sentry duty, sprayed the bedrooms with their tommy guns, and left the dynamite bomb—which did not explode. Trotsky escaped with a slight wound in his right leg.

Eitingon's follow-up plan was more subtle. It was designed to work from the inside.

Ramón Mercador, the son of a Spanish communist woman who had worked with Eitingon in the guerrilla operations set up by the KGB in the Spanish Civil War, had been provided with a forged passport under the name of "Jacson." Under the direction of the KGB legal resident in New York, Mercador was accepted in New York's left-wing circles and became friendly with Sylvia Ageloff, a devoted follower of Trotsky whom Mercador had met in Paris. She became his common law wife and through her he gained entrée to Trotsky's household, making several visits to his villa.

On his last visit, on August 20, 1940, he entered Trotsky's study to have him criticize an article he had written. He was equipped with a revolver, a dagger, and a short ice ax in his raincoat pocket (Mercador was a mountain climber). Arrangements had been made for a quick getaway, with his mother in one car around the corner and Eitingon in another a block away.

As Trotsky began to read the article, Mercador crushed his skull with the ice ax. Trotsky did not die at once, and his screams brought in the guards, who seized the assassin. Trotsky died a day later. Mercador spent the next twenty years in prison. Eitingon and Mercador's mother escaped. She was decorated by Stalin himself on her return to Moscow.

Mercador/Jacson never talked. He died recently of cancer in Cuba and, according to his brother in Moscow, was publicly buried in Khrushchev's cemetery with KGB officials in attendance.

By the early fifties, when the KGB resumed its liquidation of émigré politicians, the techniques of murder had become more refined.

Within a few months of Stalin's death, KGB chief Beria gave "wet affairs" two specific assignments directed against the NTS leadership in the summer of 1953. Planning was suspended with Beria's dismissal and execution, and everyone sat tight until the "investigation" of Beria was completed and a new boss might give new orders. Planning began again in September with the choice of candidates for a hit team (in Khrushchev's phrase, "trustworthy combat operatives").

The first of the two operations, the kidnapping of a senior NTS official in Berlin in April 1954, succeeded. The second, the assassination of the NTS operations chief, backfired with global repercussions.

The target was Georgi Sergeevich Okolovich, the man in charge of the NTS's secret operations, who lived in Frankfurt. The designated assassin was Captain Nikolai Khokhlov, an experienced KGB intelligence officer.

Khokhlov and two assistants had been trained in Moscow for the mission, but by the time he arrived in the West he had apparently made up his mind not to go through with it. He visited Okolovich on February 18, 1954, introduced himself, and told him the story of his assignment.

Khokhlov's story, and his description of the Special Bureau (from 1954 the Thirteenth Department of the First Chief Directorate) and its activities, were made public in a press conference he gave on April 22, 1954, a month before I left Munich. Moscow's counter-propaganda could not minimize the enormous impact of his revelations of the KGB as an official Murder Inc.

A target of equal, if not greater, interest to Moscow was Stefan Bandera, the most effective and charismatic of the Ukrainian leaders. Karlshorst made its first attempt to kill Bandera during my Munich tour. It aimed at a simple shooting.

Karlshorst selected a highly suitable assassin: a champion German sharpshooter who toured East Germany competing in local shooting tournaments. A married man with nine children, he was recruited on the promise that his family would be allowed to go to West Germany if he carried out his mission.

He was sent into the Munich area via West Berlin, and in the course of the next six to eight months, he found lodging and a cover job. He was not told his target. Once settled, he was instructed to locate Bandera, who was living under an assumed identity. His only clues were a series of pictures of Bandera taken from a West German illustrated magazine. He finally identified Bandera, and traced him to his address. The sharpshooter's case officer, who kept in touch with him through an East German courier, decided the time had come, supplied him with a high-powered rifle, and gave him the final order to liquidate Bandera.

The sharpshooter's family had been released by degrees as he made progress on his assignment. By the time he was given the go-ahead, his entire family was safely in West Germany. They all disappeared with the help of two CIA case officers who had handled him from the start of the mission.

The KGB persisted and five years later succeeded in killing Bandera.

Among the Karlshorst officers specializing in operations against the Ukrainian émigrés was Bogdan Stashinsky, a native Ukrainian.

Stashinsky began his career against the Ukrainian resistance at home—where he was recruited at the age of eighteen as an informant in his native village to penetrate the local group of Ukrainian nationalists. After building up his cover as a German in East Berlin, he ran several agents in the Ukrainian emigration and focused on collecting information on Lev Rebet, a Ukrainian editor known to be in touch with CIA. In September 1957 Stashinsky was assigned the job of killing Rebet by a "man from Moscow" and the next month killed him.

His next assignment was to locate and kill Bandera, still living in Munich under an assumed identity. In October 1959 Stashinsky killed Bandera inside the apartment house where he lived.

After being given the Order of the Red Banner by KGB chief Shelepin for his deed, Stashinsky was assigned to Moscow for further training, and was given reluctant permission in April 1960 to marry an East German girl with whom he had fallen in love. Assigned to the Second Chief Directorate, he saw no prospect of fleeing to the West as his wife urged him, but he was permitted to fly to Berlin to attend the funeral of his child. Although his wife had been under constant KGB surveillance for fear she would talk about her husband's work, and Stashinsky was kept under equally close surveillance during his visit, the two managed to run away from the funeral into West Berlin and turned themselves in to the German police.

The murders of Rebet and Bandera displayed the technology of scientific socialism at its most advanced stage. The ideal murder is one in which there is no evidence that a man has been murdered or, even if the fact of murder is clear, the means of killing is a mystery. The Laboratory of Special Weapons in the KGB headquarters had devoted considerable effort to achieve the perfect murder—by a gas gun.

In the case of Rebet the semblance of no-murder was achieved. He was killed by a spray of prussic acid released by a seven-inch-long noiseless "pistol." The inhaled gas had the same effect as sniffing glue—the contraction of the blood vessels. Rebet's heart simply stopped, and his death was officially ascribed to a heart attack.

Bandera was killed by the same method, but a careful autopsy by the German authorities detected traces of prussic acid in his stomach. The fact of murder was clear, but there was at the time no clue to the murderer.

Khokhlov's weapon for the aborted murder of Okolovich was equally advanced. He was supplied with a noiseless pistol concealed in a cigarette case that fired poisoned bullets that were effective within a range of ten or twenty yards.

With all its scientific expertise the KGB failed in the most obvious requirement for a successful assassination: the reliability of the assassin. Both Khokhlov and Stashinsky were intelligence officers who were abruptly ordered to kill. Both men had strong human reservations about committing a cold-blooded murder. Both men confided in their wives. Both wives urged their husbands not to continue in the KGB.

Their KGB superiors clearly equated their proved competence and discipline with their willingness to do *anything*. They failed to allow for the human variable, to accept the fact of the individual conscience.

Stashinsky's trial by the Germans in October 1962 became a worldwide sensation. It advertised Moscow's willingness and ability to go to any lengths to neutralize its political opponents abroad. The technical expertise reflected by the murder weapon added overtones of shock and perverse admiration. The amorality of the Soviet regime was there for all to see.

It was a severe blow to the Soviet image, and Khrushchev apparently decided that the political price of an exposed assassination was too great to pay.

There is no evidence I know of that the KGB has been instructed to murder anyone abroad since 1962. Negative evidence in secret operations cannot be conclusive, but on balance Moscow's urge to project a civilized image during the sixties and seventies and the natural thinning of the émigré ranks would appear to have made the "wet affairs" squad unacceptable as a political tool.

Émigrés and resistance groups in a police state have nowhere to go unless they act in conjunction with an advancing army that eventually links up with them. Since Allied forces in Western Europe had no plans to invade Eastern Europe, Washington's liberation rhetoric was not matched by liberating actions even when the workers revolted in East Germany in 1953. The émigré threat was finally dissipated when the West failed to come to the support of the Hungarian freedom fighters in 1956.

Today émigrés are just another reservoir for recruiting agents to operate against the countries they now reside in. They are attractive because of their national origin, (often) their language, and for any ties they may still have in their native countries. Since but few have achieved positions in government or industry that give them access to classified material, they are mainly useful as support agents—to talk to a relative in government, to make an introduction, to service a dead drop or act as a letter box.

Renegades

Moscow's intense concern over Soviet intelligence "defectors" rested, and still rests, on a two-fold anxiety. A KGB or GRU defector is in a position to provide Western services with vital information on the operations of Soviet intelligence—as well as the inside facts of Soviet life so useful to anti-Soviet propagandists. Perhaps even more important is the discouragement of further defections. If a KGB officer walks out of his service to seek asylum in the West, he must be taught a lesson: you will pay the price of treason. This lesson will not be lost on his colleagues.

During Stalin's purges of the late thirties, the ranks of both the KGB and the GRU in Moscow were decimated, but Stalin faced the challenge of luring their residents abroad to come home in order to be liquidated.

In June 1937, anticipating the problem, Stalin had a law passed subjecting the close relatives of any "non-returner" to exile in Siberia even if they knew nothing about his intention to defect. A KGB administrative decree subjected the close relatives of any KGB officer who defected to a ten-year prison term. If the officer disclosed any state secrets after his defection, his relatives were liable to execution.

The members of the Foreign Department posed a unique problem. If they got wind of the purge, they might be inclined not to return to Moscow. The word was spread that the Foreign Department would not be purged, and its chief in Moscow was left in his job to support the rumor.

Many case officers returned to Moscow when they were ordered, but the most skeptical refused. Their skepticism was reinforced by the word that came to the field that the KGB resident in France (Nikolai Smirnov), who had returned in the summer of 1937, had been executed. As his fate became known (the KGB residents were understandably most alert to the goings-on in Moscow), NKVD chief Yezhov spread the story that Smirnov had been a French and Polish agent. Since Smirnov's agent net in Paris continued to operate and the codes for the Paris–Moscow traffic were not changed, this was an obvious lie.

During the summer of 1937 about forty KGB officers were recalled from their foreign posts. Only five refused to return in the face of the threat to their families.

Two renegades who made press headlines were shot.

Ignace Reiss, a wide-ranging illegal in Europe, broke openly with Moscow in July 1937, sending a letter to the Soviet Embassy in Paris announcing his break with Stalin and urging a return to "freedom—back to Lenin, to his teachings and his cause." Stalin ordered the killing of Reiss, his wife, and child as a warning to any of his colleagues who might decide to defect.

A "mobile group," or hit squad, was sent to Switzerland and discovered his hiding place from a woman friend of the Reiss family, an old-time KGB agent who had become a confidante of Reiss. She helped the hit man, an old-time illegal by the name of Abbiate, lure Reiss into a car trip outside Lausanne. Abbiate sat in front with Reiss, the woman in the back seat. He pulled the car over to the side of the road and emptied his pistol into Reiss. Reiss's body was found on September 4.

The hit squad and the woman fled in haste, leaving their luggage at a local hotel. In it was found a box of chocolates poisoned with strychnine intended for Reiss and/or his child.

Reiss was killed so promptly that he had no time to write the anti-Stalinist memoir he had planned. He did have time for an interview with Sedov, Trotsky's son, that was later published.

One of his colleagues, Walter Krivitsky, the resident in Holland, had more time. He broke with Moscow a few months later and sought political asylum in Paris. Another hit team was dispatched to Paris to murder Krivitsky, his wife, and son, but the public intervention of the French Government saved him— for the time being. The kidnapping of a White Russian General Miller from a Paris suburb in late September 1937 had caused a wave of public indignation, and Moscow was warned not to add a murder to their Paris record.

Krivitsky had time to write his memoirs, but he was found shot to death in a Washington hotel room in 1941. Suicide? Murder? By whom?

It is in the light of this tradition that the next crop of KGB defectors in 1953 was handled with the utmost security precautions by British, American, Canadian, and Australian security services. Each defector was given a secret location for interrogation and resettled with a new identity and a means of livelihood.

The KGB has failed to exact retribution on any of the postwar intelligence defectors. Men such as Gouzenko, several post-Beria defectors of 1954, and several more in the early sixties survive to this day. The care taken by Western security services to "bury" them must have played a role, but Moscow's political sensibilities did as well.

One defector barely escaped retaliation. After his news conference in 1954, Nikolai Khokhlov lectured openly for years on the evils of the Soviet regime. Apparently the KGB had had enough. In September 1957, while Khokhlov was attending a convention in Frankfurt, Germany, he became deathly ill. His condition was finally diagnosed as the effect of poisoning by radioactive thallium, another brilliant invention of the Special Laboratory. With the help of American specialists Khokhlov survived.

Highly refined techniques of murder may seem "ridiculously sophisticated" (in Khokhlov's words), but they served two KGB purposes: to show up, or at least confuse, the Western police and security services that investigate the deaths, and to impress other Soviet émigrés and defectors with the mysterious and subtle ways in which Moscow might engineer their end.

In the bloody history of the KGB's "wet affairs," there have been aberrations. There is no question that the kidnapping and murder of prominent émigrés or defectors required authorization from the top leadership. No bureaucracy works like clockwork, and I will cite two cases where the chain of command faltered.

Dr. Walter Linse, head of the Association of Free German Jurists, was kidnapped in West Berlin on July 8, 1952. It was a messy and noisy job. Linse fought his abductors on the street until one of them put a bullet through his leg. Neighbors saw the abduction in progress, and a truck driver chased the car to an entrance into the Soviet sector. Official American protests followed. The Soviet Commissioner had to lie.

The Linse kidnapping, it emerged later, had not been authorized by the Center. KGB/Karlshorst simply sent a message to Moscow to get its approval for taking action (unspecified) against Linse, who was a thorn in their propaganda side.

The KGB chief was called on the carpet to explain, and one of his subordinates wrote up a bland report admitting that something went wrong, but that after all the operation had been a "success" and no one had been hurt. It was a clear case of lack of discipline, but bureaucrats can cover up in Moscow as well as in Washington.

The second aberration was more serious. It involved a foreigner and violated Khrushchev's ban on assassination. It occurred when Khrushchev was out of town, and the Second Chief Directorate was clearly acting on its own.

At the time when Khrushchev was trying to work out a trade agreement with Bonn, in September 1964, Bonn sent Horst Schwirkmann, a counter-audio or debugging expert, to sweep the German Embassy in Moscow. He uncovered microphone after microphone, including a broadcast mike in the code room.

On a quiet Sunday morning Schwirkmann was sightseeing at a monastery outside Moscow when he suddenly felt an intense pain in his buttocks. It turned out that he had been injected with a nitrogen mustard gas that almost took his life.

There is little question that the KGB (Second Chief Directorate) had taken this action at some level without getting Party authorization. It was a stupid move, and the Soviet Government apologized for the act more than a month later—on the day, October 14, when Khrushchev came back from vacation and was fired by his colleagues.

It is perhaps fitting that the most Stalinist of the East European regimes recently revived the practice of assassination.

Georgi Markov, a famous writer and natural rebel, defected from Bulgaria in 1969 and found a place on the Bulgarian desk of the BBC. He also gave weekly talks on Radio Free Europe on life at the top in Bulgaria. His personal and inside knowledge of the Communist Party and government elite obviously hit a sensitive spot. In September 1978 he was jabbed in the thigh at a bus stop, developed a high fever, and died of heart failure.

Ten days before the attack on Markov, another Bulgarian, Vladimir Kostov, who worked for Radio Free Europe, felt a sharp pain in his back and developed a high fever for three days—which he overcame.

In both cases the poison had been introduced by a small pellet no bigger than a pinhead made of a rare platinum alloy with four miniature indentations to hold the poison (an extract from the castor oil plant) that led to cardiovascular collapse. It was seventy times as potent as the same amount of cyanide used by Stashinsky in killing Bandera in 1959.

The decision to kill these men was clearly made at the top Party level in Sofia and not at the whim of the intelligence service. Bulgarian intelligence has always had an émigré section and an adviser from the KGB in the front office. It has several murders on its record, from that of a Bulgarian rocket technician in Vienna to the editor of an émigré newspaper found dead in 1974. These actions must have had the approval of the KGB and its cooperation as well in supplying the refined techniques of poison-killing.

ON LEE HARVEY OSWALD

Although the events leading to President Kennedy's assassination promise to remain controversial issues for decades to come, it might be useful to examine Oswald's role from the perspective of the KGB.

Only a small fringe of conspiratorialists still ascribe the President's murder to Moscow. Their arguments violate both political and professional common sense.

Moscow has never, so far as we know, ordered the assassination of a native political leader in a foreign country. Nor has any even faintly persuasive scenario been devised by specialists in political fantasy to explain Khrushchev's motives for embarking on such a hazardous undertaking.

If the KGB had been given the assignment of killing President Kennedy, Oswald would not have been their assassin—an American repatriate on record in American security files. In such an enormously delicate operation the KGB would have found a totally anonymous assassin whose identity could not be traced; a highly trained and tested killer who could be relied upon not to bungle the job; and a careful operational plan focused on practical opportunities and a reasonable chance for escape.

A still unclarified incident relating to this problem was the defection of an officer of the Second Chief Directorate (Internal Security), Yuri Nosenko, who offered himself to the Americans in Switzerland in June 1964. He had, he asserted, read through the file on Oswald in the Soviet Union, and maintained in effect that the KGB had nothing to do with the assassination. There were many grounds for suspicion in his overall story, ranging from outright lies about the KGB and his own role in it to countless errors of fact and areas of ignorance. It was decided by most of his interrogators that Nosenko has been sent out by the KGB as a bogus defector for the purpose, among others, of dispelling American suspicions that Oswald was their hired killer. If the Soviets sent Nosenko to us with an avowel of their non-complicity in the Kennedy assassination, was it because they really had nothing to do with it or because they did?

The issue of Nosenko's bona fides remains controversial among professional intelligence men to this day. The arguments are complex on both sides, but the following perspectives are pertinent.

I know of no previous or subsequent example of a senior KGB intelligence officer being delivered to the West to carry out a deception mission. This is understandable, for it is a high-risk enterprise. Once the KGB loses control of its man, anything may happen: What will he say? Only what he is told to? What does he give away from his past career? Why will he not make the best of staying in the West by telling everything he knows—including the bogus nature of his mission?

The KGB knows that the Western services have wide resources to check out all aspects of any misleading information a defector might bring along. However much true and useful build-up data the KGB gives him, what other sources are available to check out and isolate his false information? The KGB does not know.

To assume that the KGB will "give away" one of their own officers for whatever purpose requires that we ascribe to it a gamble that flouts the record of its caution.

Furthermore, the grounds for suspicion in Nosenko's story can equally well be cited as proof of his bona fides. Would the KGB send a man on a unique high-level mission so badly prepared to handle his anticipated interrogation? Nosenko's lies and errors were, in my opinion, most likely due to his understandable urge to exaggerate his own importance and range of knowledge, his only asset in the West.

By any measure, he would have been an extraordinarily bad plant.

It can be assumed that the assassination of President Kennedy caused real anxiety in the Politburo: the President killed by a man who had recently resided in the Soviet Union. Had Khrushchev anticipated a hysterical American reaction inflamed by charges of Soviet complicity, he had other means than sending out a bogus defector to take off the heat. The KGB could have used its global inventory of agents and channels to let the British and Americans know, directly and indirectly, that Oswald was not its man.

Only slightly less realistic than a KGB association with the President's murder is the notion that Oswald was recruited by the KGB before he left the Soviet Union to carry out an intelligence mission (always unspecified) in the States.

Was Oswald a KGB agent?

Here again it is easy to underrate the professional competence of the KGB.

The recruitment of Oswald for a mission, any mission, in the United States makes little sense either from an intelligence or from a security point of view. Here is an American, psychologically unstable at best, whose behavior has brought him to the attention of the American Embassy in Moscow, Western journalists, and the Federal Bureau of Investigation. He is, even before his return to his native country, a conspicuous person. He is, of course, suspect to the FBI simply as a man who has lived in the Soviet Union for several years. He is married to a Russian woman. The KGB would assume (incorrectly) that he would be carefully interrogated on his return, and that his Russian wife would add to American suspicions.

Even if there were no security drawbacks, there are no conceivable intelligence benefits from an agent like Oswald—a loner, a neurotic, a man with no friends or organizational affiliations that might make him a useful source for classified information of any sort.

There is nothing in Oswald's behavior after his return to the United States to indicate that he was acting under Soviet tutelage. His erratic behavior with various Cuban groups, his visit to Mexico City, his letter to the FBI about the harassment of his wife do not reflect the actions of a recruited agent. In any event, there is no evidence that the KGB recruited and trained him during his stay in the Soviet Union, no evidence that he was given a legend, or cover story, no evidence that the KGB tried to resume contact with him after his return to the United States or had any plans to do so.

Hundreds of questions remain open on the "Oswald case," but the search for a conspiracy is unlikely to be advanced even by an opening up of the KGB files in Moscow.

VII

THE THIRD MAN
AND OTHER
TRAITORS

Like any service, the KGB wants to recruit agents already in positions that will yield an immediate payoff: a Defense Ministry official or a Foreign Service officer. It is, however, unique among modern services in that it makes investments in gifted young men with a promising future and "grows" them into place by guiding their careers and steering them into sensitive positions. Its greatest return on a long-term investment came out of the recruitment of at least five young Britons at Cambridge University in the early thirties. Among them was H. A. R. ("Kim") Philby, the most notorious Soviet spy of his generation.

From those of us, American and British alike, who were occupied with operations against the Soviet Union in the early days of the Cold War, the name and face of Kim Philby are bound to elicit highly mixed reactions. Here was a highly competent colleague close to the heart of British operations, a man who in London and Washington worked closely with his American counterparts and betrayed to the KGB every secret that came into his possession. He destroyed Allied operations before they were started. He protected Soviet agents from exposure. He gave the KGB an inside picture of the Allied intelligence establishment in a crucial phase of the East-West conflict. The damage he did is incalculable.

Yet, as an agent for "the other side" for over twenty years, his performance was brilliant. He played his double role without a slip. Sober or drunk, he was always the man we thought we knew. A professional to his fingertips, he exercised his talents against us with quiet efficiency. He made hundreds of secret meetings and serviced countless dead drops—in Vienna, Spain, London, Istanbul, Washington—and not one was observed at the time. He did what he did, like it or not, for his cause, not ours.

I lunched several times with Philby during my Washington tour. These were routine lunches with an affable Britisher who was our liaison to London. My official contacts with Philby were, in retrospect, more lethal. He attended several British-American meetings to coordinate our respective operations into the Soviet Union and to prevent any confusion or overlap in our air-dispatch of agents into the Baltic states and the Ukraine.

The meeting I now recall most clearly dealt with operations into Lithuania. Philby sat at one corner of the conference table flanked by the British Soviet experts from London. At one point I raised the question: Can we determine whether or not the British agents then reporting by radio from Lithuania were under KGB control? Philby did not offer an opinion in the ensuing discussion.

The immediate events that led to his exposure occured before I left Washington for Munich in May 1952. Precisely one year earlier two British officials, Guy Burgess and Donald Maclean, crossed the English Channel and vanished into thin air. Maclean had been scheduled for interrogation the following Monday as a suspected leak to the Russians. Their flight caused a worldwide sensation—and speculation: someone must have warned them. The search for the Third Man was on, but it was not until 1963 when Philby found safe haven in Moscow that the public learned of the KGB's most talented postwar agent in the heart of the Western establishment.

The Cambridge Trio

The KGB reaped its richest harvest of "ideological" recruits among the undergraduates at Cambridge University in the early thirties. At least five became Soviet agents, and the story of their exposure covers almost thirty years. Dr. Alan Nunn May was the first to be caught in the Canadian spy case. Burgess and Maclean fled to Moscow in 1951; Philby, in 1963. A year later Sir Anthony Blunt (now deknighted) confessed to the British authorities to being a Soviet agent during and after the war, though he was not publicly named until 1979.

The three men whose careers were most productive for Moscow were Philby, Maclean, and Burgess. Each was recruited independently and each was handled separately by KGB officers throughout their careers: the Cambridge trio was not a net.

All three joined the Communist Party of Great Britain in their college days at Cambridge University, Burgess and Maclean as open members, Philby as a member of a secret cell. Philby went up to Cambridge in October 1929, Burgess in 1930, Maclean in 1931. In April 1931 David Guest, back from a sabbatical year in Germany where he had seen Nazi brutality at close hand and spent some time in a German prison, started a Cambridge University Party cell.

Communism had become popular among the British intellectuals in the early thirties. Some of the most brilliant scientists, writers, and academics joined the Party or worked closely with it. The best minds were Marxists; some flirted with the Party as a phase of political maturing, and later became respectable figures in the establishment. Others were totally committed for life: some were killed in Spain, others became leading members of the British Party, a few became publicly "disillusioned" but kept their faith.

Philby was always quiet about his politics, and did no political writing. Maclean wrote openly about "the whole crack-brained criminal mess" of capitalist society, and talked about going to Russia to help the Revolution. He changed his mind and opted for a career in the British Foreign Office. Burgess, a professed homosexual, heavy drinker, and brilliant conversationalist, flaunted his communism, visited Russia in 1934, and came back "disillusioned": he resigned from the Party.

All three, now clean and respectable, were to wind through the heart of the British foreign affairs establishment for the next twenty years: Maclean as a first-class Foreign Service officer until he collapsed from drink in Cairo in 1950; Burgess as a hard-drinking clown with high-level connections in London; the

steady, imperturbable Philby as a journalist and a senior member
of British intelligence for the seven years from 1944 to 1951.

Philby's Career

Unlike Burgess and Maclean, who became open members of
the Communist Party, Philby must have been spotted from the
start as a highly eligible candidate by either a local Party official
or a KGB contact from London. He spent his first year after
graduation in Vienna, and it was here, probably, if not at Cambridge, that he was recruited by the KGB through the good
offices of his new bride, an Austrian communist. From then on
his career was guided by the KGB: his shift of political coloration to a pro-Nazi sympathizer and his assignment as a journalist
on the Franco side of the Spanish Civil War must certainly have
been their idea. It was during his assignment with the British
forces in Europe that he was instructed, according to Philby, to
direct his efforts toward getting a job in the British Secret Service. He succeeded within a year.

By that time he had become a professional KGB agent trained
in secret communications. His meetings with his Soviet case
officers in France, Germany, and London—and later in Istanbul
and Washington—went unnoticed by others. There is no clear evidence of who handled him or who arranged his escape. The only
equipment that he needed throughout his career was a small camera and a strong light—and when his career was about to come
to an end on his Washington tour, he buried his camera and tripod on a wooded hill near the Potomac.

In 1945, before the war in Europe had ended, Philby got his
first prize assignment for the KGB: as head of the newly formed
Section IX directing and coordinating British operations into the
Soviet Union, against Soviet intelligence abroad, and against the
major Communist parties in Europe. Even the existence of this
section directed against their Soviet ally was considered top secret. Ironically, when Philby became its head, the Chief of the
British Service reportedly instructed him to stay clear of any connections with the Americans, who might leak the news to the
Russians.

During Philby's two years in Section IX, Moscow not only
monitored the beginnings of the discreet British efforts against

the Soviet target—a matter of some political significance—but also the identity and personality of British intelligence officers, a closeup view of its file system and office procedures (with samples), its budget and table of organization. All these homely internal details provided the KGB with a sense of intimacy and understanding—for future operations, for interrogating British agents and defectors, for protecting their own activities in London. Once he became the senior British counterespionage officer, Philby also sat astride the anti-Soviet security work of the domestic service, MI5, and maintained close contact with his "opposite number," Roger Hollis. His berth on the Joint Intelligence subcommittee on communist affairs enlarged even further Philby's reach in the British intelligence community.

Yet Section IX was only the core of Philby's take on the British service.

Any senior bureaucrat, corporate or governmental, has indirect access to many sectors of his organization's work beyond his own precise function. The compartmentation at the lower working levels of a secret service is never matched by a "need to know" restraint at the upper policy levels.

Philby's unwitting sources were innumerable: members of committee meetings exchanging facts and views on their sectors of interest; colleagues and friends exchanging shop-talk at relaxed luncheons; retailers of bureaucratic gossip about rivalries with MI5 or the Foreign Office. Facts and opinions alike are grist to an alert agent's mill.

More concretely Philby could, and did, use the central files. He had the habit of requesting from the Registry specific files outside his immediate area of responsibility—whether under Soviet instruction or his own keen sense of matters "of interest," is not known. He was to worry about this in the later investigation since the check-out lists could provide tell-tale evidence of his non-professional curiosity.

His access went even further than British intelligence matters, for across the desk of any senior official in any foreign affairs bureaucracy come memoranda and policy papers from other agencies. Philby had access to hundreds of classified documents from the Foreign Office, the War Office, the Admiralty, and the Cabinet secretariat. Add to these sources his friendships and conversations with senior officials from these ministries, and his value as a political source for Moscow becomes apparent.

Philby also served a protective function. Both from his own

shop and from his necessarily close liaison with MI5, he was in a position to warn Moscow of any threat to their operations both on the Continent and in the United Kingdom: of impending arrests or active investigations of Soviet suspects, about the details in their files or their interrogations, on Soviet agents doubled by the British.

His most valuable service—both to himself and the KGB—came in the Volkov affair.

In August 1945, while Philby was in charge of the counterespionage desk in London, Konstantin Volkov approached the British consulate in Istanbul with a request for political asylum. He identified himself as a KGB officer under cover as a Soviet vice-consul, and proposed to provide the British with secret information on KGB operations. As proof of his identity and evidence of his inside information, he supplied his British contact with written reports on KGB agents operating in the West.

Among these agents he included three agents in Britain, two in the Foreign Office and one in British intelligence, whom he did not identify by name. He also warned that the British diplomatic code had been broken by Moscow.

The report, pouched to London, naturally came to Philby's desk for action. The one man in London who knew that the three agents Volkov mentioned were Maclean, Burgess, and himself was assigned to handle the case. He naturally informed his KGB contact in London that night of the Volkov approach, and arranged to handle Volkov personally. By the time he reached Istanbul to interview Volkov, after several contrived delays, Volkov had been forcibly returned to Moscow. It was Philby's closest call.

In 1947 Philby was considered ripe for a field assignment and became chief of station in Istanbul. In his memoirs he talks vaguely about operations into the Balkans and across the eastern frontier into Soviet Georgia. What he learned here of Turkish or American operations into both areas we do not know, but however marginal his knowledge, Moscow at least had an on-the-spot observer in this southern base for anti-Soviet operations.

It was with his Washington assignment as British liaison officer to the CIA that Philby reached the apex of his KGB career both as a counterespionage and as a political agent.

Official Washington was a lively and intimidating bureaucratic scene for Moscow. The Cold War had been heightened by the Korean War, and Washington "politics" became a serious focus for the KGB. The Central Intelligence Agency had become not only an anti-Soviet and anti-communist espionage outfit, but since 1949 the instrument for carrying out covert-action operations—against Poland and Albania, as well as against the French and Italian Communist parties. It was still sending agents into the Soviet Union, beefing up its radio transmissions and propaganda operations, supporting the anti-Soviet emigration—the center of the Western conspiracy to weaken the Soviet state.

The CIA was the threat abroad—and the FBI at home. It was a peak period of the spy scandals, with the FBI hard at work gathering evidence against the Rosenbergs and following up the leads supplied by Harry Gold. The KGB's prime agent at Los Alamos, Dr. Klaus Fuchs, they learned from Philby, was under suspicion. In addition, KGB officials in New York and Washington were under close surveillance.

Philby was able to help the KGB in both cases. As liaison man with the CIA, in constant intercourse with CIA division and desk chiefs across the geographical board, in close collaboration on matters of joint interest with the counterintelligence staff, in occasional meetings with the CIA director and his senior subordinates on both the intelligence analysis and secret operations side, countless CIA secrets came his way, both official matters of joint interest to the SIS, and unofficial shop-talk over lunch and cocktails with his American colleagues.

The KGB's main targets were obviously CIA operations into the "Soviet orbit," as we then called it, the same kind of anti-Soviet actions Philby had reported on as head of Section IX in the early days. Moscow could now read the cable and pouch communications between Washington and London, reports on Washington committee meetings, background notes to Philby on actions being taken in London, mutual requests for traces, and the progress of joint investigations. He was able to provide such basic data as CIA organization and personalities, as well as specimens of its letterheads, memorandum styles, and signatures.

What Philby passed, and how, is not known. He had a camera and tripod in his house for photographing the documents he took home at night, and he handed over the microfilms—directly to his case officer in quiet meetings in the Maryland or Virginia suburbs, or placed his cassettes in a convenient dead drop. All we can see clearly is what he had access to.

Though Philby's production on British and American secret

operations was the core of his work, his value as a political source to Moscow cannot be overestimated.

The major payoff of a political source comes when he can report the intentions of the other side during events of great moment. As first secretary in the British Embassy, as a bright, personable, and politically astute member of the diplomatic community, Philby mixed socially with senior members of the American establishment, and with the diplomats of other nations equally interested in Washington's military and political plans and foreign aid decisions. He could also report on the temper of Congress and policy conflicts in the White House and the Department of State.

Of greatest interest to Moscow, however, was the fact that both Philby's assignment in Washington and Maclean's position on the American desk of the British Foreign Office in London straddled the outbreak of the Korean War. No agent, even at the highest levels in Washington, could have warned Moscow of President Truman's overnight decision to intervene, but both men were in a position to report on the fateful decisions of that fall— to counterattack, to reach the Yalu, not to "roll back." Since Moscow was presumably in close touch with Peking in the fall of 1950, Stalin's intelligence grasp of the Korean situation reached into the two key capitals.

All of this political reporting, passed orally to his case officer or summarized in written memoranda, may have been confusing to Moscow (as it was in Washington), but Philby's expert judgments and evaluations à la Sorge in Tokyo would have made these crucial events plainer for the American desk of the KGB and the Politburo staffers in the Central Committee.

With his excellent sources, Philby was again able, in Washington as in London, to monitor Allied counterespionage efforts against several valuable Soviet agents—including himself. He kept Moscow informed of the progress made by the FBI and MI5 in investigating a leak from the Los Alamos atomic installation. Although the trail got closer and closer to Dr. Fuchs, there was apparently nothing the KGB could do to save their man without imperiling Philby.

Philby was more successful in saving himself and Maclean.

Maclean's greatest contribution to the KGB came during his tour in Washington when he was for a time the secretary of the Combined Policy Committee (the United States, the United Kingdom, and Canada) dealing with nontechnical aspects of the atomic energy program such as the availability of and requirements for uranium ore. He also had—against the rules—a no-escort pass to the headquarters of the Atomic Energy Commission, which he visited fairly often after office hours.

Before leaving London for his Washington assignment, Philby had been briefed on a highly confidential investigation of a leak from the British Embassy in Washington sometime in 1945–46. Again, as in the case of Dr. Fuchs, he saw the list of possible suspects (including clerical and housekeeping employees of the embassy) gradually narrow down to the point where the prime suspect was Maclean, who was then in England recovering from an alcoholic breakdown in Cairo. Maclean had to be warned.

The denouement reads like a spy story.

Burgess, who had been assigned as first secretary to the Washington embassy in August 1950 and lived for a time with Philby, became his courier. Still the controlled drunk, Burgess managed to have several run-ins with the Virginia police, and was sent back to London, where he arrived, via the *Queen Mary,* on May 7, 1951.

A week later, on the weekend before Maclean was scheduled for interrogation, the two men boarded a Channel steamer: Burgess' decision to join him in his flight appears to have been at the last minute, presumably but not certainly at the KGB's direction.

Philby was recalled from Washington the next month. The evidence against him was circumstantial—his close association with Burgess, his remote connection with Maclean, an old report that had been unearthed implying some sort of Communist Party connection during his stay in Spain. Philby, sure of his ability to handle the "evidence" against him, withstood the genteel interrogation of his colleagues. Asked to resign, he was on his own for two years until he became a correspondent for the *Observer* in Beirut, Lebanon. What tasks he performed for the SIS or the KGB during these years is not known, but when he was again questioned in January 1963, he made a partial confession, stalled for time, and then escaped to the Soviet Union on January 23, 1963. He now works there as a "consultant," and in July 1980 was awarded the highest Soviet decoration available for foreign citizens.

Why?

With the Third Man now in the open, the public query shifted from Who to Why. Why would a well-born and educated member of the British establishment work for the Russians—against his own country, of course, but more significantly against his own class?

After his exposure Philby's psyche became the object of wholesale comment and analysis unique in the history of espionage. The press (naturally), his former friends and associates, amateur and professional psychologists, and Western intelligence services all speculated on the deep-seated motives that carried him through almost thirty years of his brilliant dual life. His "alienation" from class and country were attributed to the model of his loner-expatriate father or to the inadequacies of the father-son relationship; to an incurable and immature urge for romance and adventure; to "the self-hate of a vain misfit" or "mad idealism"; to character flaws ranging from a natural rebelliousness to an instinct for deception to sexual ambivalence. As Philby noted in his book written in Moscow,* "Explanations of extraordinary silliness were offered in preference to the obvious simple truth."

My Silent War, though a KGB-sponsored effort to sharpen American suspicion of their British allies, includes his own analysis of his motives which I am inclined to take as genuine—insofar as any man can recall precisely his earlier states of mind.

The simple truth was that Philby had become a convinced communist in his Cambridge days and had never faltered in his faith. He left Cambridge in 1933 "with the conviction that my life must be devoted to Communism," and he kept to that conviction in the face of the ugliest features of Stalinism "in the confident faith that the principles of the Revolution would outlive the aberration of individuals, however enormous."

A political animal from his adolescent years, Philby was an intellectual in the true sense of the term: a man who thought for himself, who arrived at his convictions by reading, and thinking, by observing and arguing, who sought "the truth" above the limitations of class and nation. He sought and found his own Absolute.

Philby came to Cambridge already dedicated to the socialist formula for society: capitalism was clearly breaking down in the Great Depression, and social injustice was visible in breadlines and hunger marches. His transition from the Cambridge University Socialist Society to the communist formula came from his disillusionment with the British Labour Party: ". . . the real

* *My Silent War* (New York, 1968).

turning point in my thinking came with the demoralization and rout of the Labour Party in 1931." And he began to question "the validity of the assumptions underlying parliamentary democracy."

His conversion to the communist faith was "a slow and brain-racking process" that lasted two years. Though gradual, it was complete and enduring, and he spent his life in the service of his cause. His KGB career he characterized as a "struggle against reaction."

Other intellectuals have documented the intensity of emotion and thought that can accompany the conversion to revolutionary Marxism.

Arthur Koestler became a communist in 1931 at the age of twenty-six (he left the Party in 1939). After reading Marx, Engels, and Lenin, something clicked in his brain and shook him "like a mental explosion."

> To say that one had "seen the light" is a poor description of the mental rapture which only the convert knows. . . . The new light seems to pour from all directions across the skull; the whole universe falls into pattern like the stray pieces of a jigsaw puzzle assembled by magic at one stroke. There is now an answer to every question, doubts and conflicts are a matter of the tortured past. . . . Nothing henceforth can disturb the convert's inner peace and serenity—except the occasional fear of losing faith again, losing thereby what alone makes life worth living.

When Whittaker Chambers, equally an intellectual, joined the Party, it made him "happy and healthy with a feeling of singular well-being." He had achieved an "organic attitude toward life." In explaining the appeal of Marxist-Leninist doctrine he so much admired among the radical Jewish students he met at Columbia, he not only stressed its theoretical appeal as an explanation of the Depression, but its emotional appeal as "a program for action. The very vigor of the project particularly appeals to the more or less sheltered middle-class intellectuals, who feel that there the whole context of their lives has kept them away from the world of reality."

In his confession Dr. Fuchs underlined a theoretical appeal that was also a formula for self-fulfillment:

The idea which gripped me most was the belief that in the past man has been unable to understand his own history and the forces which lead to the further development of society; that now for the first time man understands the forces of history and he is able to control them and that therefore for the first time he will be really free. I carried this idea over to the personal sphere and believed that I could understand myself and that I could make myself into what I believed I should be.

The road to Moscow started for all four men in their twenties. They were "born again" into a faith that gave meaning and purpose to their lives.

It is easy for a non-communist to underrate the appeal of Marxist ideas or Party membership to the Western intellectuals of the thirties. But for them, and for many today, Marxism provides a religious faith that gives meaning to life and history. It offers a man a Bible in the writings of Marx and Lenin and a humanitarian ideal of an earthly paradise, however unrealistic (like all paradises). The Party gives him a church, where he is part of a community of true believers working toward an end beyond their narrow egos. And, for those, educated and uneducated alike, who need a "devil," it provides the capitalist system as a focus for their frustration and a channel for their hatred.

For radical and impatient temperaments, the Party offers action and the conspiratorial satisfactions that come out of any secret or semisecret organization. Yet it is the doctrine that counts most, the higher principles to which a man dedicates his life. In the late forties I extracted an exuberant, and clearly sincere, excerpt from a speech of welcome made by the director of a GRU training school to a new class of trainees: "A nation without a doctrine is a nation which has nothing. . . . There is nothing more beautiful, more wonderful, more sublime, and more just than the Communist doctrine. . . . It is more powerful than nationality or race. . . ."

This quasi-religious appeal was fortified in the thirties, both in England and the United States, by the hard facts of political and economic life. In both countries the Marxist critique of the capitalist system was documented in the streets. In America there were more than ten million unemployed, with breadlines, soup kitchens, hobo camps, bonus marchers, foreclosed mortgages, bankrupt bankers. The social structure of society was collapsing.

Businessmen and bankers sought a formula for reform within the system; the radical Marxists sought a restructuring of the system. Even the New Deal reformation of the system could not stave off a recession in 1937 which left seven million unemployed.

European politics intensified the communist appeal to men of goodwill—to liberals and radicals alike. Hitler became Chancellor of Germany in 1933, and the menace of fascism became focused on the Spanish Civil War that broke out two years later. In Spain, for those who were interested, the polar opposites were fixed: Communism versus Fascism. It was an either/or choice propagated by Moscow, the Communist parties, and independent intellectuals. Moscow led the anti-fascist coalition in action as well as words. The entire Left, from communists and socialists to radicals and liberals of every persuasion, lined up on the Loyalist side in Spain—and the Loyalist side was the Soviet and communist side. There was no alternative. British, French, and American inaction—neutrality, nonintervention, appeasement, call it what one will—was for them a retreat from the Enemy. Out-of-hand nationalism, German, Italian, and Japanese, was pitted against the world order—and the democracies. Outright internationalism, at its head the Soviet Union, could alone stave off the fascist threat.

The American Spies

In England the theoretical, economic, and political appeal of communism and the Soviet Union made its strongest dent among the upper class, on the sons of the elite in Cambridge, Oxford, and the London School of Economics.

In the United States the attraction was strongest among the intellectuals and labor organizers who emerged from the ghetto. Communist cells sprang up, not at Harvard, Yale, and Princeton, but in Manhattan—at Columbia University and the City College of New York. Most of their members were the sons of immigrants, many of them Jews from Eastern Europe, first-generation Americans entering the mainstream with college and advanced degrees. Some of the most talented intellectuals, writers, and artists of the thirties—and the sixties—came out of this tradition. They were Party members for a time, or for life, Party sympathizers, liberals and radicals in the Party's anti-fascist fronts. This group also produced some of the most fervent anti-communists and anti-Stalinists out of the believers who lost their faith.

There were, of course, some "old" Americans in the Party ranks, and some heavy WASP contributors, but the American image of the Party as a "bunch of foreigners" prevented its acceptance by the American middle and upper classes as a native institution. The British Communist Party *was* a party of true-born Englishmen.

Measured against the Cambridge trio, the American spies of the Chambers, Bentley, and Rosenberg nets rank low in social status, official access, and the length of their espionage careers. No figures with social status comparable to the British trio came out of the American establishment—with the possible exception of Harry Dexter White and Alger Hiss. White died three days after he had been accused and denied the charges. Hiss denies to this day that he was a Party member or a Soviet agent.

Hiss has been often equated with Philby as "a traitor to his class," but both as a man and as a spy his nearer equivalent is Donald Maclean. They are alike in their social origins and their government careers.

What will always remain elusive, of course, is Hiss's state of mind during 1937–38 when he was passing documents to Chambers.

A secret agent is marked in his own mind by acting like a secret agent: photographing documents, placing microfilms in a dead drop, skulking to secret meetings, playing with recognition and danger signals.

A "source" can feel himself less an "agent" (not *per se* a flattering word) by acting more normally: taking home classified documents, digesting or copying them, giving the material to a friendly visitor in the living room. Rid of its clandestine abracadabra, the act of spying can become an almost normal part of life, an act a man can justify with only minor rationalizing. It is, contrasted to the professional actions of men such as Rosenberg and Philby, a very genteel form of espionage.

Giving inside information to the Party is even more palatable than being a "spy."

Why give it to the Russians?

The motivation of Julian Wadleigh is pertinent. Wadleigh, another of Chambers' "pipelines" into the Department of State, supplied hundreds of documents from his Trade Agreements section to a Party contact, and later to Colonel Bykov, during 1937–38. The son of an Episcopal minister, an educated economist, with an M.A. from Oxford, Wadleigh volunteered to help the fight against fascism by helping the Russians. He knew he was acting illegally, for he violated both his secrecy oath and the espionage laws. In retrospect he found his delivery of documents a "distasteful" affair, but in his own mind he insisted that he felt no conflict of loyalties, no "treachery," for the reports he supplied "were to be used against Germany and Japan." If his words are taken at face value, he clearly acted on principle.

There can be little doubt that a man such as Hiss would do whatever he did on principle.

What is impressive about Hiss, granted his guilt, is his capacity to stand up to the accusations against him in open face-to-face interrogation. Though he changed his story on specific items, there were no crucial slips or breakdowns. His coolness and control matched those of Philby, though the material evidence faced him with a greater challenge than the purely circumstantial evidence against Philby.

Acting on principle became the justification of many of the scientist spies of the forties, for after 1941 the urge to help the Soviet Union became more powerful for even non-communists. It now became a matter of helping an ally against a common enemy.

It is an axiom in advanced societies that science is an international quest for truth that makes all scientists kin. The true scientist knows no national boundaries, for his goal is the advancement of human knowledge and the betterment of the human race. Scientists crop up with some frequency in the Canadian and British nets because the Soviet target was atomic bomb research. Were they also as scientists peculiarly susceptible to Soviet recruitment? Were they all "internationalists" spying for a Higher Cause?

Scientific internationalism is a dignified, if not noble, reason for spying, but in the cases we know the basic motivation was communist, and not scientific, ideology.

When Dr. May was exposed by Gouzenko's documents and was brought to trial in 1946, he professed as his main motive his conviction that an American monopoly of the atomic bomb would work against the human interest. Other scientists defended him, some on grounds that secrecy in science was itself an evil force, others because he was helping an ally against the German and Japanese enemy. Implicit in his, and their, defense was the somewhat arrogant notion that scientists are entitled to exercise special judgments beyond the authority of ordinary men.

These appear to be rationalizations. Dr. May had been a member of the British Communist Party. He either volunteered to work secretly for the Russians or simply followed Party orders to cooperate. In either case any scientific internationalist impulses he may have felt were subordinated to the Party's aims.

A minor technician in the Canadian net put the case most simply: ". . . it was not put to me so much that I was supplying information to the Soviet government. . . . It was more that as scientists we were pooling information." A more senior scientist, Professor Raymond Boyer, supplied information to promote "international scientific collaboration." In these and other cases it is clear that the GRU simply used the nobler pitch to bolster its own narrow national interest.

It will be recalled that Rosenberg employed the same political-scientific rationalization in persuading his brother-in-law to supply information from Los Alamos.

Rosenberg's motivation is readily understandable. The son of a Russian immigrant brought up in the tenements of Manhattan's East Side, he became a radical and a Marxist in his teens. He joined the Party to fight against social injustice. The failure of the capitalist system was easy to see in the days of the Depression. In the absence of an autobiography, his personal conversion to the Party and his transition to working for the Russians can only be guessed at.

Both Alger Hiss and the Rosenbergs have been controversial figures for thirty years. Books have been written proving their guilt and their innocence. The publication of thousands of FBI documents has not settled the controversy. Human emotions, political partisanship, "investigative" zeal, all play a role. What the historians will eventually make of it is hard to predict.

The British historians, are, in a way, better off. They have, in the Cambridge recruits, straightforward Soviet agents to deal with, persistent self-conscious traitors. Neither Alger Hiss nor the Rosenbergs can be given the same unequivocal label.

The Split Mind

As I recall the image of Philby across the conference table and think of my British colleagues who worked closely with him for over a decade, I am again struck with the awareness of how impenetrable is the mind of a complicated man even to his closest friends. I can understand how Philby could go through life without uncertainty or guilt—once devoted to a Higher Cause, the moral (if not the legal) judgments of national values become irrelevant. What is mystifying was his extraordinary capacity to play two roles with such skill.

Faith and dedication are not enough to make an intellectual into a good spy. There is an additional prerequisite: the ability to harbor in the mind two sets of purposes and reactions without letting one interfere with the other in any observable way.

Dual lives are a familiar occurrence in any society: the very proper bank embezzler, the married man with a (secret) mistress, the closet alcoholic. There are poseurs: the doctor without a medical degree, the con artist of a dozen roles. These are actors, playing a second role, often briefly, on the margins of their "normal" lives, or new players who reject their past and take on a full-time second role.

The ladder of deception can be roughly graded even in the secret world: from the secret communist who meets his cell-comrades once a week, to a government official who takes home a few documents each night. Some small part of the mind keeps its secrets from the rest of the world, as Whittaker Chambers put it rather simply to the House subcommittee:

> Americans are not conspiratorial by nature and tradition, and they cannot understand how conspirators work. Now this whole set-up here was conspiratorial . . . I had two compartments, Whittaker Chambers on one side, which is a more or less private compartment, and Carl in these [Communist] groups here, and I did not want to make any bridge between them. . . .

This compartmentation is an easy task for simple conspirators or secret agents working in a laboratory, as it is for racketeers, dope smugglers, and the run of common criminals.

The real challenge comes to an intelligent and sensitive man acting as a spy in the midst of his equally intelligent and sensitive friends and colleagues. He must, day in, day out, play his normal or front role with fellow workers, friends, and drinking companions, and all the while be aware of his own secret self. A single slip can be fatal.

The voluble Dr. Fuchs, a man who like Philby spent his days

in close contact with sophisticated fellow professionals, analyzed his own split mind in his confession.

> I used my Marxist philosophy to establish in my mind two separate compartments. One compartment in which I allowed myself to make friendships, to have personal relations, to help people. . . . I could be free and easy and happy with other people without fear of disclosing myself because I knew that the other compartment would step in if I approached the danger point. It appeared to me at the time that I had become a "free man" because I had succeeded in the other compartment to establish myself completely independent of the surrounding forces of society. Looking back at it now the best way of expressing it seems to be to call it a controlled schizophrenia.

Outside of not quite understanding how "Marxist philosophy" helped Fuchs achieve this split, I find "schizophrenia" an odd term for his state of mind. The schizophrenic is not a split mind or personality, as Dr. Fuchs should have known, but a mind split off to some degree from external reality. The true schizoid lives mostly inside his own head. Neither Dr. Fuchs nor Philby can be accused of any detachment from the real world around them.

However we label them, the two compartments existed for thirty years in Philby's mind, both alertly operating at the same time. In working with his colleagues—at his desk, in conversation at lunch, around the committee table—one part of his mind did the work and socializing, the other noted facts, document references, and policy statements that would be of interest to his KGB boss. And it was only in his secret rendezvous with his case officer that Philby could let himself go and be his true self.

What is impressive is the strength of the will, the controlling mechanism that kept his bicameral mind in tandem and maintained it as an effective instrument for action and observation on two planes. There were no slips—and he led most of his professional life among perceptive, notoriously skeptical members of the intelligence fraternity. Only a deeply bred sense of caution and an extreme self-discipline beyond the reach of most men could have survived those long years of action-filled duplicity.

He made no slips even in his cups. Like Sorge and Trepper, like Burgess and, later, Maclean, Philby was a heavy drinker. Yet large quantities of alcohol were not enough to dissolve that iron steersman at the helm.

ON GRADES OF TREASON

Most spies are not traitors. The pilferers of industrial secrets; the penetration agents of political parties; the Rumanian oil technician who sells NATO secrets to the Russians; the Frenchman who seduces an American Embassy secretary in Paris; the German businessman who briefs his Soviet contact on an upcoming negotiation cannot be accused of betraying their countries. Many spies are not even criminals—in places where there are no laws against espionage directed at another country (both Krivitsky and Trepper settled in Belgium as a safe base for spying against Germany and Great Britain).

Treason is a crime directed against the nation-state and is defined by that state. It applies only to its own citizens—by birth or naturalization. Sorge was a traitor (to Germany). Trepper, a Galician Pole, was not. Philby was a traitor. Dr. Fuchs's citizenship was unclear.

Since treason is a national crime, it always bears two faces. One nation's traitor is another nation's hero. Sorge and Philby are heroes in the Soviet Union, Oleg Penkovskiy, a traitor in Moscow, is a heroic figure in Washington. Soviet renegades ("defectors" is the polite term) become admirable fighters for freedom in the West.

There is also a politics of treason.

Is a traitor less a traitor when he spies for a wartime ally? For the Soviet Union during World War II? When he contributes to the Allied victory?

Or does it depend on the ally? Would the Rosenbergs have been less culpable if they had been working for the British or the French?

Is a man less treasonous if he works against a particular regime and not against his country? Were the plotters against Hitler patriots or traitors? Are Ukrainian resistance fighters traitors?

Beyond politics there is a morality of treason. What is the state of mind of the traitor? Why does he spy?

For the ignorant, thoughtless, or neurotic temperament "treason" can be a meaningless concept: an illiterate corporal in Berlin handing over scraps of Army documents, a mixed-up adolescent working near a missile site. What he does in most cases he does for money. In treason, as in murder, the level of intelligence of the criminal and his personal history are relevant to the crime. Is the alcoholic sergeant the worst kind of traitor—or the most pardonable?

Is the man who spies on principle the lesser or the worse traitor? Penkovskiy worked for the good of humanity, Philby for a Higher Cause than the nation-state. The more intelligent the man, the more clearly he knows what he is doing. Does that mitigate his crime? Is he better or worse than the man who is recruited under pressure—by threats to his family, by sexual blackmail, by brainwashing in a POW camp?

Is the man who shows remorse for his crime the lesser traitor, or is the man who seeks immunity with a full confession implicating his fellow criminals? Or is the spy who keeps his mouth shut to the end?

However vague or quibbling these questions, they affect the moral judgment of an act of treason. Small men, ignorant or neurotic, can become traitors with no real awareness of what their acts mean. Naked treason is unequivocal. It is a conscious act against the state by an intelligent native citizen who knows what he is doing. Philby and Hiss, however disparate the level of their achievements, have become symbolic figures for our generation, heroes in some people's eyes, for doing what they believed in. It is the high-minded duplicity of educated, self-conscious men that will always challenge the moral analyst of treason: are there honorable traitors?

VIII

THE
GERMAN-NATO
SIEVE

For thirty years the Federal Republic of Germany has been the primary focus of Moscow's European diplomacy, propaganda, and intelligence operations.

Germany has always had an ambivalent place in Soviet foreign policy. On the one hand, an armed Germany has posed the major military threat to Soviet security. In a single generation German troops twice invaded the Soviet Union, brought death to tens of millions of Russians, and destroyed the Soviet industrial base west of Moscow. During the Cold War, with Germany rearmed and the linchpin of NATO, a third invasion threatened. The Soviet military threat to Western Europe in the minds of Bonn, London, and Washington has been matched in Moscow's mind by the German-American threat to Eastern Europe. Anyone who questions the genuineness of Soviet fears of a rearmed Germany misreads the mentality of the Soviet leaders from Stalin to Brezhnev.

On the other hand, Germany has been a natural partner of the Russians from the Treaty of Rappallo in 1922 to the secret military cooperation during the thirties. Stalin's pact with Hitler was a defensive alliance designed to draw the teeth of the German tiger. His conviction that direct dealings with Hitler would neutralize the German threat led to his blindness about the impending German invasion.

There is another, increasingly crucial consideration: the economic one. Even in 1917 Lenin hoped for, and helped incite, a communist revolution in Germany, for he was convinced socialism could triumph only in a highly industrialized society. During the past ten years West Germany has been a major source of capital and technology for the strengthening of the Soviet economy. The breakthrough in the East-West stand-off came in Bonn with the victory of the Social Democrats in the 1969 elections and the start of Chancellor Willy Brandt's *Ostpolitik,* or opening to the East.

For twenty years after World War II the KGB focused its talents on Western Europe, above all on the heart of the capitalist threat, West Germany, and the North Atlantic Treaty Organization. It directed against them the most concentrated wholesale intelligence barrage in the history of Soviet intelligence.

At no time and place has the conjunction of high-priority targets and easy access to the area of operations been so ideal for any espionage service.

The statistics of agents caught in West Germany stretch the imagination. They sound more like military casualties in war than *secret* agents caught in the act. During the fifties this espionage free-for-all was reflected in the arrest and trial records of the German courts. There were almost two thousand convictions in 1950–53, more than eight thousand in 1959. And these were the agents who were caught. A serious estimate of resident Eastern agents operating in West Germany during the mid-sixties placed their number at over five thousand.

After the erection of the Berlin Wall in 1960 and the beginnings of a German-Soviet détente in 1969, the rate of arrests and the number of spy swaps have diminished somewhat, but it is only sensible to assume that over and beyond the high-level penetrations we shall look at, hundreds if not thousands of routine Soviet and East European agents still operate in the German Federal Republic.

The reservoir of potential agents during the early postwar years was almost inexhaustible.

The richest haul of Soviet agents came from the German prisoners of war in the Soviet prison camps. Many had joined the Free German League of Prisoners of War, some of whose members had been parachuted into Germany at the end of the war to report on the American occupation forces. Over the following year German prisoners were granted early release if they agreed to work for the Russians on their return to the West.

Many of them did not follow KGB instructions and remained passive or turned themselves in to the German authorities. Yet the men who had welched on their agreement were carefully registered in the Moscow Index.

One German POW, a former accountant who volunteered his services as an agent, was trained and parachuted into Germany before the end of the war to spy on the American forces. He did nothing to carry out his mission or maintain contact with the Russians. Sixteen years later a Soviet commercial attaché called on him and threatened to expose his past unless he cooperated.

Another POW, trained as a radio operator, was released in 1948 and failed to make contact after his return to Germany. Thirteen years later he also received a visit.

Men with an unsavory Nazi past were especially prone to blackmail. The KGB's painstaking search through captured German records gave it handles on thousands of men and women residing in West or East Germany. Again, through the fifties and sixties, a knock on the door of a now respectable burgher and a brief chat often brought a new agent into the KGB net.

And there was an even richer target close at hand for KGB/ Karlshorst: West Berlin. It was an easy hunting ground—for German as well as American agents.

I had visited Berlin several times since my illegal trip of 1945, and watched it change from an accumulation of rubble to the spy capital of the world. By the time of my visits during my Munich assignment (1952–54), West Berlin had become prosperous. The German "economic miracle" itself was supplemented by the salaries of spies and counterspies to which KGB/Karlshorst contributed its share. In the scores of nightclubs and restaurants, high-class cabarets and a profusion of low-class dives and brothels, Russians, Poles, and East Germans mixed with the British, French, and Americans in common enjoyment of the German fleshpots and in quest of new agents.

The KGB concentrated on American officials and servicemen, on the Berlin representatives of Soviet émigré groups, and on American and West German intelligence agencies in West Berlin itself. It also dispatched couriers and agents into the British and American zones to handle the heavy work load of making contact with the agents the KGB had recruited in Russia. Berlin was also the gateway to the rest of the world: to the channel ports, to Paris and Brussels, to New York and Rio de Janeiro. Like the old West European Bureau of the Comintern, Karlshorst gave training in communications, concocted legends, and forged identity documents for its own and for Moscow's agents on Western missions. Many of the illegals trained in Moscow were serviced in Karlshorst on their way to the West.

The volume of Karlshorst's work is hard to describe, but the work of only one of their staff officers, an Austrian national trained in East Germany, will give some notion of its infinite variety. Here are some of the tasks assigned to Rudolf Sigl, a reluctant employee who defected in 1969:*

—Locate two German officer POWs who had been "recruited" in the Soviet Union but had not made contact.

—Visit Bremerhaven and describe its port facilities and procedures.

—Reestablish contact with a former KGB agent in Cologne.

—Post money and letters from West Berlin and pay allowances to wives of jailed KGB agents.

—Monitor and cultivate visitors to the annual Leipzig fair in East Germany, and recruit East German students to study in Moscow and work on officials and clerks in the West German Embassy.

—Handle a well-known East German TV announcer who made frequent trips abroad.

—Handle an official of the Ghanaian trade mission in East Berlin who was later transferred to Bonn.

—Direct a researcher on German minorities abroad and assess the potential for penetrating them.

—Handle a Moroccan journalist who, among other tasks, visited Morocco to spy on American air bases and to assess his chances for joining the Moroccan police.

—Meet and assess young African diplomats, government officials, and labor leaders who came to East Germany seeking political or financial support, and debrief them on the personalities and organizations in their home countries.

* His book, *In the Claws of the KGB* (Philadelphia, 1978), is more factual and sober than the title might suggest.

The growing handful of Soviet officials stationed in West Germany during the early years operated independently of Karlshorst, and as their numbers swelled, the KGB's Bonn residency became Moscow's main operating arm against the Federal Republic. In 1970, when I last had a reliable estimate, about two hundred KGB officers were operating under official cover in the Federal Republic.

The wholesale Soviet onslaught against the German and NATO targets was materially assisted by the work of the East European intelligence services.

The Six Sisters

The satellite regimes shared with Moscow its hatred and distrust of the West Germans and its concern for the military threat posed by NATO. The Polish and Czech services are manned by citizens who have good cause to hate the Germans even without the inspiration of a twenty-year anti-German propaganda barrage. For many East Europeans it is as "patriotic" to work against the Germans as it is, or was, for Americans to work against the Soviet Union.

As the years passed, the satellite services became a highly effective and integrated component of Soviet intelligence. Staffed and trained by the KGB, first for internal security work on their own terrain against Western agents, these services eventually carried out ad hoc assignments for the KGB abroad, each exploiting its own natural targets: Polish and Czech émigrés in Germany, France, and Great Britain, Rumanian-French contacts, Bulgarians in Turkey. In the early years KGB "advisers" directed these operations, screened the intelligence produced for items of interest to Moscow, and took over the direct handling of any agent of interest to KGB, whether it was a British diplomat recruited by the Poles, a German parliamentarian recruited by the Czechs, or the scores of West German officials recruited by the East Germans.

It took the KGB more than ten years to organize this collaboration into a strategic intelligence system with basic missions assigned to each service against both European and global targets. By the early sixties each service had its allotted tasks based on formal understandings reached in Moscow. A concerted and formidable attack on NATO began in 1964.

The Czech service was particularly helpful.

The Czechs recruited a German-Czech member of the West German parliament with access to classified military information, and ran a British MP for nine years. Among the chandeliers they supplied for the Turkish parliament building, they bugged one for the office of the parliamentary chairman. In their work against NATO they concentrated on installations in Greece and Turkey.

They recruited Germans living in Czechoslovakia with relatives in West Germany, and sent them west to make contact with their relatives. They infiltrated the German Social Democratic Party by recruiting a low-level functionary who had lived in Czechoslovakia before World War II and who recruited a member of the West German parliament with access to classified military information.

Farther afield, they penetrated a group of former Czech intelligence officers (post-1948 refugees) employed by British intelligence in order to collect data on personnel, addresses, and license numbers of the British intelligence and security services—a useful supplement to the KGB's own take. In Washington they did routine investigative work on CIA employees: their education, home addresses, car license numbers, language classes. Their ultimate search was always for someone born in Eastern Europe, someone who might be susceptible to the family approach.

They recruited an agent in Britain's Royal Air Force who supplied photographs and manuals on an anti-missile system. Their arrival in Moscow in 1960 elicited a personal letter of thanks from Khrushchev.

The most valuable "national" assets of the sister services are their own émigrés in Europe and the Americas. In the postwar flight of political refugees from Eastern Europe, many persons were permitted to escape to the West in return for a promise to cooperate. Those who confessed to Western authorities gave the same story: they were imprisoned, forced to cooperate, but they had no intention of keeping their promise. Some, of course, had every intention of cooperating, but they were difficult to screen out in the interrogation centers. Some of these "refugees" were trained agents and gave plausible stories to their interrogators.

The periodic flow of new emigrants is exploited in the same way: after the Hungarian uprising in 1956, the post-1968 flight of Czechs, the Jewish emigration of the seventies. The East European services not only monitor the correspondence of emigrants with the homeland, but take the same double approach as the

KGB. They penetrate foreign intelligence services that seek to use émigrés for espionage operations and to recruit as intelligence agents those who have achieved some degree of status in their new homeland—in New York, Chicago, Mexico City, or Buenos Aires.

Other sister services have made their contribution over the years. Perhaps the most notable Polish contribution was the recruitment of a British clerk in Warsaw, Henry Houghton, whom the KGB took over and ran for years within the British naval establishment. Rumanian intelligence, focused on the French target, had a net in the French Foreign Office in the late sixties and had penetrated the French atomic energy program. They also ran for some years NATO's financial comptroller, Nahat Imre, a Turkish citizen.

The close interlocking of the KGB and East European services made it possible for the KGB not only to read and select their intelligence reports, but to read the operational files of any agent who might be of interest to them—and to take over the agent if it wished.

German Versus German

The most valuable of the sister services against the West German target was naturally the East German one.

The ease with which North Vietnam infiltrated South Vietnam in the sixties (including the South Vietnamese intelligence services) is matched by the ease with which the East Germans penetrate the more complex institutions of West Germany. Any split nation is still in most vital respects a single nation: in blood, language, and social tradition, if not in political and economic structure. There are no foreigners on either side. There are blood relations on both sides. Each service knows the other service intimately as both services operate almost wholesale in the other's territory. What varies is the control system, and here the advantages, of course, lie wholly with the East Germans.

East Germans sent into West Germany were ideal recruits. They could be carefully selected, trained, given communications, and assigned specific targets. The facilities of East German intelligence were comparable to those of the KGB in the Soviet Union. Many candidates could be tested as informants within East Germany itself. Many were easy victims of pressure: men with Gestapo or SS records, minor war criminals, ordinary felons or political prisoners. Others among the innumerable Germans uprooted by the war, careerless, often hungry, could be lured by money or the prospect of setting up a business in the West. Most had relatives in the West.

Greater care had to be taken in recruiting agents within West Germany itself. Here the KGB records on Germans with Nazi or SS backgrounds were most fruitful. The threat of exposure to a man with a secret past works wonders: a little cooperation and you can keep your position in society—we will even help you advance your business or career interests. Hundreds of middle-class Germans have been recruited through this kind of simple blackmail.

All these are the bread-and-butter of Soviet intelligence, a kind of hack-work in which the loss of some agents, the arrest and trial of others, or the ejection of KGB officers under diplomatic cover, produced no decline in volume. They represent a kind of continuing tactical reconnaissance of the German scene, a blanketing of political, industrial, and military life in the heartland of European power.

These are the little people, ordinary men and women of ordinary talent, inconspicuous in their appearance and habits, shopkeepers, guards and janitors, salesmen (who make good couriers), safe-house keepers. They are no index to the KGB's true exploits against the German target.

The wholesale Soviet campaign of recruiting or sending in low-level, mostly untrained, agents into a complex society appears wasteful if not ridiculous. Yet the KGB knew what it was doing. Even if only one or two out of a hundred such agents turned out to be useful—either for the friends they had or the jobs they got —the investment of limited man-hours in a routine effort would be justified. This wholesale effort also gave its green case officers useful experience in the mechanics of espionage. We, of course, do not know to this day which of the agents planted in the fifties and sixties are still in place. Little agents can grow into big agents, just as college students can grow into scientists and diplomats.

The Establishment

Little agents are a routine long-term investment for the KGB. Big agents pay off at once with political and military intelligence reports of immediate strategic value. The KGB and the East German service have had a rich quota of well-placed agents in the West German establishment.

In Bonn, as in the major capitalist countries, the KGB priority was and is the penetration of the executive bureaucracy, above all the Foreign Office and the Defense Ministry, and especially their code rooms and communications. It wants agents in the upper reaches of the establishment, in its executive or legislative branches, in the domestic security and intelligence services, and in the embassies of its major allies.

The Foreign Office in Bonn has been sporadically penetrated since the fifties, mostly through women employees. As in Moscow, sex has been the handle.

One of the more colorful figures of the fifties was a sixty-year-old businessman, the "Red Casanova" of the headline writers, who bedded innumerable secretaries and clerks, both for his own pleasure, for profit to his own commercial (cover) interests, and for the East German service. Carl Helmers was on the East German payroll for over four years until he was arrested in February 1958. Among his sexual conquests was a forty-four-year-old married woman with two children, Irmgard Roemer, who deserted her family for love of (father-figure?) Carl. Her job in the Foreign Office was to handle communications with its embassies abroad. Carbon copies of all in and out communications flowed regularly to East Berlin.

One of the most productive, and pathetic, victims of KGB seduction was an unmarried secretary in the Foreign Office, Leonore Heinz, who was thirty-five when the operation started in the summer of 1960.

A man under the name of Heinz Suetterlin called on her at her home out of the blue with a tall story. In his hand he had a (bogus) reply to a lonely hearts advertisement giving her address. A handsome man in his mid-forties, a highly suitable match, he was invited to come in. Within months he had wooed and won her hand in marriage.

Once married, Suetterlin persuaded his wife to bring home Foreign Office documents for him to photograph. The operation literally worked by the clock. She simply took them home at lunchtime in a handbag with a secret compartment.

Suetterlin was in one-way touch with the Center through the official Moscow radio. It would play his call-tune ("Moscow

Nights") to alert him and provide instructions to service a dead drop where he deposited his film and received orders.

Marital fidelity proved highly lucrative to the KGB. It yielded more than three thousand documents, almost a third secret and top secret. They included not only Foreign Office cable traffic and NATO and German defense and intelligence information, but personnel files on other foreign service employees and notices to the Foreign Office on security investigations of Soviet and East German agent suspects.

For Mrs. Suetterlin the price of her marriage was tragically high. When she discovered that her husband had married her on KGB orders, she hanged herself in her cell.

The saga of Frau Suetterlin has been repeated scores of times since. In a country where World War II killed off an enormous number of young men, many of its women who were unmarried found careers in business and government in the fifties and sixties. They were patriotic West Germans and many occupied responsible posts as secretaries in the German government—in the Foreign Office, in the Ministry of Defense, and in NATO installations.

As late as 1978–79 a series of female agents were uncovered in Bonn. One was a thirty-eight-year-old Foreign Office secretary who was wooed and won by a handsome German who finally confessed to her that he was spying for British intelligence—and introduced her to the "chief of the British service." After she had passed some secret documents, he told her he was spying for East Germany, but she kept up the supply of documents in order not to lose him.

Other women trained as agents posed as political refugees from East Germany and were given the task of getting a classified government job. In 1979 the defection of an East German intelligence officer sparked the flight to the East of several women whose identities were known to him.

Direct penetration of a Foreign Office or Defense Ministry produces the quickest, and usually richest, intelligence payoff, though the hazards are greatest in a high-security installation. There is, in parliamentary democracies, an indirect but less hazardous avenue to the same secrets: a member of the legislature.

Anyone can join a political party. A zealous worker can become a party functionary and, given the right qualities, can run for local office. His own talents will determine his future career, and he can be unaffected by security interviews, file checks, or investigations. All democratic parties are loose organizations in terms of security.

The KGB and its sister services have exploited both major West German parties, the Social Democrats and the Christian Democrats, from the early fifties to the present. Their major interest is in members of parliament who sit on defense committees.

There are two alternatives: to recruit a man already in parliament, or to invest in a young man with good prospects for becoming a member.

The prototype of a highly productive sitting member is the Social Democratic Party MP, Alfred Frenzel, who was recruited by Czech Intelligence in Vienna in 1956.

A Sudeten German (with a Czech mother) born in 1899, Frenzel had a checkered political career between the two wars. First a socialist, then a dedicated communist and full-time Party worker, again in 1934 a Social Democrat, he escaped to England after Hitler's takeover. In December 1946 he began his career with the Social Democratic Party that brought him election to the Bavarian parliament by 1950 and a seat in the federal parliament in 1953. He became a member of six parliamentary committees, including the Defense Committee.

During an official visit to Vienna to discuss German-Czech relations with a Czech representative, he trapped himself by accepting 3,000 marks from the Czechs for his trip expenses. For a time he met with his Czech case officer regularly, mostly in western Austria, smuggling his documents across the border interleaved in newspapers. Soon he was given a local contact by the name of Altmann who met him in his parliamentary office in Bonn or a local hotel, stuffed the documents into his briefcase, and returned them after he had photographed them. Theirs was an active enterprise: twenty-two meetings in one year.

Following a report from a German agent in Prague that the Czechs possessed up-to-date knowledge of German and NATO defenses, an investigation led to the parliamentary Defense Committee and to the arrest of Altmann (already suspect), Altmann's courier, and then Frenzel. Frenzel was tried in April 1961, convicted, and later exchanged.

The defense secrets Frenzel had access to and delivered to Moscow via Prague included the German defense budget and defense plans, the organization of the Army and Air Force, reorganization plans for the German Navy, German rocket and aircraft projects, and data on items of NATO equipment.

Frenzel made a complete confession at his trial and blamed his own weak character for his crime. A small, self-made man, he had worked up the ladder to achieve status, money, prestige, influence, and a sense of power. Being a spy apparently added to that sense of power, for he clearly did not spy so zealously for the paltry sums of money he was paid. Merely on the record, of course, he was suspect. He had a Czech mother, he was a former communist, a member of the Czech Legion, an immigrant into West Germany with relatives in Czechoslovakia. As a member of parliament he was exempt from any security requirements.

The Front Office

The use of a political party as an avenue to Bonn achieved its most brilliant success with the dispatch of an East German agent as a political émigré in 1956. The arrest of Guenter Guillaume on April 24, 1974, in his apartment in Bad Godesberg, a fashionable Bonn suburb, forced the resignation of his boss, Chancellor Willy Brandt, shook the NATO alliance, and caused a parliamentary investigation of the West German security services. Its political impact was far greater than the exposure of Kim Philby, who was, after all, only an intelligence official.

Guillaume was employed by a publisher in East Berlin when he was tapped for his mission in the West. After four years as a freelance journalist, he was employed during 1951–55 in the photographic department of the East German firm Volk und Wissen, occasionally traveling in West Germany under his publishing cover. He resigned from his job six months before he was placed in the stream of refugees and arrived in the Emergency Refugee Relief camp in Giessen under his true name in 1956.

His political career began the next year when he joined the Social Democratic Party. He became a party functionary, worked hard, gained the confidence of his bosses, was promoted. The political views he expressed were right of center. From the early sixties he worked on the monthly journal of the party's South Hesse district.

In 1970 he was recommended by his party superiors for an opening as an assistant in Chancellor Brandt's office. He was praised for his "diligence and devotion," his "reliability," and his "unbounded trustworthiness."

In Bonn, Guillaume became Brandt's personal aide with the principal task of conducting liaison between the Chancellor's office and the Social Democratic Party headquarters. His precise relationship with Brandt, what his boss talked to him about, above all, what classified documents he had access to—all these have been much argued about. What is clear is that an intelligent agent in this position could not help but be a valuable source of the highest level political intelligence—the tone and mood of the front office, the essence of the informal discussions and chitchat, the personalities and roles of the chief aides and Cabinet members, the general business going on. During a period when Bonn's relationship with Moscow was passing through a vital phase, this must have given Brezhnev a valuable insight into the mind of his adversary-partner.

What concerned the government, the press, and the public, of course, was what "state secrets" Guillaume passed to the KGB. Here the evidence is necessarily fragmentary, and the following items are only samples of the KGB take: copies of nineteen secret and confidential Telex messages made with Guillaume's photographic equipment covered the substance of a secret NATO conference, German Foreign Office discussions with President Nixon and Secretary of State Kissinger in the United States, Western positions on the Berlin Four-Power agreement, two Nixon letters on U.S. relations with Europe.

During Brandt's vacation in Norway in July 1973, Guillaume had access to the classified Telex traffic sent to Brandt from Washington concerning NATO matters.

On Brandt's campaign trips in a chartered train, Guillaume handled the classified traffic coming to the train's communication car.

Nor can the value of Guillaume's more routine reporting both before and after 1959 be discounted. He had access to internal Social Democratic Party politics, details on party discussion of domestic and foreign policy, and internal security reports (mostly on leftists) from the West German security service to the party.

What stands out as a brutal fact is that Guillaume spied for the East Germans (and the KGB) for almost twenty years, in constant communication with his superiors in East Germany, sending in a steady stream of intelligence by dead drops, live mail drops, couriers (including his wife), and personal meetings with his case officer. It was a first-class operation, carried out by precisely the right kind of man: a colorless, hard-working party bureaucrat who made no mistakes. The credit for the choice goes to the East German service, the profit from the choice to the KGB.

Again, we have "the Philby effect." The exposure of Guillaume shattered the confidence of the NATO powers in the reliability of a key ally and created suspicion and distrust among its security and intelligence services. *Any* dissension among the Western Allies is grist to the Soviet political mill. Any discrediting of a Western security service gives a working advantage to the KGB. How could the Germans any longer trust a service that had been so flagrantly duped?

The Chancellor's office did not remain leak-proof. In 1977 a secretary and several other members of Chancellor Schmidt's office were arrested on suspicion of working for East German intelligence.

Service Versus Service

In the vast espionage arena of the two Germanies, counterespionage operations took on a singular importance. Hundreds of agents were caught on both sides not only through the doubling of each other's agents, but through the penetration of the other side's field offices. At various times from the fifties to the present both services ran agents inside each other's headquarters where all the secrets were conveniently available. Intelligence defectors from both services supplied lists of agent names that led to wholesale roundups. Both broadcast the names of each other's exposed agents over the Berlin radio. The exchange of captured agents between West and East Germany became a normal diplomatic enterprise.

The major blow to the West German security service, the BFV,† came in 1954. Its chief, Otto John, came to West Berlin in July 1954 to attend a celebration of the 20th of July putsch against Hitler, in which he had participated. He vanished into East Berlin and showed up at an East German press conference a few days later.

Had he defected or was he abducted? The issue is still contro-

† Politely labeled the Bundesverfassungsschutz, the Office for the Protection of the Constitution. The term "security service," or Sicherheitsdienst, had unpleasant Nazi overtones.

versial. According to John, he was drugged and abducted. John remained in East German hands until December 1955, when he reappeared in West Berlin, and was tried and sentenced to four years in prison.

However John got to the east, what he told his interrogators we do not know. Both the mystery of his disappearance and of his behavior after his flight only added to the scandal.

A decade later it was the turn of the German foreign intelligence service, the BND (Bundesnachrichtendienst).

Karlshorst's primary counterespionage target was the headquarters of General Reinhard Gehlen's federal intelligence service located in Pullach, a Munich suburb. It was the one point at which the KGB could gain access to the entire range of the BND's anti-Soviet operations. Karlshorst had worked on this target since my early days in Munich, and it was only later that we realized that another Philby had been operating in Pullach from 1951.

The Cambridge trio in England was matched in numbers, but not in quality, by the Dresden trio in Bavaria. The German trio that stood in the dock on July 8, 1963, were uneducated, low-class opportunists who had made it in the service of the Nazis. They were wartime comrades, buddies who had worked for the SS during the war and for Allied intelligence after the war. The KGB was their third boss.

The oldest man, a former SS captain, Hans Clemens, was the key to the operation. Unemployed after being charged and acquitted as a war criminal in Rome in September 1949, he paid a visit to his wife in Dresden. Here she had developed a circle of Soviet friends to whom she introduced her husband. A KGB officer recruited him to carry out two tasks: to try to join a Western intelligence service and to recruit his friend Felfe for Soviet intelligence.

Heinz Paul Felfe had been imprisoned after the war for his SS work and sent to Canada, but he was released in 1946 and took up his old profession in Germany—as a counterintelligence investigator for the Ministry of All-German Affairs and as an informer for British intelligence. When his old friend Clemens brought up the KGB offer, he visited Karlshorst in August 1951 and readily agreed to work for the KGB.

Clemens then went to another ex-SS comrade, Krichbaum, who worked in the personnel section of the BND (Gehlen's service was notorious for the number of former Nazis and SS men in its ranks).

Clemens got a job in the BND: the first man was in.

Clemens then recommended Felfe, who was hired for a field job in November 1951 and assigned to Pullach headquarters later. A real pro, a hard worker, he became the head of the Soviet counterintelligence section: neatly matching Philby's key assignment in the British service. His career was apparently helped by his successes in uncovering East German agents (with some leads supplied to him by the KGB).

For the next ten years Felfe put on film every useful document that passed over his desk or was accessible in the files: index cards on BND personnel and agents abroad (and copies of their intelligence reports), lists of suspects and Eastern agents under investigation in West Germany, and monthly counterespionage summaries. He supplied Karlshorst with profiles on his colleagues (for possible follow-up), minutes of committee meetings, material on BND relations with domestic security and military intelligence services, headquarters squabbles, operational plans, and budgets. He was entrusted at one time with the BND's own investigation into a possible Soviet penetration of the BND.

Over 15,000 photographs and tapes poured into Karlshorst in suitcases with false bottoms, in cans of baby food, and through the third man of the trio, Tiebel, who played a crucial role as courier. Some of Felfe's reports were placed in dead drops, or delivered to live drops for forwarding. Hot reports went by radio.

Felfe made several secret trips to Berlin and Vienna for discussions with his KGB case officer. On two of these trips KGB generals came from Moscow to meet Felfe. He was shown a letter of appreciation from Alexander Shelepin, then head of the KGB, a common ego-massage for the KGB's top-level agents.

Felfe was exposed as the result of two investigations. The first was the follow-up to a lead supplied by a CIA agent in the Polish intelligence service to whom a KGB officer had boasted that one of several BND officers who had made a trip to the United States was a KGB agent. The other was the result of an investigation into the leak of a top-secret report from Pullach with a very narrow distribution. When Felfe was arrested, he was caught with the goods.

I had never met Felfe during my Munich tour. Unlike Philby, he was in no position to know anything about our own operations into the Soviet Union, for these were kept rigidly insulated from Gehlen's men. It is, however, impossible to assess what remote facts a curious intelligence officer can discover.

Felfe was a competent, businesslike desk officer, a hard-working paper bureaucrat with no social graces, qualities of equal interest to the BND and the KGB.

He was particularly proud of his Karlshorst showpiece: a detailed map of the KGB compound, a layout of the floor plan for each building, the number of each office and its occupant. Felfe even knew what KGB officer went to what men's room. It was an ironic piece of ego-serving showmanship.

Though Felfe's trial was discreetly handled, the man inside the traitor emerged with some clarity.

Felfe asserted that he spied against his own government out of principle based upon hostility toward the Western powers (for the bombing of Dresden and his own "ill-treatment and torture" in Allied prison camps). But the principal motivation for his treason apparently lay deep in his own self-image. He enjoyed intelligence work and knew himself to be good at it. As a professional, he considered the British, Americans, and Germans sloppy. Moreover, they did not appreciate him. He wanted to be a number 1 professional and wanted to work for a number 1 professional service. He gladly accepted Moscow's offer, and became in his own mind a number 1 agent in the number 1 service. Moreover, his services were greatly appreciated. Dedicated primarily to his profession, he was above nationalism and patriotism. He was a true egocentric without an ideological bone in his body.

Felfe's decade of treason had a devastating effect on the BND, for his reporting to the KGB included not only detailed coverage of the BND's own operations, but it also neutralized the domestic security efforts of the BFV. Chasing down East European spies became a self-defeating enterprise.

Totally exposed in its most secret workings—agent names and locations, missions, communications—the BND had not only lost a decade of apparently effective work, but it was compelled to start again from scratch in building up its support capacity. It needed new codes and ciphers, cover offices, safe houses, and border-crossing points. The BND damage report must have run into tens of thousands of pages. Not only were agents and addresses compromised, but ten years of secret agent reports had to be reevaluated: those fabricated by the other side, those subtly slanted, those from purely mythical sources.

The compromise, of course, extended even further: to Allied documents and secrets made available in Pullach and to that vast corpus of German government political and military information to which a senior intelligence officer has both proper and improper access.

Within the intelligence services and the government the damage to pride and morale was incalculable, but the KGB must have seen as a greater profit the Philby effect: the shattering of confidence among the Allies. How could the Americans or the British or the French continue to rely on the German services, or trust them with American secrets? How could Allied military commanders feel secure in entrusting their own highly classified information to a German command that could not guarantee the security of its own intelligence or security services?

Both the Philby and Felfe exposures served Moscow well in its long-standing political mission of promoting friction among its enemies.

Felfe is not dead. After serving six years of his fourteen-year term, he was exchanged in 1969 for some West Germans in East German prisons, and later made a visit to the Federal Republic to do research for a book he is purportedly writing. Again, aping Philby, an ace spy may write his memoirs, and, if he does, the KGB will be able to rekindle old doubts and suspicions by promoting its own brilliant image and dirtying the waters of Allied cooperation. For the KGB, blown spies have an enduring literary value, for they can write a persuasive mixture of fiction and fact that makes for the best propaganda.

Cracks in NATO

For Moscow the armed forces of the North Atlantic Treaty Organization have posed the most immediate military threat to Eastern Europe and the Soviet Union. From NATO's inception as an organized force with fixed locations in the mid-fifties, both its headquarters in Paris, and later in Brussels, and its field installations throughout Europe have been the priority KGB target in Europe.

NATO has been an open book for Moscow since the late fifties.

The low-level penetration of NATO and American field instal-lations has been a routine exercise by the KGB for over twenty years, utilizing French and Italian workers in shipyards, arsenals, and port areas, Greek and Turkish laborers and enlisted men. Scores of Italian workers have been recruited in and around American bases in Milan. Two KGB officers were expelled from Italy in the late sixties for their illegal contacts against these tar-gets. These field installations remain persistent objects of interest to both the KGB and the GRU.

One of the most colorful operators used by the KGB against NATO installations was an Italian, Giorgio Rinaldi Ghislieri, who had been recruited by Soviet intelligence in 1956 to spy on U.S. military bases in Italy. By profession a parachutist and stunt man, he operated for over ten years before his arrest in March 1967.

During these years he and his wife, a "Countess Zarina" who ran an antique shop, set up and managed a network of agents and informers who reported on NATO bases in Italy and U. S. Air Force bases in Spain. His sources apparently extended into France, Greece, and Cyprus. Although his claim that he had sev-eral hundred agents in his network may be exaggerated, he clearly had eyes and ears in scores of NATO installations.

The penetration of NATO headquarters has been almost as simple. The reasons are clear. Any multinational enterprise offers a wide choice of potential recruits of various nationalities: in this case ranging from Germans, Americans, and British to Italians and Turks. A large headquarters requires a large staff of clerical, communications, and logistics personnel, many of whom have ac-cess to classified documents. The military staffs and defense ministries of each member nation are an avenue into the head-quarters of the alliance. It can be worked on from Copenhagen to Ankara.

Soviet facilities for operating against these fixed targets are ex-tensive. The KGB and the GRU have in this case the unstinting cooperation of the civilian and military intelligence services of the Warsaw Pact countries, which share Moscow's concern for the NATO threat. Their embassies and consulates throughout NATO Europe supplement the work of the Soviet services. The Poles and the Rumanians as well as the Russians have placed agents in NATO headquarters, some of them in central positions with across-the-board access to NATO's classified papers.

One of the earliest, and most damaging, penetrations of high-level NATO documents and communications was carried out by an American sergeant in the late fifties. The KGB's brilliant manipulation of Sergeant Robert Johnson's assignment as a guard at the Armed Forces Courier Station at Orly airport is outlined in the next chapter.

Year in and year out Germany and Germans have been the steadiest and most productive avenue to the Brussels headquarters. As we have seen, secrets purloined from the German parliament, from the Chancellor's office, and from the German intelligence service all contained highly classified items on NATO. The German Defense Ministry stands high on the list.

In the fifties a Christian Democratic Party functionary agreed to work for the East Germans out of an urge to revenge himself on his boss, whom he hated. His greatest asset proved to be his wife, who worked in the Defense Ministry.

A senior civil servant in Defense, Peter Fuhrmann was ironically the government's expert on military secrets and had testified in several espionage trials. When he was arrested in November 1961 in the act of passing a classified document on German rearmament, it emerged that he had been delivering defense secrets for the past seven years.

The most senior Soviet agent within NATO was West German Rear Admiral Luebke, who retired because of ill health in September 1968. Up to January 1968 he had been deputy chief of NATO's logistics division. Confronted with the proof of his photographing top-secret NATO documents for Soviet intelligence, he disappeared a few days later (he called the evidence a frame-up), and was found dead, a victim of either suicide or murder. The results of the subsequent investigation have been kept secret, leaving wide room for speculation on the damage he had done—and why. The admiral apparently had a kinky twist: a married man with five children, he gained a particular pleasure from photographing nude girls.

On the same day as Luebke's death, BND deputy chief Major General Horst Wendland committed suicide, apparently for personal reasons. Several other deaths on the same period and the sudden flight of several high-ranking scientists and physicists originally from East Germany set off a storm of indignation and speculation. One scientist, Dr. Harald Gottfried, a physicist at the Karlsruhe atomic center, did not run, and upon his arrest more than eight hundred pages of classified documents were found in his home.

The biggest German spy scandal in recent years blew into the open in December 1977. Three persons had been arrested the previous year: Renate Lutz, principal secretary to the Defense Minister; her husband, Lothar, also a Defense employee; and Jurgen Wregel, who worked on the administrative staff of the Navy. The intelligence take was understandably broad: German Army organization and planning, the Western analysis of the defense situation, estimates of the 1975 maneuvers, etc. More than one fifth of the take involved NATO information, including material on its nuclear weapons.

A year later an East German couple, Horst and Marie-Luise Schadock, were arrested. Both had worked for several years in German and NATO defense installations.

Though, on the surface, Bonn has been the major avenue into NATO, all the capitals of the NATO allies lead to Brussels.

Perhaps the most productive of these external sources was a former French professor, George Paques, who had been recruited by the KGB at the end of the war. He occupied various senior positions in the French Government until 1958, when he was assigned to the general staff of the Ministry of National Defense. In 1962 he became deputy director of the press and information service of NATO in Paris, where he remained until his arrest in August 1963.

Among the most conspicuous Soviet successes in the sixties were two agents within NATO headquarters itself who had access to a broad range of NATO documents.

Francis Roussilhe, a Frenchman working for Rumanian intelligence, headed the registry of NATO's International Secretariat and had access to almost all NATO documents. During his career he passed more than five thousand documents to the Rumanian service for transmittal to Moscow.

Another senior NATO employee, Nahat Imre, a Turkish official married to a Hungarian wife, worked for years in the finance department and in December 1967 became financial comptroller in the international staff. Since all requests or authorizations for major expenditures went over his desk, he had direct access to the most highly classified NATO activities. When he was arrested in 1968, he had scores of photographs of NATO documents in his possession. He confessed that he had been working for various East European services from the late fifties on.

What is impressive about these cases is the length of time the agents operated successfully before they were caught: six, eight, ten, twelve years.

Scores of other penetrations were uncovered in the sixties: hardly a year went by without another NATO spy making the headlines in Europe. The NATO sieve leaked through the seventies, and the tempo of disclosures reached a climax in 1979.

In March of that year a German secretary, Ursel Lorenzen, who had been working in NATO headquarters since 1966, was recalled to East Germany to save her skin. Her identity had been blown by a defector from the East German service. She obligingly gave a TV interview in East Berlin in which she outlined some of her take on NATO contingency plans and military exercises. A bevy of German secretaries followed in her wake.

There is not much to be said for NATO security. In the face of this persistent onslaught—and the known cases, it must be assumed, are only a fraction of the total—it would be fatuous to consider NATO secrets at any level "secure." The superiority of Warsaw Pact forces over the NATO alliance is compounded even further by the Warsaw command's intelligence grasp of its potential enemy. There is little reason to assume that NATO will do any better in keeping its secrets in the eighties.

ON DOCUMENTS

The KGB wants documents, classified records on paper: blueprints, operating and repair manuals, tables of organization and equipment, military contingency plans, charts of electronic and chemical processes, records of experiments, minutes of meetings, correspondence within and among military and civilian government agencies.

Far more than any Western service the KGB focuses on documents. For the British or American services the best penetration of a Soviet or East European target is a man on the inside, a knowledgeable man who can deliver orally or in writing the information he gets from his job. *He* is the producing agent, the live source whose secret reports become a trickle in the enormous river of information pouring into Western capitals. Documents are desirable but not essential.

Moscow is skeptical of information filtered through the human head, Soviet or foreign. For the KGB a human agent at any level is not himself a source but an instrument for getting or copying documents. An agent's knowledge, his judgments and opinions, his second-hand information are soft. They are subject to limitations of memory or judgment, to faulty oral transmission, to the need for evaluation. Documents are hard facts: a NATO contingency plan, a wiring diagram of the Concorde, minutes of Cabinet meetings, the correspondence between the Pentagon and Brussels, the records of a laser experiment, letters written by a German chancellor or a French defense minister, the floor plan of a California defense plant. These items speak for themselves. Their meaning is clear and unequivocal—like Dr. May's sample of uranium or a stolen Sidewinder missile or the early jet engine smuggled out of Great Britain.

Its focus on documents both complicates and simplifies the job of the KGB. Many agents are willing to tell their handlers what they know, and what they learn, even in the most sensitive of jobs. Most are unwilling, or emotionally unable, to take classified documents out of the files and film them on the spot or at home. They are, in either case, spies for a foreign power, but when they are in the possession of documents improperly, when they photograph them, and when they pass on the microfilm, they are creating tangible evidence of espionage. They can proclaim the innocuous nature of their conversations with a Soviet official to whom they report orally. They cannot refute the evidence of a document they pass to him directly or deposit in a dead drop. Most Soviet spies who have been caught have been caught in the act of transmitting documents—and the evidence stands up in court.

Yet there are clear advantages in stealing documents. With simple equipment (a Minox camera) an agent creates an inconspicuous "report" easily hidden and easily transported to the point of delivery—and it can be delivered without any visible contact with his case officer. The charm of microfilm, and even more so of microdots, is the total insulation of the agent from his KGB contact. He can mail his film to an address, or place it in a dead drop, and never see the man who gets it. An agent cannot give away an anonymous case officer.

Agents who report orally, of course, must meet with their case officers to report. Hence the employment of trade-craft practices of secret rendezvous, danger signals, and recognition signals which at best can only minimize the insecurity of their face-to-face meetings.

Documents have an even greater attraction: The age, experience, education, or sensibilities of the agent do not affect the value of the stolen documents. He (or she) may be a twenty-year-old secretary or a senior government official. He may be a corporal on night duty in an intelligence headquarters or a major general. He may be a machinist at Los Alamos or a scientist on a research project.

Nor are any demands made on the professional competence of the responsible KGB officer. All he needs to do is to service a dead drop, or pick up a letter at a specific address, return to his office, and put it in the diplomatic pouch to Moscow. He may be an old hand or a young officer on his first tour. His only concern is to guard against surveillance.

IX

AMERICAN INNOCENTS ABROAD

Soviet intelligence has recruited more American citizens to work as agents than Western services have recruited Soviet citizens.

The reason has nothing to do with a lack of patriotism.

Americans have littered the globe since the early fifties: in Western Europe and Japan, in the southern rim of Asia, in Latin America and Africa. Each one—soldier, clerk, diplomat, businessman, student—is a potential agent for the KGB.

There are hundreds of thousands of Americans living outside the United States who are relatively unscreened for emotional stability or loyalty. They live fairly open lives, even in a military command, and are accessible to local citizens or East European officials assigned to the area where they are stationed. The percentage of the unstable or greedy among them may be no higher than in the cross-section of other societies, but since there are far more Americans abroad, the gross number of potential recruits is higher.

Not only is the number of Soviet citizens abroad at any one

time far smaller, but they are screened with infinite concern for
their loyalty before they are given a foreign assignment. Access to
the run-of-the-mill Soviet officials abroad by foreigners is
difficult, in most cases impossible. Only a relative handful, the
top diplomats and intelligence officials, are permitted to act freely
in their new social environments. And these are the most carefully screened and most trusted.

Since the mid-fifties the KGB's attention to American civilian
employees stationed abroad has been systematic and persistent.
Throughout the Third World and in European capitals, more and
more "American specialists" have shown up under official Soviet
cover and now work assiduously on the American target.
Throughout the sixties and into the seventies more than two hundred direct approaches by Soviet case officers have been reported
each year by American Embassy employees. How many approaches have not been reported, we do not know. The recruitment of an American official or clerk is the pinnacle of KGB success.

In every capital of any size the KGB residency has an American section targeted on the personnel of the American Embassy.
It maintains a network of informants and agents in and around
the American colony who conduct a continuing reconnaissance of
the personalities, movements, and contacts of American diplomats, clerks, journalists, businessmen, and students.

In New Delhi, for example, during my five-year tour
(1957–62) as chief of station, it was the basic housekeeping job
of the KGB residency to run a circle of paid informants who were
in a position to report on resident foreigners. They ranged from
realtors and airline officials to black marketeers and junior Indian
journalists.

A second outpost of the residency was formed by "confidential
contacts," men such as journalists, third-world diplomats, native
and foreign businessmen, and indigenous embassy employees who
had direct access to resident or visiting foreigners. These "access
agents" are able to furnish information on the personalities, social habits, and political attitudes of the Westerners they come in
contact with in their normal occupations.

The American section of the residency included at least three
American specialists, all personable, sophisticated, and fluent in
(American) English. Its sector of confidential contacts covered a
wide spectrum: a scattering of Indian employees in the American
Embassy and other official installations; at least four young In-

dian journalists, two of them on the staff of the left-wing weekly, *Blitz;* the Sikh owner of a restaurant in Connaught Circle, the hub of New Delhi; a Czech second secretary, also fluent in English, who avidly sought out Americans for lunches or picnics.

The main job of these contacts was to spot likely recruits, make their acquaintance, and turn them over to an officer of the American section.

One of the most active, and conspicuous, spotters was the Sikh restaurateur. He was a handsome, engaging bachelor of thirty who catered to an international clientele. He particularly liked Americans, and his restaurant became a popular spot for young Americans to visit for after-hours disco-dancing parties with the young set: Indian men, and a few liberated women; junior diplomats from the Polish and Czech embassies and the British and Canadian high commissions; and American secretaries and file clerks.

It was an obvious setting, and the routine was simple. In one case the Sikh spotted a likely American candidate, singled her out for special attention, and passed the word to his KGB case officer. At the next party a Soviet third secretary (attractive, excellent English) showed up and cultivated her friendship. When he proposed a private date, the contact was broken off.

In spite of their persistent explorations the KGB had only one success that we know of—and it is not even clear whether the American, a State Department code clerk, was recruited in New Delhi or on a subsequent assignment in Southeast Asia. What we do know is that the code clerk, John Disco Smith, somehow ended up in Moscow as the tool for an anti-American propaganda campaign by the unofficial Peace and Progress radio. The preliminary Moscow broadcasts exposed some of the vile episodes the CIA had supposedly been guilty of in southern Asia, including the imaginary exploits of the CIA station chief in Delhi. The broadcasts also promised a further cloak-and-dagger series in which I was apparently to be the hero, but they never came off. Perhaps the audience reaction to the pilot did not achieve a high enough rating.

Sex and the Single Woman

The KGB takes capitalist sex very seriously. It is a business to be studied, not a game to be played. Among the classified studies now in KGB headquarters is a dissertation on the effect of education on American sexual mores.

For the KGB, sex is a dual weapon. It can be used not only to entrap a man by pressure, as in Moscow, but to seduce a woman abroad into voluntary cooperation. Blackmail is the rape of the will. Persuasion is the seduction of the body and the spirit. The unmarried American woman working abroad has been a rich target for persuasion—through purely physical sex, through love, or through marriage.

Unmarried American women and girls working in our overseas embassies have had more than their share of KGB-sponsored sexual advances in the past twenty years. They are prized objects for KGB attention: secretaries, code clerks, and heads of registry have normal access to classified documents. They know their bosses well, and what their bosses are up to. They can place a bug with ease.

The KGB is aware, as every service is, that government employees assigned abroad are more easily compromised than in their domestic milieu. They tend to let their guards down in a foreign environment: they talk more freely, mix more easily with "foreigners," seek out new friends. They often take a more open approach to pleasure and adventure.

The unmarried woman is doubly susceptible. Living in a community of older married couples, without old friends or acquaintances, she is often bored or lonely in her off-time. She is ready to meet strangers, American or foreign. Socially active or a loner, good-looking or homely, she is in the KGB book ready for fun or for love, and an affair of the loins or of the heart is one more avenue to the documents to which she has access.

The role of seducer can be played by a KGB officer, a non-Russian intermediary, or a Soviet illegal masquerading as an American civilian.

The KGB approach to an unmarried female clerk or secretary is direct if a specific handle is available.

An official Soviet visitor to a West European trade fair telephones a secretary of the local American Embassy and delivers a letter from a distant cousin of hers in Latvia. The Russian is an attractive man, accomplished in his work. They have dinner, several dates, then a brief affair. When it is time for him to return home, he introduces her to a local friend as a channel for keeping in touch with him in Moscow. The friend, of course, is a KGB officer assigned to recruit her.

Another "introduction" attests to good file work in Moscow.

A Soviet third secretary calls on an American clerk and brings her a message from a mutual acquaintance, a Soviet civilian whom she met on a Black Sea cruise five years earlier.

In the absence of such excuses for direct contact, the KGB station employs its local resources to meet the right girl.

Embassy singles often spend their off-duty time with each other, and possibly a few local citizens, at their favorite bars, cafés, or discotheques. As in New Delhi the KGB can easily identify these hangouts and just as easily recruit some young local citizens to join the embassy crowd. These spotters are then in a position to size up the clientele, find out what they do, spot likely candidates, and arrange to introduce into the group a young Soviet or Polish diplomat with good English and good manners who is also out to enjoy life.

When a woman appears both susceptible and worthwhile, the KGB will invest considerable time and talent to construct a persuasive scenario.

The mark is an attractive twenty-five-year-old clerk in the American Embassy in The Hague with an equally attractive job in the central registry, the repository of all classified embassy cables, documents, and memoranda.

Eleanor had obviously been spotted in a previous assignment, and her personality, habits, and tastes were already on file in Moscow.

Soon after her arrival at The Hague, Eleanor met an attractive young American named George at a "club" dance for embassy singles and young Dutchmen.

George was a Soviet illegal carefully prepared in Moscow for The Hague assignment: identity, legend, forged papers. He was a very American American, with a taste for baseball and hamburgers. He had previously been assigned to the Washington residency under diplomatic cover.

George told Eleanor he was born in Singapore and became a naturalized American citizen after World War II. He had worked since as a construction laborer in the States and as a merchant seaman, and got off his ship at Amsterdam to look for a job in Europe. He was precise and detailed in recounting his life story. He clearly liked her.

George rapidly cultivated Eleanor in a whirlwind romance, and the two became engaged. She agreed to marry him at the end of her embassy tour.

So far the plot is routine.

George then went to *West* Berlin, ostensibly to get a temporary job through a friend of his, but actually to make contact with his Soviet case officer in East Berlin and discuss the further "development" of the case.

The loving pair stayed constantly in touch by phone and mail, and Eleanor visited him twice in his West Berlin apartment (a Soviet safe house).

An accident intervened: George was badly banged up in an auto accident in *East* Berlin, and Eleanor rushed up to visit him in the hospital. Before she left, George gave her a roll of film and asked her to leave it at his apartment in West Berlin. The preliminary trap was then sprung: on her way out of the hospital she was arrested by the East German police, frisked, and accused of spying. The police interrogated her, with occasional slaps in the face; and she finally admitted George gave her the film.

She was now not only properly intimidated but concerned for the welfare of her lover.

Her confrontation with George was carefully arranged in a compound to which George had been brought in his hospital bed and apparently under guard. The room in which they met had a peephole (in this case no TV cameras were required).

In a brief exchange when the guards were looking the other way, he told her he had been working secretly for a Western intelligence service and begged her forgiveness for involving her. This was just the right note: her love for him was deepened.

Then came the pitch.

The KGB officer who had monitored the meeting from the next room then entered in full uniform. He discussed their problem and promised to let both George and Eleanor go free if she would work for Soviet intelligence in Holland. Eager to save her lover, she agreed and was released.

Eleanor never got around to supplying the KGB with any documents, but the adroitness of her development, as well as the selection of her seducer, reflects favorably on the KGB's psychological perception.

The KGB's exploitation of sex as a hook for the unmarried Western woman is now in its fourth decade. Its greatest known successes have come, as we have seen, in West Germany, with its disproportionate number of war widows and single women. Its successes with American women can only be guessed at. Whether or not the modern liberated woman of the West is a harder or an easier target for the KGB is an open question.

The Cash Nexus

Money is the KGB's main handle for the recruitment of men, especially for those brought up in a capitalist society, where money is not only a means to good living but a symbol of success. Greed, and the ambition for success that goes with it, ranks with sexual need as the most powerful drives in the KGB's view of the capitalist psyche—and who will challenge its judgment?

Soviet intelligence rates money especially high in the recruitment of Americans. A GRU manual from the early sixties* stresses that many Americans have just one desire: to make more money. "It can be said that Americans encourage any method of getting rich." Paying an American agent for his work increases "his personal interest in working for us. . . . This disciplines the agent and improves the case officer's authority." Money reinforces "the ideological motivation of an agent. . . . Material incentives should be used to consolidate an agent relationship, even in those cases where the basic factor motivating an American to cooperate with our Intelligence Service is ideological."

It cautions against using money as a simple "barter" arrangement, for the Americans involved realize that working with the KGB is a risky affair, not a simple business deal.

In another manual, this one from the KGB's training curriculum of the same period, the importance of money is also stressed, though somewhat more pompously:

> Correct use of the factor of material interest first of all requires an understanding of the psychological makeup of the American, who soberly regards money as the sole means of ensuring personal freedom and independence. . . . In the average American, this attitude toward money engenders an indifference to the means by which it is obtained, although sometimes involving risk. . . .

* The GRU manual is translated in Chapter 3 ("The Prikhodko Lecture") of *The Penkovskiy Papers* (New York, 1965). The KGB manual quoted in this chapter can be most conveniently found in Appendix C of John Barron's *KGB* (New York, 1974).

The KGB is also convinced that Americans like to work abroad because they make more money through higher salaries, rental allowances, and tax breaks. Junior personnel are doubly vulnerable. If they are on a low salary, especially in a high-cost capital, they need more funds to enjoy the local fleshpots. In assessing an agent-prospect, the case officer must always try to determine his income as well as his tastes.

Bribing men to spy has been used most effectively by both the KGB and the GRU in recruiting members of the American armed forces stationed abroad: they are easily accessible to direct social cultivation by local men and women as well as by Soviet intelligence officers. Noncoms and junior officers are the favorite target —the ordinary GI rarely has access to intelligence of interest.

In the roster of KGB successes are penetrations of the Joint Chiefs of Staff, of top-secret communications inside the Pentagon, of classified Air Force communications and research centers, of the Strategic Air Command, of innumerable missile sites in the United States and abroad.

At the top of the roster stands Sergeant Robert Lee Johnson, whom the KGB picked up in Berlin in the fall of 1952. He became the key man, ten years later, in the KGB's most productive military espionage operation of the Cold War.

Johnson was a walk-in with a grudge against the Army. Not very bright, a heavy drinker and a gambler, a man with no prospects, he passed over some routine papers from his job as clerk in the Berlin Command G-2. He also delivered his best friend to his Karlshorst case officer. A homosexual, and brighter than Johnson, the friend was eventually chosen by the KGB to become an agent under commercial cover in Washington, D.C.

When Johnson was transferred to a finance clerk job in France in April 1955 and then discharged from the Army the next year, he had no contact with the KGB until, in January 1957, he was reactivated and told to rejoin the Army. Johnson reported on several missile sites during his stateside assignments, and on his transfer to an Army base in France, he was put in the hands of "Victor," a Soviet case officer in the Paris embassy. Urged to get a job at Supreme Allied Headquarters in Paris, Johnson found an assignment as a guard at the Armed Forces Courier Station at Orly field near Paris.

There then began a flawless operation, a classic of ingenuity, technical competence, and coordination masterminded by Moscow Center.

The target was the "impenetrable" vault at Orly which housed, for a day or more, the top-secret-plus communications from the Pentagon to the American commands in Europe: secret and top-secret documents, cipher systems, and cryptographic equipment.

Carefully guided by Victor from Paris, Johnson broke through the three barriers that guarded the vault: a steel door closed by a metal bar with combination locks at each end, and a second steel door to the vault itself with a complicated key lock. By a combination of pure chance and alertness to opportunities, Johnson made a clay impression of the vault key and the combination of one of the locks. By the use of an X-ray-type device Johnson applied to the second lock for half an hour, Moscow was able to secure the final combination.

During the next five months, from December 1962 until April 1963, the operation worked like a clock: seven times at fifteen minutes after midnight each Saturday night Johnson, alone on the weekend, delivered his haul in a flight bag to his contact a few minutes away, the pouches were driven the twenty-four miles to Paris, opened, photographed, and resealed by a team of technicians from Moscow, driven back to Orly, and handed over to Johnson at 3:15 A.M.

The intelligence take was, of course, of enormous value to Moscow: American military cryptographic materials, crucial aspects of NATO defenses and contingency plans, Western estimates of Soviet military capabilities, and the most intimate inside details of the various military bureaucracies involved in Europe and Washington. It is not surprising that Khrushchev himself took some time off to read through the prize items.

If an intelligence service is to be measured by its best operations, the Orly affair puts KGB competence at the highest professional level. Here are some of the elements involved:

—The errorless coordination of actions by at least four European residencies—in Paris, Bonn, Vienna, and Amsterdam.

—The movement of more than a dozen Moscow technicians disguised as couriers who arrived in Paris at precise intervals via Algeria, Germany, Denmark, and Belgium.

—The careful selection of almost unobservable meeting sites around Orly that made Johnson able to be away from his post for not more than five minutes.

—The extraordinary competence of the Paris technicians in processing the documents in Paris within an hour, and Moscow's technical research in developing a sophisticated combination detector.

—A carefully prepared escape plan with forged British and American passports for Johnson and an emergency rendezvous in the Netherlands.

Credit must also be given to both Moscow and the Paris case officers for their painfully patient handling of a stupid and undisciplined agent to carry out a set of actions requiring both precision and promptness. In the seventh and last raid on the vault, Johnson went to sleep during the vital three hours, missed his 3:15 A.M. contact, and almost blew the operation.

Other members of the armed forces recruited for money range from sergeant to colonel. Here are a few specimens:

—Captain J. P. Kauffman was "trapped" during a visit to East Germany in 1960. He provided data on U. S. Air Force installations in Greenland and Japan and was debriefed on the identity and personal qualities of Air Force officers stationed in both places. Vulnerable officers were clearly to be explored further.

—Yeoman First Class N. C. Drummond was first contacted in London in 1957, and after he signed receipts for $250, he was hooked. He supplied classified Navy documents for the next several years: Navy manuals and defense data from the Newport Naval Base. He collected over $20,000 up to the time of his arrest and trial in 1964.

—R. G. Thompson, who served with the U. S. Air Force in Berlin, defected to East Germany, was sent back to his post, and later trained in espionage in the Soviet Union. He spied for six years, from June 1957 to July 1963, both abroad and in the United States. He supplied classified documents, photographs of military equipment, data on missile sites, and intelligence information in Air Force files. He used a short-wave radio to receive instructions and requirements from KGB/Moscow.

—Lieutenant Colonel (Retired) W. H. Whalen worked in the Pentagon with the Joint Chiefs of Staff, and was paid over five thousand dollars between December 1959 and December 1961. He was arrested in 1966 and sentenced to fifteen years.

—In 1970 Staff Sergeant Attardi got three years for copying top-secret plans from the document section in Heidelberg, Germany.

—In July 1973 Sergeant James D. Woods was arrested in New York City with highly classified documents in the trunk of his rental car. He had been assigned to the Air Force Office of Special Investigations since March, when he was transferred from the Travis Air Force Base in California. He was caught at a rendezvous in Queens with a first secretary of the Soviet Embassy in Washington who traveled to New York to make the meeting.

—Air Force Master Sergeant Walter T. Perkins, the ranking noncom at the Air Defense Weapons Center at Tyndall Air Force Base in Florida, had access to all the Center's classified documents. He was arrested at the Panama City, Florida, airport in October 1971 and charged with trying to smuggle out of the country documents on radar detection system and Air Force data on Soviet and East European missile systems.

Though these and other cases simply involved money, some of the military spies were neurotic to the point of psychosis. Master Sergeant Perkins, for example, pleaded not guilty by reason of insanity caused by acute alcoholism (he drank a fifth of whiskey daily). Another recruited agent, an Army deserter, G. J. Gessner, was charged in 1962 with passing nuclear secrets to the Russians after he deserted from the Army in December 1960. He was found mentally unstable and incapable of standing trial.

Other GIs were recruited under pressures other than bribery. Staff Sergeant H. W. Boeckenhaupt, who was arrested in 1966 at the March Air Force Base in California, cited Soviet threats to his father in West Germany as the reason for his going along. He had previously worked in the Pentagon with a top-secret clearance.

There are other lures for male Americans on a foreign assignment.

Dozens of American officers and men were recruited in West Berlin in the late forties and fifties with the assistance of German girls. In one case an American colonel, bald and flabby, a married man in his forties, was bent on a last hurrah. He took on a twenty-four-year-old German girl as his mistress, who delivered him to the KGB. He got her a job in his own military intelligence outfit and, later, at the Tempelhof Air Force Base in West Berlin. Both he and his mistress were able to supply useful information from their sources.

The KGB has practiced "false flag" recruitments when a direct Soviet approach seemed undesirable. In 1950 two American Jewish counterintelligence officers were recruited in Vienna by a Soviet intelligence officer masquerading as an Israeli.

Almost thirty years later an American in Canada was recruited by a KGB officer posing as a Canadian intelligence officer.

Another approach reflects an odd notion in the KGB's mind of the racial scene in America. A black third secretary in an American Embassy in Europe was considered vulnerable because he was married to a white European girl. After a few social meetings with a KGB officer, he was asked to carry out a few simple unclassified tasks. He broke off the contact.

American civilians are no less susceptible to bribery than the members of our armed forces. Indeed, capitalist businessmen are considered fairly easy marks by the KGB, for they can be bribed not only with cold cash but with business opportunities. The means used to "help out" an American (or German) businessman cover a broad range: providing a "loan" to set up a private business; briefing a salesman on how to make the right contacts in Moscow (and paying the airfare, if he is agreeable), or promising a lucrative contract with the Soviet trade mission or a Soviet market for his products. As commercial contacts have grown between East and West, these opportunities have multiplied. The contacts are in a nebulous field of semisecret espionage, for in most cases the initial relationship does not involve classified information, but the industrial and commercial intelligence that Moscow needs to act effectively in the complex world of capitalist business. The restrictions placed upon West-East exchanges after the Soviet invasion of Afghanistan are unlikely to affect business as usual at this level of commercial intercourse.

American students are also a global target from Tokyo to Latin America. Their recruitment in almost all cases also involves a cash nexus. A KGB "fellowship" covering the cost of four or more years of education is, in effect, a salary being paid to an incipient agent during his training period.

Eastern Europe is a particularly easy locale for operating against American students, not only those studying in Berlin, but visitors from abroad. During the Vietnam War a local journalist held seminars in East Germany on behalf of the anti-Vietnam War movement. Among the Americans who attended, one was recruited by the seminar leader himself and several others cultivated for future contact by other "guests" at the conference.

An American student in Paris married to an East German girl visited her relatives and was sized up by East German intelligence. He wanted to become a journalist, and was offered the money he needed for his future education in return for the modest task of spotting his student acquaintances in Paris (and later in Rome) who were "sympathetic" to East Germany or the Soviet Union. On his return to the United States, contact was resumed.

The KGB will go to great lengths to spot likely student candidates. In England, for example, the London residency took pictures of the anti-war demonstrations in Grosvenor Square during the late sixties, ran down the identities of American student participants, spotted some in the hard sciences, and approached several after their return to the States.

The KGB has also apparently determined that the only way to recruit a CIA officer in the field is to bribe him with a tidy sum of cold cash.

The CIA Target

The CIA's interest in recruiting a KGB (or GRU) official abroad is matched by the KGB's focus on CIA officers in our overseas stations.

There was, by the late fifties, no problem in establishing the identity of most KGB officers under diplomatic cover—just as the KGB found it a simple matter to identify the CIA officers under official cover from the telltale biographical listings in open State Department publications (an "exposure" later practiced by organized anti-CIA Americans). The *primary* concern of both KGB and CIA officers is not to hide their own affiliation, but to guarantee the security of the agents they meet. Identifying a CIA or KGB officer is barely a first step toward identifying any one of his agents, for the training of both is devoted to equipping them for secret work in a hostile environment.

The first step in the KGB game involved direct social contacts with the CIA officers in the embassy.

In New Delhi, during the late fifties, I encouraged our more experienced officers to get to know the "American specialists" in the KGB residency, to accept invitations to lunch, tennis, or hunting, or to enter into a family-to-family relationship. Our own purpose, of course, was the same as the KGB's: to size up the opposition, to fill in the personality dossiers at headquarters, to look for a vulnerable spot.

My own closest contact was, by happenstance, the head of the

GRU residency whom I met through a mutual Indian friend. After some casual social encounters I invited him to lunch at my home, and for over a year we had private lunches almost once a month featured by serious discussions of such contemporary matters as the Bay of Pigs (he thought it a pretty sad exercise), the Chinese development of communes (he thought them premature), the Sino-Soviet split (he thought the Chinese would pose no problem to Moscow for at least another twenty years), etc. Up to the time he left, he made no impolite advances—nor did I.

These "friendships" served our purpose in giving a handful of Soviet intelligence officers a friendly face and a telephone number that one of them might find useful in the future, if for whatever deeply personal reasons he decided to change sides. We were not so naïve as to expect a KGB officer to be persuaded by money or American charm to work for us.

Nor has the KGB depended on Soviet charm or Marxist ideology in the attempts it has made to recruit a CIA officer. The crux of every offer has been money, lots of money—up to a quarter million dollars.

Once a KGB officer has decided that the CIA man whom he has been cultivating may be open to an offer—he may be very friendly, sympathetic in his remarks about the Soviet Union, or critical of Washington policy—he follows a simple scenario.

After several social engagements or a year's "development," the KGB officer invites his CIA friend to a private lunch—at home or in a restaurant—to meet "someone you'll be interested in." The third man, sent from Moscow headquarters, is a KGB expert in handling delicate situations with Americans. His visit has a second purpose: anonymous in the area he visits, any incident or noisy turndown will not involve an accredited Soviet diplomat. I know of several such ploys that ended in turndowns.

One of the most amusing took place several years ago in Berlin. A Karlshorst officer had met and developed an employee of the CIA's Berlin base. On their last social contact before the KGB made its offer, the conversation centered on a single subject: how much it cost to live in America. The KGB officer had one simple query in mind: what is "a lot of money" in the States. He went up the ladder: $25,000, $50,000, $100,000? The CIA man agreed that $100,000 was a lot of money. The KGB man asked how much *he* earned.

At their next meeting in a West Berlin restaurant, the third man was introduced, and after a time the KGB friend left the table with a lame excuse, and the two were alone. The offer was

$150,000. Our man refused. "If that is not enough, name a figure. Money is no object with us." Since our man refused to name a figure, the conversation was over.

On another occasion, in a Near East capital, a third man was brought in to a meeting in a residential suburb. After drinks, caviar, and Russian dumplings, he made an offer of $250,000. The CIA mark turned it down without indignation but proceeded to make a counter-offer: half a million if you work for us. Again the conversation was over.

In some of these cases the KGB tries to impress the target with its extensive knowledge about him: we know all about you. The KGB officer will cite small facts about his past life, discuss his hometown with familiar references to local landmarks, or show him a picture of his car in front of his house in the District of Columbia. Apparently this omniscience is designed to soften up the candidate for a job with an omnipotent service.

The question arises, of course, in these two-man confrontations: who is doing what to whom? Who profits?

We hear, on our side, only of those propositions that have been turned down. Out of all these KGB hits, has one been quietly accepted? We do not know.

What we do know is that the KGB does not fool around with CIA officers in the field—no psychological persuasion, no ideological talk, no small hooks. Cold cash is their only weapon against men they consider otherwise impregnable, for even CIA officers are products of the capitalist system.

The face-to-face association of CIA and KGB officers has given rise to some silly myths. The two services do not "collaborate" on espionage or counterespionage missions. They do not exchange information of mutual interest—say, on the Chinese. They do not fall in love with each other as fellow professionals looking down on the naïve and ignorant herd. They are not infected by an international camaraderie that cuts across national loyalties.

They would otherwise not be so intent on recruiting each other.

Is there, or has there been, a KGB agent in the Operations Directorate of the CIA?

I have lived through, at first or second hand, several investigations of suspected KGB agents in the CIA, most of them sparked by vague assertions or imprecise leads from KGB defectors (a man named Tasha or one whose name began with "K"). An extraordinary effort was, of course, devoted to following up *any* allegation of a mole in CIA ranks at headquarters or abroad. The European pattern—top KGB agents in the British, French, and German services—was for some counterintelligence experts persuasive, though the prewar and postwar circumstances of the European services were far different from the American. In any event the most thorough search did not come up with an accredited KGB agent during my tenure up to 1970, though the search itself for some years created a climate of suspicion that seriously hampered efforts to recruit Soviet intelligence personnel and fully exploit the KGB defectors who came our way.

The question, of course, must remain open, for no one can prove a negative in matters of this sort. No one can categorically assert that there is no KGB agent in the CIA—or in the Congress, the Department of State, or the White House.

Only one convincing negative would appear possible: reports from a Western agent in the American desk of the KGB's Foreign Directorate in Moscow, or the testimony of a KGB defector with recent experience on that desk. Yet even a KGB defector of high rank who assures his interrogators that the KGB does not have a penetration of any of these offices will still not convince the paranoid observer: was he sent out to lull the FBI into a false sense of security?

Vigilance, as the Russians say, is essential, but that will not be enough to quiet some people's nerves.

ON THE NURTURE OF AMERICANS

The proper handling of agents must be suited to their temperaments. Some can be barked at or threatened—within limits. Others require softer treatment: wheedling, cajolery, flattery, praise. The prescription will vary with the age, ego, education, and national origin of the agent.

Americans, for example, are prized as agents by Soviet intelligence for some of their national traits. It is their "efficiency, resourcefulness, boldness, and perseverance" that, in the words of the GRU manual, makes them good agents. In addition, the familiarity of the average American with machines and appliances facilitates his training in, for example, the use of radio communications.

Yet other national traits demand some caution in handling Americans.

Since Americans "are distinguished by their efficiency and resourcefulness," Soviet case officers must be precise and efficient in *their* handling of the operation.

Since Americans have a sense of humor, the case officer is advised to tell jokes and be witty in his contacts in order to establish an easy rapport with his agent.

Since Americans are very patriotic, the case officer "must be careful not to indiscriminately criticize things American like making disparaging remarks about 'American culture.'"

Since Americans, "to a larger degree than representatives of many other peoples, have a natural love of freedom and independence, and do not like discipline," the case officer must not be rude in word or officious in manner: "he must not order the agent around."

Americans have a serious negative trait: they "make poor conspirators" and are often careless. An American agent must accordingly be briefed with extreme care on coming to a secret meeting or filling a dead drop.

Money is, of course, a crucial factor in recruiting Americans, but a highly delicate matter as well.

The KGB manual recognizes that ". . . Americans of interest to the Soviet Intelligence Service are financially well off and are antagonistic toward the Soviet Union. Consequently, these persons can be developed successfully only when the American sees that he can earn good money by collaborating with us."

The manual goes on to urge caution:

> Despite the acquisitiveness of an overwhelming majority of Americans intelligence operations based on material incentives should not become a simple "barter" arrangement. Americans understand that unlike commercial activity, agent relationships with Soviet Foreign Intelligence subject them to great risk, and they appraise any relationship which has developed with our workers very carefully. Therefore, considerable tact must be used in giving money, and account must be taken of the degree to which the agent has been prepared for this.

For the KGB money is not only a hook for recruiting an American male (few women have spied for cash), but a lever for controlling his performance.

Hooking a man is relatively simple: paying him for doing an innocuous piece of research, for writing an unclassified article for a magazine "back home," for giving English lessons, for buying (for "my friend in Moscow") a piece of electronic equipment a Soviet citizen cannot buy.

Once taking money becomes an acceptable habit, the agent-candidate is more easily led to supplying classified information he has access to. He has accepted an obligation to the donor, a business obligation, and he has committed himself to doing further business. If he is not aware of what his acceptance of cash or a gift means, he can be gently reminded.

When he is fully recruited, a paid agent has the same cash-nexus with his case officer that any employee has with his employer.

The KGB is a business concern: it wants a return on its investments. The agent must earn his money. He must carry out his boss's orders. He can be fired for poor performance.

Money now becomes an instrument of manipulation. An untested agent can be paid by piecework, or he can be promised a large bonus for delivering a particular document. When an agent is on a regular salary, he can be promised a raise to inspire better performance, or his regular stipend can be cut down for poor work. If he is shifted to an unproductive job, he can be put on leave without pay.

A problem arises with principled agents. Soviet intelligence may rate principle higher than pay, but it wants to pay even "ideological" agents a salary to reenforce its control. When Colonel Bykov wanted Whittaker Chambers to pay his Washington contacts and was told that taking money would violate their principles, Bykov settled for the gift of some Bokhara rugs.

Sometimes subtlety is demanded. An American agent, the KGB manual noted, "still works effectively, but even now always likes the transfer of money to be preceded by a discussion of his unselfish aid to Soviet science."

X

PLAYGROUND
U.S.A.

From the days of Chambers, Bentley, and the Rosenbergs New York City, not Washington, has been the principal center for the KGB's American operations. It is the largest residency in the capitalist world. During the past ten years, there have been at any one time from two hundred to two hundred and fifty Soviet intelligence officers on its staff (out of a total, now, of less than eight hundred Soviet diplomats). The GRU residency ranges in size between fifty and seventy-five officers.

Moscow's ability to supply official cover for these men is almost unlimited: the Soviet consulate, the trade mission (Amtorg) and news agencies, the Soviet quota of permanent employees in the United Nations, and the Soviet mission to the United States.

There is a special bonus for KGB operators in New York. Not only do they have secure cover positions within the United Nations itself, but the more than one hundred permanent missions to the U.N. contain innumerable third-world diplomats of interest to the KGB, especially young African and Latin American diplomats. Here, in the daily workings of the U.N. and during the sessions of its General Assembly, the enterprising KGB officer can spot and study prospects with ease. He can develop a colleague into a friend and pass on the contact to a Soviet colleague in Accra or Rio when the young diplomat finishes his U.N. tour.

African and Spanish specialists in the KGB residency are also available to pick up contacts with diplomats already recruited as agents in their home countries for whatever information they can report on the business before the U.N. or in their own delegations. KGB agent contacts have been noted in the U.N. corridors and, in one case, in a stairwell.

For three years, in the late sixties, I had the opportunity to see their work close up. As chief of the newly formed U.S. station, my principal concern was the recruitment of Soviet and East European diplomats in New York and Washington. Up to 1963 the intelligence officers among these diplomats were of greatest concern and the main FBI mission was to uncover and neutralize their work against American targets. Finally, in 1963, the CIA was authorized to carry out intelligence operations designed to recruit them as intelligence agents for use abroad—either after they transferred to another foreign post or to their own headquarters. Our recruitment efforts required the closest coordination with the FBI's counterespionage effort, for the same man—a Soviet or Czech intelligence officer—could now have a double interest as a security target for the FBI or as a prospective intelligence agent for the CIA. We were at last able to exploit the advantage of operating on our own home ground—as the KGB had been for fifty years in their operations against Western diplomats in Moscow.

For the KGB, Manhattan is an easy, inviting playground. With its big banks, its big corporations, its stock exchange and commodity markets, it is the power center of American capitalism. It is the residence of diplomats from over a hundred countries assigned to the United Nations. It has close ties to Washington, where the secrets are.

Manhattan and its environs are a picnic spot for open and secret meetings. It is congested, exuberant, and fast-moving. Its congestion is more attractive than that of Calcutta or Tokyo, where a white face stands out. Its inhabitants offer a smorgasbord of faces and accents. A Slavic face, a Russian or Polish accent, a tweed suit with broad lapels are lost in the crowd.

There are thousands of spots in close range where one can post a signal for a meeting: subway entrances, street-level billboards, sidewalk construction tunnels. There are thousands of places for a brush-contact or the exchange of a few words: street corners, crowded restaurants, buses, ferries, subways.

It is an ideal locale for throwing off a surveillance: office buildings with scores of floors and banks of elevators, department stores with innumerable entrances and exits. There are narrow cross-town streets with loading bays, takeout food shops, and office-building lobbies from which one can watch for suspected tails.

There are also the neighboring boroughs, above all, Brooklyn and Queens, easily accessible, more remote from the vigilant eyes in midtown. Here the secret trysts can take place in open spaces. They almost always take place in open spaces, for the KGB has an instinctive claustrophobia. It does not like inside meetings, nor does it ever employ the "safe houses" favored by Western services. There is Prospect Park, or the Bay Ridge waterfront, or the deserted streets around the cemeteries in Queens.

And beyond the city are the suburbs.

Since the late fifties the KGB has joined the flight to the suburbs—and to the countryside of New York, Connecticut, and New Jersey. During thirty miles along a limited access highway it is not difficult to detect and throw off a tailing car. Getting off the highway, winding around a few country roads, the KGB man can be assured his meeting will be secret, whether it is at a crossroads or at a picnic table on a bluff over the Hudson.

And if he wants congestion, he can meet his man on the parking plaza of a huge shopping center in New Jersey or Long Island.

In New York it is the already recruited agent who must be given the most careful handling—someone, most likely, recruited abroad and transferred to local handlers on return to the United States. The transfer of an agent, say, in Europe or Japan to the KGB residency in New York is carried out with the greatest caution. Only after he has been thoroughly tested for discipline and competence in his overseas work will the Center authorize his transfer—and always with the usual tradecraft. In dozens of cases on record the instructions for an agent to meet his first New York contact follow a simple pattern. "Ten A.M. on June 4 at the corner of Madison and 48th. You will have a pipe in your mouth and a copy of *Time* under your left arm. A man will come up to you and ask: where do I get the train to Hoboken? You will reply: there is no train to Hoboken." If the KGB officer notes anything suspicious, he will not make the contact, and the agent must come to a prearranged second meeting site.

Agents met in this way have ranged from a small-time theatrical producer or a New York municipal employee to direct penetrations of the Pentagon.

The main KGB job in New York is to recruit new agents, and here Manhattan offers a rich variety of ordinary people easily met in bars, night spots, student unions, theater lobbies. The KGB follows a simple rule: one man can lead to another. Only against this rationale can one begin to understand why the KGB makes so many apparently random and valueless contacts and has so many low-level spotters in the various segments of New York's population—low-income Americans, resident aliens, recent immigrants. It is not who they are that counts, or what access they have to classified documents, but whether they can become a link to a person of greater interest. Here is a sampling of ordinary people who have led to bigger game:

—a young Ukrainian to his uncle in Washington (*any* relative of any federal government official is of interest);
—a taxi driver to a daily pickup fare on Park Avenue (Who is he? When does he go to what office?);
—an IBM secretary to her technician boyfriend;
—a homosexual picked up at random in Greenwich Village who has a "friend" in the United Nations;
—a bartender on Third Avenue to a steady customer from the Chase Manhattan Bank ("I'd like to meet him").

The list could go on for pages: they are all grist to the KGB mill. They may someday pay off.

And, in greater depth, the KGB runs a more broadly ranging support structure characteristic of every residency in a major Western Capital: agents who are in a position to report on other men in their circle who might make productive agents. These spotters are easily recruited (they violate no laws), and they save time and reduce the exposure of the KGB officer. Five spotters can come up with a dozen leads a year. Screened by the case officer, checked out with Moscow Center, some will become targets for professional development. The residency will pursue:

—any journalist, however low level. He meets people, picks up personal gossip, can bring along a contact to have a drink with his Russian friend.

—a first-generation American of Russian extraction who moves in émigré circles and can report on the activities and attitudes of recent Soviet immigrants;

—*any* laboratory technician, or any employee of a research firm, chemical, medical, or pharmaceutical;

—*any* employee of a defense plant.

And sex can be exploited in New York as well as in Moscow, though without the elaborate scenarios of bugged and televised hotel rooms and apartments. One handsome and debonair KGB bachelor had the not unpleasant assignment of meeting, wooing, and bedding as many female secretaries as he could find time and energy for. United Nations and large-corporation employees stood at the head of his list.

The New York Residency

All these operations, secret and open, are run out of the various branches of the residency whose chief, or resident, is housed with his front office within the headquarters of the Soviet Permanent Mission to the United Nations. Here, sealed off from the rest of the mission, with their own independent communications to Moscow, their files immune from search, the branch chiefs and their most active case officers go about their daily business in and out of the office.

The main branches of the residency are the scientific and technical, émigré, counterintelligence, and illegals. Its officers are distributed among the United Nations itself, the Soviet Permanent Mission to the U.N., the Soviet trade mission, and the official Soviet news agencies.

These officers must, for the most part, carry out their cover duties with reasonable efficiency. A U.N. official or a Tass correspondent has a job to do, and he cannot spend all his time away from his normal work. At one time in the fifties the chief of Amtorg, the trade mission, became fed up with the general sloppiness of his KGB officers. They were out of the office too much of the time, did not return their telephone calls, and failed to make meetings with American businessmen. One Amtorg chief got in a fight with the KGB resident on the issue and took his case to Moscow, where he won: Soviet-American trade is a serious matter and cannot be sacrificed for the benefit of a few spies. The new rule for the KGB officers under Amtorg cover: do your spying on your own time.

These KGB officers under official cover are readily identifiable —in New York, as in New Delhi or Bonn. Except for those on their first assignment abroad, most KGB officers have been tagged by the Western services from a wide variety of sources: from Western citizens who have been approached by a Soviet official; from Soviet agents who have turned themselves in to Western security services; from doubled Soviet agents; from the hundreds of KGB officers who have been caught in the act; from KGB defectors in the past thirty years, each of whom has identified scores or hundreds of his colleagues. Western files accumulate each year: age, grade, specialty, personality and private habits, favored methods of approach, etc.

Yet the identification of a KGB officer in the field does not curtail his secret actions. His job is not to hide himself, but to hide the identity of his agents. He is equipped by his training and experience to elude any kind of surveillance when he makes a personal meeting with his agent and to make air-tight arrangements for communicating with him indirectly through dead drops. His challenge is: catch me at it.

The men operating out of the New York residency are, for the most part, highly competent professionals, often with previous assignments in English-speaking countries.

The KGB officer at his best is a cautious and well-trained expert in studying people and in arranging the mechanics of secret communications with his agents. He is himself almost immune to the normal investigative methods employed against him: physical surveillance and electronic interception.

The talent for countersurveillance is naturally at a premium in Manhattan, where he anticipates intense, if sporadic, FBI surveillance. He will take the most elaborate precautions to make certain no one is following him, and if he fails to elude his tail, he will simply skip the meeting. Only rarely has he been traced to a secret rendezvous, unless the agent he meets has been doubled against him.

He may take hours to reach a Manhattan rendezvous: changing subways, buses, walking in and out of drug and department stores. He often plays subway tag. One man approached his meeting in Chelsea by going uptown on the subway, changing at an express stop to catch a downtown train, again going uptown and downtown once again to throw off a tail. He may drive around the deserted Bowery on a Sunday afternoon making quick turns to throw off the tailing car. When he feels free, he stops off at a telephone kiosk to make his call. He may drive out on Long Island or up along the Hudson in the daytime or at night watching his mirror. He may go on a Sunday picnic with his family and meet a "friend" in a nearby wooded area. His ingenuity in countering surveillance is his prime asset.

His telephone security is absolute. It is almost instinctive, a built-in caution that does not permit slips. Years ago I patiently read through two years of telephone intercepts of the Soviet Embassy in Havana under Batista. Not a single hint of an agent contact was detectable in the steady stream of calls to and from caterers, laundrymen, and travel agents. A counterintelligence colleague whose dull fate it was to screen thousands of such transcriptions found only a single case in which an outside caller implied an agent relationship—and he, of course, was not identifiable.

He is close-mouthed even in his own living room and in the company of his colleagues outside the office. He keeps his professional life strictly within the confines of his own "clean" premises. There is never a hint, in those conversations we have overheard, of shoptalk. And with the agents he runs there is no professional chitchat that might give away any of his other activities. When a self-confessed Soviet agent seeks to ingratiate himself with us by reporting the "secrets" his case officer has been chatting about, we know he is lying. It is a simple litmus test.

Lest he be looked upon as a paragon of perfection, it is worth noting that, being human, he can make mistakes.

An otherwise competent case officer, who consistently eluded surveillance in making his meets in the metropolitan area, went out of town to meet an agent in upstate New York. Before the set time of his rendezvous he went to a village bar, got drunk, had a fight, and was picked up by the police. He had given away at least the approximate location of one of his agents.

Another officer, assigned to make a meeting on the West Coast, took a bus to Philadelphia and there boarded a plane for San Francisco under an assumed name. When he reached his destination, however, he used his own credit card to identify himself to the hotel registry clerk. With his true name on record, his further movements could again be investigated.

Office accidents can intervene. A senior officer, quiet and imperturbable in his demeanor, normally took three or four hours to get to his meet, but one afternoon he was detained in his cover office by a series of telephone calls. He came dashing out of the U.N. mission and rushed straight to his meeting on the west side of Central Park.

The KGB officer in the field is under constant pressure to produce—and this pressure can sometimes lead to error. Since his performance is measured by the number of contacts he makes, and the number of agents he recruits, he can become too busy. He is not assigned a specific quota (an unrealistic myth), but his fitness reports depend on the amount of his activity outside his office (a pressure not common among the Western services I am acquainted with).

One overzealous KGB officer in New York, clearly a man of energy and ambition, behaved like a jitterbug making over a dozen "secret" contacts almost every week. Not as careful as he might have been in judging the value or reliability of his agents, it was relatively easy for the FBI to feed a few controlled agents into his net. Their subsequent exposure diminished his reputation and slowed down his antics.

The pressure to produce can also breed abuses, but not for long. One inept case officer who needed some recruits simply visited a local bar, struck up conversations with the barflies, and got their names. Paraded as suitable candidates for "study," they would not have fooled the boss for very long.

There are also, of course, some lemons in any elite bureaucracy open to privilege. A notorious case in New York was the nephew of a Soviet Cabinet minister whose stupidity was a free topic of conversation among his colleagues. There are also men who do not have the requisite guts: an officer who has to get drunk before he musters the courage to make an approach, or falsifies his contact report to describe a social contact as a recruited agent.

Although the KGB has a few stupid or obtuse officers who are professionals only by dint of having learned the techniques of clandestine tradecraft, Moscow sends its best men to New York (and Washington) to avoid the kind of foul-ups they have run into in less politically sensitive capitals. Some of their brightest recruits come out of the Soviet-American student exchange program. Some of the Soviet students are already marked for future KGB employment, others are assessed on their return. The most qualified, with excellent English, surefooted in the American environment, with a circle of acquaintances on and off campus, are occasionally assigned to the New York residency on their first foreign tour.

The Technical Target

The largest section of the New York residency is its Scientific and Technical Branch. It is the key collector of both open and secret information on American technology, a top KGB priority for the past thirty years. It is a fair though rough estimate that 80–90 per cent of the KGB's budget and manpower spent on American targets has been devoted to scientific and technical intelligence, both industrial and military.

The job of the S&T branch of the New York residency is to fill this maw of requirements from any available sources.

Much of the take comes from completely open sources. Trade and technical magazines are shipped to Moscow by the thousands. Technical developments reported in the press are clipped.

Soviet officials attending industrial fairs and exhibitions come back with shopping bags full of sales brochures, photographs of exhibits, technical layouts. When instructed, they buy pieces of equipment that Moscow wants.

S&T experts visit the many factories, laboratories, and research institutes that are open to them. They develop and maintain personal relationships with professors at Columbia and the Massachusetts Institute of Technology. They attend, and give, lectures to specialized academic audiences.

All of this activity is quite public and proper. No one needs KGB training to be affable, curious, and knowledgeable in his field. All the while, however, the trained S&T officer is mixing with the right people, making friends, sizing up the men he meets. Here are some scenarios:

—A young corporation executive likes his Soviet friend and is happy to invite him to dinner, introduce him to his circle of acquaintances, and do him a favor now and then by opening doors otherwise closed to him. One man leads to another.

—A laboratory assistant is pleased to be invited to dinner by a visiting Russian, talks freely of his work and his boss, and agrees to meet him next time he is in the neighborhood. The blueprints are within reach.

—A professor of biochemistry meets a knowledgeable Soviet

"fellow scientist," invites him for a weekend, discusses the literature in his field, professes interest in a visit to the Soviet Union.

—The salesman for an instruments firm with a booth at a scientific conference chats with a Russian who gives him his card. Six months later he receives a call from the Russian, who invites him to lunch.

Multiplied a thousand times, these carefully reported contacts place the Center in a position to select the right man in the right spot for what it wants and to instruct the residency to "study" him.

Recruited agents carry out a wide variety of missions.

They have been useful in circumventing the restrictions of the strategic embargo list on exports to the Soviet Union. In one case a KGB officer cultivated the acquaintance of a shady businessman in Queens, New York, and asked him to buy a computer tube for $50,000. They met, both using station wagons, in the far corner of a parking plaza for a shopping center in northern New Jersey. They parked their station wagons back to back and lifted the bulky wooden crate from one car to the other.

Scores of items on the strategic list have been sent over the years by American businessmen to individual addresses in Western Europe supplied by their KGB contacts. These transshipment operations are relatively easy for the KGB to arrange, for they involve no open violation of federal law.

Recruited agents range from an amateur sewer expert who studied sewers all his life and had a firsthand acquaintance with all the sewage systems of California, to an engineer with an American oil company who passed on the technical information available to him.

The richest haul of classified data has come from factory and laboratory research workers in the more than ten thousand companies and plants that have access to defense information ranging up to top secret. Now that Congress had directed the publication of the names of firms that have classified defense contracts, zeroing in on valuable targets has become simpler. The S&T desk men in New York check over the list for firms and locations: whom do we have in the Minneapolis area? Any lead to the Bridgeport area? However long it might take, some laborers, technicians, or engineers will be recruited for what they know or can learn.

Other branches of the residency carry out equally specialized tasks but with fewer men. The KR, or counterintelligence branch, focuses not only on the penetration of the FBI and the CIA, but the old-line federal agencies like State and Defense. It is also responsible for monitoring the security of the "Soviet colony," running informants and checking the contacts of all Soviet officials from the ambassador to the Tass journalist.

The illegals branch does not run illegals, but provides the Center with the material required to dispatch illegals to the United States. It keeps the Center up-to-date on changes in the immigration laws and procedures for getting a social security number or driver's license. It supplies birth certificates and passports when it can, and probes for vital statistics when requested by the Center.

The residency also has a steadily dwindling émigré branch.

Émigrés

It may appear curious that at this late date the KGB still maintains an émigré directorate in its Moscow headquarters and sends out émigré specialists to its major residencies. Most of the wartime Soviet émigrés have died, and nowhere is the emigration an organized group of any consequence. Moscow's forty-year pathological concern with the political and security threat they posed has clearly died down, if not out. What has taken its place is a sensible and businesslike view of their usefulness as agents in their countries of residence.

These émigrés, in New York or San Francisco, many of them second-generation Russians, Ukrainians, or Lithuanians, offer the KGB a pool for possible leads to émigrés in government, industry, or commerce. KGB officers handling support agents in these groups constantly talk about people—about friends, relatives, American acquaintances. Who does what where? Their émigré contacts may be of no use whatever for espionage purposes—clerks, shopkeepers, doormen—but on the solid thesis that one man can lead to another, they might come up with a name (and an introduction) of value to the KGB. Many of these "agents" are short-term: if they can supply nothing useful, they are simply discarded, and new ones found in their place.

Some émigrés, of course, have made it in American society. The émigré section in the San Francisco consulate pays considerable attention to the large White Russian colony on the West Coast, many of whom have done well in business and have good connections with locally prominent Americans. The KGB émigré specialists know the names and backgrounds of the most recent émigrés and they can meet and choose the ones that might be useful. They are, of course, useful as support agents, but some eventually reach positions in which they have access to the kind of information the KGB wants.

An Armenian, Sahag K. Dedeyan, worked for a defense research organization and brought out classified documents on NATO and U.S. defense matters and delivered them to his cousin, S. O. Paskalian, a diamond cutter. Paskalian photographed the documents and passed them to two Soviet United Nations officials. Both were arrested in 1975.

Two years later Ivan N. Rogalsky, a resident alien living in a Soviet émigré community in Jackson Township, New Jersey, was also arrested for espionage. He had recruited another émigré, an engineer by the name of Nekrasov, who supplied him with classified documents on satellite communications from the RCA Space Center in Princeton, New Jersey. Fortunately, Nekrasov had not been "recruited" but had reported the approach to the FBI. Rogalsky was caught in the act of passing his photographs to his case officer in the Soviet Mission to the United Nations.

Thousands of Soviet émigrés are still coming in to the United States. Many of them are educated in special fields and can hope to get responsible jobs. A handful are well-known intellectuals, both writers and artists, and make high-level contacts on their arrival.

The KGB has a threefold interest in these more recent arrivals: the nature and content of the interrogations they are subject to by American intelligence; monitoring their eventual location and jobs; and making support agents out of the more useful ones. Some, again, may eventually get jobs of interest to the KGB.

It also goes without saying that the KGB in Moscow makes every effort to recruit some of these emigrants before they leave the Soviet Union. Some have been groomed to become agents: in one case a young Central Asian Jew was trained for two years before he was granted an exit visa. *Any* emigration—Soviet, Polish, Czech, or Cuban—is normally exploited by the home service for the legal entry of a trained agent into a target country.

The Washington Residency

The GRU manual quoted before gives a (1961) operator's view of the nation's capital: ". . . the organization and utilization of agent communications in Washington are full of difficulties because of the city's small size, its limited number of public places, lack of subways, and inadequate public transportation system, especially in the suburbs." Though much changed in the following twenty years, Washington is in many ways still a large small town, not a metropolis.

The KGB residency in Washington, D.C., is by contrast with New York City modest in size (probably fewer than fifty officers) and, again probably, less active in the recruitment of government servants than the GRU residency within the Office of the Military, Air, and Naval attachés whose cover gives them ready access to their colleagues in the Department of Defense.

Operating conditions, as the manual points out, are not healthy. Washington's white residential neighborhoods are small and compact, their streets (in Georgetown, Cleveland Park, and Wesley Heights) sparsely populated at night. The Federal Triangle is densely packed with government officials who, for the most part, live in the suburbs. There is both static and mobile surveillance by the FBI.

The biggest obstacle is the high security consciousness of government employees in the Pentagon and State Department. Built-in caution is even higher among CIA and NSA employees (both located just outside Washington).

For the most part the KGB arranges its agent meetings not in the District, but in the suburbs (as in New York), in places like Shirlington or Springfield on the Virginia side of the Potomac. Philby, for example, apparently never met his handler in the District itself. Stretches of highway ensure effective countersurveillance by both case officer and agent. Meetings in the open air permit a critical survey of the surrounding terrain.

Yet the KGB residency appears to be reasonably active in recruiting and handling agents on the local scene. A Soviet attaché managed to meet a CIA employee in Washington who still had relatives in the Soviet Union. After threats against his relatives failed to pressure him into cooperation, the KGB brought his brother from the Soviet Union to Washington to help in his recruitment.

Both the KGB and Czech intelligence have worked on desk officers and clerks in the Department of State. Nor are the old-line agencies the only focus. The KGB has gone after employees of the General Accounting Office, since its files include budgets for all government projects—and the budget for a major classified project involving military research, development, or production can provide a compact answer to the most precise questions. It has attempted to recruit employees of the Department of Transportation. Why is not clear.

Yet intelligence agents are not the KGB's main concern in Washington.

A poor area for recruiting or handling secret agents, Washington is ideal for making social contacts. Its concentrated schedule of "official" dinner parties and receptions offers easy opportunities for Soviet (or Polish or Czech) officials to meet top-level government employees, senators and congressmen, foreign diplomats, the cream of American journalists. But they act in a fishbowl, a small-town assembly of people who know and recognize each other. To extract an agent from this assemblage of attractive intelligence targets is a daunting professional task. To make friends is a simpler one.

Agents of Influence

New York and Washington are the power centers of the American establishment. Their elites, corporate, governmental, and political, make the decisions that directly and indirectly affect the Soviet interest in dealing with the Main Enemy. It is a crucial part of the KGB mission, second only to its espionage function, to influence these decisions.

It is a solid fact that many of the KGB officers in the New York and Washington residencies are not engaged in espionage. A large fraction of these legals—it is impossible to fix the fraction—do not recruit secret agents, do not have secret meetings, do not collect classified documents. Their task is simply to make friends and influence people.

The term "agent of influence," a literal translation of the Russian term *agent vlyiyania,* is both elastic and misleading. Many so-called KGB agents of influence are by no means "agents" in the conventional sense: men hired to carry out work assigned them by a case officer. Many are not aware that the Soviet diplomat they are in touch with is a KGB officer. Many have no notion that their Soviet contact is anything more than a proper diplomat. Only a few ever become "agents."

These agents of influence cover a broad spectrum of social relationships from casual luncheon partners to close personal friendships. They may be politicians, government servants, industrialists and bankers, journalists, and professors. Their only claim to be singled out by the KGB for personal cultivation is the fact that, in one way or another, they can exert some influence in their own societies.

The KGB has been assigned this essentially diplomatic function for the simple reason that the Soviet Foreign Ministry is not up to the task. For twenty years the KGB has recruited the brightest young men, given them the most intensive language and area training, and converted them into "specialists" (American, German, Latin American, even Turkish) by appropriate field assignments. Meanwhile, the Soviet Foreign Service languished during the Cold War (it did not have much to do) and is only now being built up in size and quality. Among the KGB ranks today are men as fluent, sophisticated, and knowledgeable as any foreign diplomat. KGB careerists have become ambassadors, senior U.N. officials, and top Soviet negotiators.

In Washington, the KGB men about town focus on meeting the right people: government officials, legislators, journalists, and lobbyists.

An increasingly active circle of Soviet interest is the growing array of congressional staffers. In the past few years the Soviet Embassy has taken to lobbying on the Hill, a legitimate enterprise for any foreign diplomat. The purpose is not, as often suggested, to recruit congressmen or their committee staffers because Capitol Hill is off limits to the FBI, but to put forth the Soviet point of view on pending legislation from trade agreements to SALT treaties. They also get to know the staffers and develop social relations off the Hill: a lunch at the Hay-Adams, a drink at a downtown bar. They are not recruiting spies but influential contacts. One staffer regularly consulted his Soviet friend on Moscow's point of view on pieces of upcoming legislation.

They are, of course, more active in New York City (as they are in espionage work), where they have a far larger official representation and where the density of "influential people" in the American corporate, financial, and media world is higher. Even in the late sixties the KGB officers' social calendars featured people from bank vice-presidents and senior corporate officials to influential journalists, professors in New York and Cambridge, stock brokers, and (from what emerged later) grain dealers. Each KGB officer moves in his own proper circle determined by his personality and his cover job: the U.N. diplomat, the member of the Soviet Mission to the U.N., the consular or trade representatives, the scientific and technical specialists, the Tass man. Each meets and cultivates compatible New Yorkers. Each has the job of making friends and exerting influence on them.

During the late sixties, for example, the KGB line to their bankers and businessmen friends in New York was a simple one. The Europeans are getting ahead of you in trade and investment in the Soviet Union. If you do not get moving, the Europeans will monopolize the rich opportunities available.

The KGB conversational line shifts as Moscow's interests shift: on SALT, the Jackson Amendment, troops in Cuba, Afghanistan, Poland.

This kind of routine work simply reinforces the official Soviet line carried out by the ambassador and his legitimate staff. Yet it can be far more effective when it is articulated by a fluent, knowledgeable, and sophisticated Soviet officer at a private lunch or dinner party of people who count. It is most effective when it appeals to the self-interest of the men around the table.

The KGB man about town always has his eye on the main chance: he is a diplomat-plus. His job is to spot, and study, his acquaintances, to keep an eye out for any influential friend who can be recruited as a proper agent. He writes up in detail all his contacts and sends them to Moscow. He assesses the men he deals with: their character, capacities, interests. He can have them invited to the Soviet Union, or facilitate their introduction to Soviet trade officials with whom they would like to do business. Those who go to Moscow can be assessed by KGB officers under suitable guise.

In these personal contacts the KGB does not exceed the limits of diplomatic propriety, but its officers can quickly size up and exploit any one man's susceptibility to a more confidential relationship. How willing is he to export items on the strategic list? How eager is he to get in on a specific contract? How open is he to bribery?

The KGB seeks to establish influential contacts not only in New York and Washington, but in all the major capitals of the West. It has been particularly active in Bonn, Paris, Rome, and, up to 1973, when the British threw out more than a hundred KGB officers, in London.

These contacts cannot be tabulated any more precisely than those of any active Western diplomat: it would take a questionnaire addressed to thousands of influential New Yorkers or

Washingtonians to determine their nature and range. Since these contacts are normal and legal, it is not the business of the government to question them.

The simple educational value of the KGB's corporate contacts should not be discounted. For a regime that lived in almost total ignorance of the capitalist world for forty years, Western business methods, corporate structures, commercial communications, and government regulations are matters that have to be learned, and they can best be learned from its business and banking practitioners.

Further, Moscow has great respect for the power of the large American corporations, and as seats of power they demand attention. In developing social contacts even with junior employees, KGB officers not only learn about the strange ways of corporate life, but they may be in touch with a man who will grow into an executive position in later years. One mid-level corporate executive had been in steady contact with a series of KGB officers for over six years—at no time was he asked to do anything improper.

It is difficult to nail down a true "agent" of influence, a man recruited and paid (in one way or another) who will carry out Soviet instructions. Those who have come to light include such varied types as a British businessman helpful in evading export restrictions, one of the German negotiators on a truck-plant deal with the Russians, a New Zealand Cabinet minister, an Italian TV director, the wife of a West European Prime Minister. The French ambassador Dejean, whose story I have told earlier, was not the target for espionage but for an influence operation. What the KGB wanted was a sympathetic voice in President De Gaulle's entourage, not a pilferer of documents.

The only case I know of a Soviet agent of influence's being arrested and convicted of a felony was that of Pierre-Charles Pathé, a seventy-year-old French journalist who had acted as a KGB agent for twenty years before his arrest in 1980. His work for the KGB included printing KGB articles in his confidential political newsletter, reporting on the personalities of French journalists and politicians, and analyzing French political developments. His main job clearly was to influence the climate of enlightened French opinion in the Soviet interest. He received a hundred thousand francs and five years in prison for his services.

The run-of-the-mill influence agents recruited by the KGB in the capitalist world must by now run into the hundreds. Most of those we know about are in the world of commerce and trade, sectors of ever-increasing importance to Moscow. It is difficult to determine in many cases the variety of motivations that induce them to "cooperate" with their Soviet friends. Political and commercial opportunism plays a part. Some may have genuine political sympathies with the Soviet side of the Cold War confrontation that remains under détente. Some no doubt have been blackmailed.

Telephone Espionage

The location of Soviet official installations and apartment houses in New York and Washington places the KGB in an ideal position to monitor both private and government telephone conversations. More than half the long-distance calls within the United States and from the United States overseas are made by microwave. These radio signals can be intercepted by antennas located on or in the Soviet Embassy in Washington, the Soviet Permanent Mission to the United Nations, or the Soviet apartment house in the Bronx.

Interception is a simple matter. The selection of calls from or to a specific telephone is far more complex, but recent computer technology has made it possible for the Russians to select from these microwave circuits individual calls that match a list stored in the computer. These calls are automatically taped.

The KGB is interested in both military information from government calls and economic information that can be gleaned from monitoring calls made by corporations, banks, and businessmen.

After the Cuban missile crisis of 1962, Khrushchev complimented the GRU for having provided him with information from telephone intercepts in Washington clarifying the events and discussions in official circles that led to the final resolution of the crisis. Always the creative imitator, the KGB instituted its own monitoring equipment and went heavily into the intercept business. It was, for example, in a position to monitor Pentagon circuits to its overseas commands, including operational instructions to Saigon during the war in Vietnam.

Perhaps the most lucrative contribution in the economic field was its monitoring of telephone calls into and out of the Department of Agriculture in the early seventies. The KGB did a great deal of spade work (mostly involving perfectly legal contacts) in preparing Soviet negotiators to pull off the "Great Grain Robbery" of 1972, but the KGB coverage of telephonic reports by the grain dealers to the Department of Agriculture clearly helped Moscow time its purchases before the full extent of U.S. grain requirements became apparent in Washington. As a colleague of mine put it, "The Russians knew more about events in the American grain market than the White House did."

The grain deal is an excellent example of the KGB's cash value to Moscow. Without secret agents, through legitimate contacts and telephonic intercepts, the KGB helped Moscow get the data required on grain crops, grain dealers, and government reporting requirements that made it possible for its negotiators to carry off this well-coordinated purchase mission. A KGB officer appeared at the final negotiating session in New York, but he was thrown out by the Moscow team on the grounds that grain-buying was none of his business.

Only in the late seventies did Washington take steps to seal off this economical and useful source of both classified and commercial information: sensitive telephone circuits within the United States to be carried by underground cable; the use of ciphers in the traffic of defense contractors; the addition of scrambler devices to render unintelligible more and more official and private circuits in the air—these and other devices costing millions will slowly, but only slowly, cut down the semi-open information available to the KGB.

The Land of Opportunity

The American target can be attacked not only from within, from New York, Washington, and (since 1975) San Francisco, but from outside as well. The United States as a piece of operating terrain is wide open to Soviet intelligence.

With its two long, poorly policed frontiers in the north and the south, illegal entry from Canada or Mexico is child's play. A native Canadian or Mexican national (never a KGB officer) can cross the frontier, have a meeting with an American, and return safely to his case officer.

More than forty American ports are open to Soviet ships, each with a KGB security officer aboard. In New Orleans or San Francisco he can go ashore, service a designated dead drop, and return safely to his ship within a few hours. Any one man among the tens of thousands of Soviet and East European officials and tourist visitors who come to the United States each year can perform the same simple service without imperiling a member of the KGB residencies.

The United States is also a natural target for so-called third-country operations run by the KGB residencies in Ottawa and Mexico City.

These third-country operations (Trepper working in Belgium against Germany) help protect an agent or case officer from the security services in their country of residence. It is common practice in Europe, where the narrow geographic range makes servicing an agent in another country convenient as well as safe. A KGB officer stationed in Copenhagen, for example, made periodic visits to various European capitals to meet George Blake, then working in British intelligence headquarters in London. One of the KGB tasks in New Delhi was to meet agents working in Pakistan. These are common practices, though the notion that legals only operate agents in other countries is far off the mark.

Canada is of major interest to the KGB in its own right, though the Ottawa residency has occasionally served as a support point for operations in the United States. Although the wartime GRU residency in Ottawa was originally set up by a GRU officer coming up from New York, and Colonel Zabotin's agent network included sources with contacts in the United States, in the following years the connections with the United States thinned out. There are cases where an agent of the New York residency traveled to Canada to make contact, but the growing alertness of the Royal Canadian Mounted Police apparently reduced the value of this practice.

Canada has also been a convenient staging area for illegals destined for assignments in the United States. Almost one third of the present Canadian population, French and English, are not native-born but immigrants from all quarters of Europe: French-speaking Rumanians, English-speaking Poles and Czechs. They provide excellent cover for East European illegals like Colonel Abel transiting Canada for an American assignment.

The exposure of Colonel Zabotin's net in 1945 probably still reverberates at the Center, but its main concern is the competence of the Royal Canadian Mounted Police who wrapped up an uncomfortably large number of Soviet agents in the sixties. In the mid-sixties more than fifty KGB officers worked in Ottawa in support of Canadian operations (more than a score were caught in a ten-year period) and of Cuban operations (the shipping of matériel from Moscow to Cuba and of Cuban trainees to Moscow). In 1978 eleven Soviet diplomats and officials were expelled from Canada for plotting to penetrate the Royal Canadian Mounted Police. One of its officers was offered "unlimited funds" to work for the KGB. Large cash offers are not limited to CIA officers.

Mexico, not Canada, is the principal base for third-country operations against the United States.

In Mexico the operating atmosphere is much more permissive, and from the late forties on, the Mexico City residency has always been staffed by a large quota of American specialists who eye the North. Communications across the northern border are easily carried out by legal or illegal border crossers and by crew members of airlines flying to U.S. cities. These men can act as couriers or pick up material from dead drops at their various destinations. The Mexican police have never gone out of their way to irritate the Russians—or Cubans. In addition, Mexico City is a safe and accessible place to meet sensitive Americans or agents who have hot documents to turn over.

When Sergeant Rhodes, who had been recruited by the Russians in Moscow, came to the end of his tour, the KGB instructed him to send anti-Soviet newspaper clippings to the Soviet Embassy in Washington as a signal for a meeting with his new Soviet contact in front of a theater in Mexico City.

In 1977 an agent from Washington, D.C., took a week's leave for a Mexican vacation, and handed over his material to a Mexican intermediary at a prearranged meeting. Since Mexican espionage laws do not concern themselves with classified American documents, neither of the two men were committing even a misdemeanor.

Some years before an aide to Senator James Eastland who had been developed and recruited by the Washington residency managed to get his hands on a number of CIA documents from a friend in the Agency. He was instructed to take a vacation in Mexico City and there handed them over to a Soviet case officer. Later, after the operation broke off and the KGB decided to reactivate him, it arranged a meeting in Mexico City which he did not attend.

Air Force Master Sergeant Perkins, whom I mentioned in the previous chapter, was arrested at the Panama City, Florida, airport with a satchel of documents he had been instructed to take to Mexico City for delivery.

Mexico is also a convenient escape hatch for Soviet agents on the run in the States. Julius Rosenberg's escape plans called for an exit to Europe via Mexico City. His agent got as far as Mexico City before he was caught. Had Rosenberg not dallied in New York, he would probably have made it all the way to Moscow.

The main task of the Mexico City residency is to recruit agents in Mexico against domestic American targets. The field is a fertile one and includes American students and (earlier) oil company employees, technicians and engineers on vacation from West Coast laboratory and production jobs; Germans and other Europeans already recruited abroad or developed and recruited in Mexico City; and bright Mexican students, especially graduate students who are encouraged and helped to pursue their education across the border and get a job with an American firm at home or in Mexico.

Its main target is close at hand: the heart of American research and development country in California, the back door into classified government secrets. It has worked against the scientific and technical target since the early fifties: electronic and air research laboratories, defense production firms, not to speak of key Navy installations and aircraft production centers (the latter a low priority since the Soviet aircraft industry is highly advanced).

Mexico City now supplements the work of the Soviet consulate in San Francisco, about a third of whose forty-odd officers in 1978 were attested Soviet intelligence personnel, most of them S&T specialists. They are a new breed of highly educated young men with good manners, excellent English, and specialized competence. They carry on an active public routine, visiting industrial installations and laboratories, attending scientific conferences, and meeting men in their own field of expertise. They are prospecting for recruits. Mexico City's job is to recruit agents outside to work inside the United States. Its success in the past thirty years can with few exceptions only be guessed at.

The Soviet Embassy in Mexico City is easily accessible for Americans who want to get a Soviet visa inconspicuously (like Lee Harvey Oswald) or who want to make a buck by selling the Russians the secrets they have or think they have. At various times in the past ten years, several military personnel, including a retired colonel, have walked in to the embassy to sell their wares.

Every service treasures a legitimate walk-in. He must have some samples of what he has to offer, prove his bona fides, and be persuasive about his access to the secrets he wants to sell.

Sergeant Robert Johnson's penetration of the vault at the Armed Forces Courier Station at Orly was, as we have seen, a technical operation of the highest order. The Mexico City residency penetrated the vault of a top-secret communications center on the West Coast without effort. It started, as the Johnson operation did, with a walk-in.

Assault on the Black Vault

In the first week of April 1975, Andrew Daulton Lee, scion of a well-off family living in a Los Angeles suburb—drug addict, pusher, and smuggler—walked into the Soviet Embassy in Mexico City with information about "spy satellites" from a "friend." He brought some samples: computer programming cards and a piece of paper tape from two cryptographic machines. Vice Consul Vasily Okana, the KGB officer who interviewed him, was of course interested and had nothing to lose by exploring this odd walk-in further. No harm could come to him in Mexico's permissive atmosphere—in New York or Washington Lee would probably have been thrown out as an FBI provocation.

Lee had six more contacts with KGB officers until the end of 1976, bringing with him a vast treasure of highly classified information from the communications vault of the TRW Systems Group, working on classified defense and space projects for the CIA and the Pentagon.

His friend, Christopher Boyce, a college dropout, got a job at TRW through a friend of his father's, and at the age of twenty-one in July 1974 was cleared for "Special Projects," which included a CIA-funded electronic surveillance satellite, the monitoring of Soviet and Chinese telecommunications, and of Soviet missile tests and radar systems.

Boyce became one of six people cleared to work in the Black Vault, the code and communications room linking TRW with CIA headquarters in Langley, Virginia, and ground stations in Australia. The vault was "impenetrable," with a steel bank-style door with a three-number combination and an inside door with a key lock. It was heavily guarded with sign-up sheets for entries and exits.

Boyce had become an alienated son of the middle class. At sixteen he had lost his faith in God and country. He had been turned off by the war in Vietnam, by the hypocrisy he saw in his own bourgeois society, by the actions of his government in Chile. He spent much of his time in an alcoholic haze. He got back by selling its secrets.

The KGB take from this simple operation was enormous. Boyce was a crucial node in CIA communications, operating two cryptographic systems between TRW and Langley, and via Langley to Australia. Fifty to sixty messages a day came in and out, and the decoded messages were kept on file for a year. They flowed into Mexico City. The computerized teleprinter and voice scramblers depended on machine settings changed each day. Computer cards for each day's setting went to Mexico City. The KGB wanted the frequencies on which these machines operated, but never got them.

The heart of the KGB take was detailed information on two top-secret American reconnaissance satellites, the Rhyolite and Argus, several specimens of advanced hardware, and the data from the satellites that passed through the vault. Among the thousands of messages Boyce turned over was one that gave the performance capabilities of most of our intelligence satellites. One of his last deliveries was some 450 frames of microfilm of the Pyramider project, a thirty-volume report on a CIA satellite communications system for global use by secret CIA agents equipped with a portable transceiver. The project, started in February 1973, had been shelved and conveniently placed on the top of a file cabinet in the vault.

Precisely how profitable this intelligence was to Moscow's scientific-technical experts cannot be assessed. It cannot have been invaluable, for in the KGB's last meeting with Boyce (Lee had finally been pressured to bring his "friend" down to Mexico City), he was instructed to give up his job at TRW and go back to college. The deal was the conventional one: the KGB would put up the $40,000 required for college and graduate school. Boyce would become a Russian or Chinese specialist, and eventually seek a job in the State Department or Central Intelligence Agency. Boyce accepted and applied for college admission in October 1976. In the KGB's eyes, "growing" another agent into place must have taken priority over continued access to the Black Vault.

Lee was obviously a weak link for the KGB. Impulsive, undisciplined, high most of the time, he persistently violated KGB instructions on the Mexico City meetings. To enforce some socialist discipline on this maverick capitalist, his handler, Boris, on one forbidden visit to the Soviet Embassy packed Lee into the back of a car and threw him out on the road with the car still in motion. Once the KGB met Boyce, of course, Lee was expendable.

Lee's final stupidity led to his arrest and the exposure of Boyce, who had already resigned from TRW. On January 6, 1977, impatient to get some money to buy drugs from his Mexican supplier, Lee tried to get Boris' attention in the embassy by throwing a Spanish-American dictionary (on which he had marked "KGB") through the fence onto the embassy grounds. Arrested by a Mexican policeman, he was later searched and a sealed envelope with microfilm strips inside was discovered.

The two were tried a few months later.

The Mexican authorities refused to let the Mexican police testify at the trials, clearly for fear of offending the Russians. Even President Carter's personal request to the Mexican president for his cooperation in the trial was turned down.

Boyce, tried in April 1977, got forty years and Lee life.*

Boyce escaped from prison on January 22, 1980, apparently through his own endeavors, and is on the loose. Had Lee not been so stupid, Boyce now could very well be on his way to becoming a Soviet specialist in Washington, another mini-Philby grown into place.

Illegals in the United States

A standing puzzle of the twenty years since Colonel Abel's arrest—and probably for the next twenty—is: How many Soviet illegals are operating in the United States? In what communities and under what guise are KGB or GRU officers living as American citizens or resident aliens? Are they active (running agents) or sleepers waiting for an assignment? Will they be activated only in the event of a rupture of diplomatic relations and the with-

* A detailed recital of this operation can be found in Robert Lindsey, *The Falcon and the Snowman* (New York, 1979).

drawal of the legals? Are some in place only for wartime contingency plans?

None of these questions can be answered, not even how many. In the late sixties, estimates ran as high as eight hundred to a thousand in Europe and North America. They were based on information supplied by Soviet defectors (who themselves had to guess), by captured illegals who reported the numbers of their "class-mates," by Soviet agents who participated in their instruction or dispatch, and on estimates of the facilities available in Moscow for training illegals. These estimates are probably much too high.

Illegals now in the United States are more likely to be counted by the score and not by the hundreds. Even the professional can only guess, for successful illegals are literally buried in a society like ours, rich in immigrants and ethnic groups.

The great value of an illegal resident to the KGB lies in his total insulation from the legal residency: ideally, the two networks act in parallel and the exposure of a KGB officer under legal cover in, say, New York or Washington cannot lead to the exposure of an illegal. Yet this classic textbook insulation of illegals from official Soviet installations cannot always be maintained. Even Trepper used the Soviet legal residency in Vichy as a means of forwarding some of his reports, and Sorge secretly met a GRU officer from the Soviet Embassy in Tokyo on several occasions.

Today the division is not always practical, for if the illegal has information of importance and has not been authorized to use a radio transmitter, he must pass it on to an embassy officer for immediate transmission to Moscow. At least one illegal on Long Island recently had several meetings with a Soviet official a few blocks from his house in the distant suburbs. Others have been contacted by officers in the scientific and technical branch when the information they secured required expert evaluation.

The most recent illegal caught in this fashion surfaced in early 1980. Colonel Rudolph Albert Herrmann had followed Colonel Abel's route to New York by crossing into West Germany under his new identity and emigrating to Canada. He arrived in the United States in 1968, settled in a New York suburb, and became a free-lance photographer.

During his eleven-year career Herrmann did not recruit agents or go after classified information of any sort. He was basically a support agent whose main chore was servicing dead drops and transmitting their contents to Moscow via accommodation addresses in Europe. He received his instructions each weekend through coded radio messages from Moscow. He occasionally visited his "homeland" Germany with his family, and went on to Moscow for sessions with his headquarters desk.

Though his duties were limited to support work, his cover was excellent. Had he not been observed servicing a dead drop already visited by a New York legal, he would have remained in place and been available for more serious work in the event of a break in Soviet-American diplomatic relations.

How useful are such active illegals in the United States to Moscow in peacetime?

We do not know, for the few illegals who have been caught are no index to the illegals still quietly active. I would assume, however, that if the KGB has a high-level mole in Washington, he would probably be serviced by an anonymous suburbanite who pays his taxes.

ON CAPITALIST FLESHPOTS

There is a long-standing myth that Soviet officials stationed in bourgeois capitals are bound to succumb to the temptations of material comforts and joys not available at home. Give them a chance—and they'll choose our side. A congressman in the late 1960s could not be convinced that $100,000 on the table and the assurance of a prosperous life in the West was not a ready formula for inducing them to defect: "What's wrong with these guys anyway?"

The KGB man stationed in the West today has a good life. No jump in the Soviet standard of living during the last thirty years has been greater than that of the KGB official assigned to New York, London, or Bonn.

In the late forties most Soviet officials in European capitals led a compound or barracks life. They lived and worked in tightly controlled premises. Each was required to sign out and in for any outside foray. Even a KGB officer had to account for his actions whenever he left the "office." Officials went out to shop only in groups of at least three or more, with one man responsible for their proper conduct and safe return.

With few exceptions up to Stalin's death, the family of each official was kept in Moscow as hostage for his good behavior. Yet even the KGB man was required to be celibate. No in-house adultery or affairs within the Soviet community were tolerated. They were puritanical in the narrowest sense and were required to set an example of good Bolshevik behavior: scandals were out.

Sexual liaisons outside the community were forbidden, not so much for fear of blackmail (sexual entrapment in London or New York, Moscow knew, was not a common practice as in Moscow), but for fear of being compromised. Girls in bars or brothels were, in the KGB view, agents of the British or American security services, and could easily rifle the pockets of their clients, identify them, and trap them into indiscreet behavior on future visits.

The first Soviet wives who came out after the war had a sorry lot: they served as cleaning women, cooks, and waitresses in a strictly self-sufficient community. A notorious fight among the wives took place in New York many years ago on the issue of who would clean up after the October Revolution celebration.

All that has changed.

Today the private life of a KGB officer in New York is like that of a middle-class American. He can eat out at a good local restaurant, see movies and plays, rent a summer cottage in Long Beach, go on picnics in the parks or the countryside, spend the day at Coney Island—and he can shop.

The Soviet official in bourgeois capitals is an inveterate bargain shopper. He scours the retail stores and makes friends with shopkeepers. He sometimes takes along a bottle of vodka as a present, and expects a *quid pro quo:* a five to ten per cent discount. He favors electronic items, hardware, shirts, and records, sometimes buying thirty or forty records at a clip. An indispensable item for his wife is a fur coat to take home to Moscow.

There is at least one case a year in Manhattan in which a Soviet official is caught shoplifting—and almost always at low-price stores.

There are no import restrictions on Soviet officials returning home on leave or permanent change of assignment. They are a major source of scarce goods for the black market, though some have become record collectors for their own pleasure.

Only a negligible number of Soviet officers have any serious interest in the arts (in contrast to their Polish and Czech colleagues). Most of them are heavy eaters and drinkers, and New York is a good place for both. Most excursions to New York restaurants are made by paired couples, congenial and Russian-speaking foursomes in which all can relax. They favor medium-priced restaurants—even when they are taking along a "foreigner" on the KGB expense account. Many reportedly are reluctant to go home after their tours, but they do—with full trunks.

Reports on their sex life are hard to come by, for the least that can be expected from an operations officer is to keep secret his own love affairs. From what we have learned around the globe, they are not restrained by a puritan sexual ethic only recently dissolving in Western society, but their fornications and adulteries are, for the most part, confined to the Soviet colony. A man can sleep with his colleague's wife much more securely than he can have an affair with an outside woman, yet most affairs on record are with single women. Some overt homosexuals are kept on the KGB payroll for their obvious operational attractions. Being overt, they cannot be blackmailed for their homosexuality.

Sex and money are the main handles for the KGB's recruitment of foreigners. Neither is an effective weapon against it.

There is a relevant footnote to this failure to be sucked in by the fleshpots.

One notable trait of the ethnic *Russian* case officer in New York I had already been impressed with in New Delhi: he takes enormous pride in being a *Russian* (not simply a Soviet citizen). There is in him a powerful and deep ethnic, almost religious faith that lies deeper than the patriotic loyalty to a state. The Russian is a man neither of the West nor of the East: Russia lies uniquely between the two, and it is to this narrower nationalism that many Russians, most of them only one or two generations removed from their villages, are instinctively bound. There is a broader sense of pride: *his* society is working, for it is making its mark in the world; and *his* service is working, the best service in the world (now that KGB officers no longer come to a lethal end, as under Stalin).

XI

ACTION IN THE THIRD CAMP

On my return to headquarters from Munich in 1954 I put in a bid for an assignment to India.

During a reluctantly granted six months' leave without pay that I spent with my family in a small fishing village on the island of Majorca to assess my past and future (I was forty-three, a good time for assessment), I realized how tired I was of Europe. Three prewar summers in England, France, and Germany, a year in Hitler's Hamburg, and two years in Adenauer's Federal Republic were enough. Life on both sides of the Atlantic had become homogenized. The cities were larger and noisier. Cars were multiplying like rabbits. There were restaurants with international cuisine and nightclubs with international acts, uniform clothes, gracious living rooms, and graceless block buildings. The monotony of political discussion in the press and in private, within the narrow limits of Cold War thinking, was even more depressing.

My own travels had ranged from Omaha, Nebraska, in the West to Istanbul in the East. I was remotely aware that the bulk of mankind lived on the Eurasian continent east of Turkey. I fixed on India as a land with an ancient cultural tradition, as one of the two potentially most powerful nations in Asia, and as an ideal English-speaking locale for getting a fresh perspective on the Cold War. My only qualification was the year of Sanskrit I had taken at Harvard twenty years before—and which I had totally forgotten.

Meanwhile I was assigned to the congenial and nonexhausting confines of the Training Division in Washington and points south. It was during that assignment that Khrushchev's New Diplomacy gave the KGB a global role.

In 1955 the Moscow theoreticians baptized a Third Camp, the nations of the developing "colonial world," to stand beside the two camps of capitalism and socialism that shaped Stalin's prism. For Stalin, and for John Foster Dulles, the neutral nations of the Third World represented a hostile force: if you are not for us, you are against us.

For Khrushchev and his colleagues they bore promise, not threat. The Third Camp was the soft underbelly of capitalism, for here lay its raw materials, cheap labor, and markets for manufactured goods. To deprive the capitalists of the economic advantages that had played a key role in the building of the great European empires would stunt the growth of the American, German, and Japanese economies, reduce the capitalist world market, and in the long term weaken the capitalist encirclement of the Soviet Union.

In 1955 Khrushchev and Bulganin went on their first Third Camp tour, Czech arms were delivered to Nasser, a Soviet steel plant was started at Bhilai in northern India, and a military-support agreement was concluded with Indonesia. Khrushchev's purpose was partly preemptive: to prevent the extension of the American cordon of military alliances around the periphery of the Soviet Union. He leapfrogged the CENTO alliance in the Mideast by his alliance with Nasser, prevented any threat of Washington's extending its position in Pakistan to India, and curtailed the extension of the SEATO alliance to the vital Indonesian archipelago. His aim was, of course, positive as well: to develop allies and trading partners for the long term, and to foster the evolution of socialist rather than capitalist economies in the emergent and emerging nations.

Moscow's New Diplomacy was formalized at the Twentieth Congress of the Communist Party in 1956 and laid the groundwork for the expansionist policies that were to bedevil the capitalist camp for the next twenty-five years.

As Moscow turned outward, Soviet embassies and consulates

proliferated and grew, and among the flood of diplomats, information specialists, and trade officials the KGB (and the GRU) assigned their officers around the world, matching the expansion of American diplomats and CIA officers after the outbreak of the Korean War.

By May 1957, when I arrived in New Delhi, India had become an amicable recipient of nonmilitary aid from both Moscow and Washington. After John Foster Dulles' death, President Eisenhower took a benevolent view of the "neutrals," made a trip to India, and praised India as the largest democracy on earth. He welcomed Soviet aid as a contribution to the development of a nation that could use all the assistance it could get. In New Delhi, and in Washington, India was competing with China, and the key question was: Can a democratic regime cope as well as a dictatorial regime with the problems of overpopulation, illiteracy, famines, floods, and disease? I recall that Prime Minister Nehru was most pleased when the American ambassador informed him that the per capita production of cloth in India exceeded that of China by a square meter.

The social and operating climate in New Delhi was ideal for the KGB. Nehru's political stance as senior leader of the Third Camp, with one hand stretched out to Moscow, the other to Washington, was reflected down the diplomatic and social ladder. Indians were eager to have their Soviet and American friends like each other, and practiced a kind of social neutralism that brought Soviet and East European diplomats and journalists into easy congress with the British and Americans—not only at National Day receptions but at private dinner parties, club tennis, and shooting expeditions. They provided a warm cul-de-sac in the Cold War.

Most Soviet activities in India were open and public. Their large-scale economic aid program brought hundreds of engineers to their major project, the Bhilai steel plant. In this, as in aid projects elsewhere, Moscow was careful not to contaminate them with espionage or propaganda functions. It was the KGB officials —in the New Delhi embassy and in their consulates in Bombay, Calcutta, and Madras—who were given the main task of cultivating friends and (legally) influencing people. Soviet officials, many of them with fluent if accented English, cultivated senior government and Congress Party officials, influential businessmen, and journalists. They built up subscription lists to Soviet/English-language journals, proffered free trips to Moscow and Leningrad, invited scientists and mathematicians for exchange visits. Information specialists visited the leading provincial newspapers and offered to take out paid Soviet advertisements in return for their printing Tass releases. The cream of Delhi and Bombay society was invited to Soviet receptions and film showings.

The Delhi residency was clearly under instructions to be discreet and highly selective, for the official Moscow-Delhi axis was much too vital to weaken with clandestine games. Yet the KGB could not totally stay its professional hand.

During my five years in Delhi, only one serious espionage operation against the Indian Government came to our attention—and it created a diplomatic uproar.

The KGB's priority target in any country of some size and political significance, friendly or unfriendly, is its coded communications. Once in control of its Foreign Office diplomatic traffic and the classified communication system of its armed forces, Moscow can keep close track of its capabilities and its plans and intentions without fear of surprise. India as the strategic hub of South Asia and the central focus of neutralist diplomacy was no exception.

The KGB penetration of the Indian Foreign Office began in Moscow with the recruitment of an Indian code clerk by the routine procedure of seduction, photographs, and the threat of exposure described in Chapter V. The more delicate operational task was to make contact with him in Delhi after the end of his Moscow assignment.

The Delhi residency cannot be faulted for taking unnecessary risks in picking up the contact, but even extreme caution failed to elude the highly efficient Indian security service, the Central Intelligence Bureau.

For several months before the clerk's arrival, the KGB resident had assigned one of his officers, a second secretary, to develop a unique and conspicuous routine: when he left the embassy at the end of the workday, he took a long constitutional, walking for several miles along the Delhi streets in a circuitous route to his residence, which lay outside the embassy enclave. The CIB naturally surveilled him (and some of the time he must have been aware of being followed), but as the weeks went by, he stopped nowhere, met no one. The KGB assumed that this proof of his innocent behavior would lead to dropping the surveillance.

Finally, on a shaded residential street, the KGB officer was observed having a brief meeting with a shadowy unidentifiable figure. The CIB surveillance persisted with the greatest care, though the KGB clearly thought it was now in the clear. At one meeting the CIB was able to follow the clerk to his own home. Confronted, he confessed and agreed to hand over some classified documents to his case officer at the next meeting. The KGB officer was caught red-handed.

Offended by this unfriendly act, Nehru called in the Soviet ambassador and ordered him to send his guilty subordinate back to Moscow. The ambassador expressed shock and surprise, disclaiming any knowledge of the operation. Nehru then sent a strong letter to Khrushchev, including the less than naïve suggestion that if the Russians wanted to know anything about the Indian Government, Khrushchev should come directly to him and ask for it. Khrushchev naturally apologized and placed the blame on the KGB—he knew nothing about the operation either and would punish those reponsible for this irresponsible conduct.

Were the ambassador and Khrushchev lying?

The ambassador's ignorance is readily understandable: the KGB resident in any embassy is under no obligation to keep the ambassador informed of his secret operations. To what extent this is a uniform practice, we do not know. We do know that before Colonel Zabotin arrived in Ottawa in 1944 to start GRU operations, he was personally briefed by Politburo member Malenkov and instructed to keep his work secret from the Soviet ambassador.

Khrushchev's ignorance is less likely. A penetration of the Indian Foreign Office would not only be a coup of some sort for the KGB, but even the KGB front office might be expected to be sensitive to its political implications for one of Khrushchev's key relationships. We know that Khrushchev was personally concerned with some of the KGB's key penetrations of the Western establishment, above all, NATO, yet it is entirely possible that the KGB chief chose not to inform him of the Indian operation until the clerk became productive and he could present his boss with a sheaf of Delhi-Washington or Delhi-Peking cable communications. Yet this is speculation.

We determined early on that the KGB played virtually no role in Moscow's connection with the active and powerful Indian Communist Party.

We were able to intercept written communications from Moscow to the Indian leaders and to procure summaries of conversations Indian Party leaders had in Moscow and Peking (these gave us our first inklings of the underlying differences that were to emerge publicly in the Sino-Soviet split).

It became clear that Party relations were strictly for Moscow to handle, and that the KGB in Delhi simply operated as a transmission point for Moscow Party correspondence. The residency kept itself completely clear of any political involvement with the Indian Party—an involvement that could have ruined the developing Moscow-Delhi axis.

KGB operations against the Indian target were clearly low-key, but occasional bits of evidence illustrated its role in supporting operations against other countries (especially neighboring Pakistan) and in supplying accommodation addresses and meetings with transients or servicing an illegal in transit. On the whole, the known KGB officers played an active and benign role in cultivating social relations with prominent Indian personalities.

Routine Political Action

The circumspect behavior of the KGB in India is almost unique in the Third World. As the linchpin in Moscow's Asian strategy, as an administratively developed country with a highly competent security service, India is not the place for playing secret games.

In the rest of the developing countries, particularly in Latin America, the KGB has been an all-purpose instrument for political action—open, semipublic and secret. Making friends is more important than espionage (there are not many secrets of consequence in most developing capitals). Supporting and, if possible, directing radical elements in their anti-regime efforts became the KGB's main mission in the Near East and Latin America: working with radical students and labor leaders, stimulating street demonstrations, spreading rumors and anti-American propaganda, funding publications and posters, playing off one political faction against another, inciting riots. All these actions, with or without the help of an indigenous Communist Party, gave the KGB its principal role as agents of disruption in organized societies from Syria and Iraq in the old days to Panama and Argentina now. Covert political action is the day in, day out occupation of KGB officers in the Third World. What else is there for them to do?

The most precise and exacting role the KGB has to perform is the preparation for wars of national liberation, and here its efforts have been mainly devoted to the decolonized and decolonizing states of Africa.

I do not pretend to have a full grasp of KGB operations in the Third World—perhaps that grasp is confined to the head of the First Chief Directorate in Moscow—but I will at least sketch out some facts and make some judgments on this forward arm of Soviet diplomacy in the increasing number of unstable societies in the contemporary world.

In India, and in many other nations of the Third World, one of the KGB's major activities is to recruit, not spies, but agents of influence.

In New Delhi, for example, the KGB officers I knew cultivated personal friendships with Congress Party politicians, businessmen, journalists, and academics. A key target, of course, was the circle of intimates around Prime Minister Nehru and leading officials of the Foreign Ministry. KGB officers promoted friendly understanding of Moscow's point of view in the Cold War, intensified Indian suspicions of the American motives in arming Pakistan, warned against American "monopolist" investments in India, and sought support for Moscow's diplomatic initiatives at the United Nations and in the Middle East.

For the developing world in general, above all for the smaller emerging nations, with few secrets to hide, the search for personal relationships with influential men plays a priority role in the KGB's work. All through Southeast Asia—in Burma, Thailand, Indonesia—and in Africa and Latin America wherever the domestic political climate permitted, the KGB men about town had lunches and dinners with the locals, invited officials and private citizens to the Soviet Union, passed on their contacts to their successors.

Much of the Third World is ruled by small elites, and one or two friendly men in the ruling elite can exert substantial influence in government decisions.

These "agents" can range, as they do in Bonn and New York, from simple friendship with a Soviet official to a continuing relationship with a Soviet intelligence officer. A Middle East diplomat, for example, was cultivated during his assignment as an ambassador in Europe. When he returned home, he became a Cabinet minister. He was soon called upon by a local Soviet diplomat who brought along a note of introduction from his old Soviet acquaintance in Europe. The two saw each other fairly regularly outside the course of formal diplomatic business. The minister was aware of a "special relationship," but he was not an "agent" in any sense.

It is these informal relationships that are hard to pin down in any society where the KGB operates, and their real value in advancing the Soviet interest can only be judged in Moscow.

A substantial investment Moscow makes in the Third World is providing scholarships to thousands of Africans and Latin Americans each year for study in the Soviet Union or East Europe. These young men, many from semiliterate societies, will be the leaders of tomorrow. Though the KGB may select a small handful of graduates each year for training as professional agents, its overall concern is to see that they get the right jobs when they go home: jobs in the media, in education ministries, and in political parties (where they exist).

Disinformation

Recruiting agents of influence is one side of the KGB effort to make friends for the Soviet Union. The other side of the coin is to spread "disinformation" about the Main Enemy, to convince third-world elites that the Americans are secretly plotting against their interests. In this respect disinformation is simply a backup to the worldwide Soviet propaganda machine, and it is carried out by the KGB because it requires technical competence to prepare forged documents and secret means for distributing them in a persuasive fashion.

False or misleading information can be inserted into the local press in a hundred ways: through recruited KGB agents or tame editors in the media, Soviet or East European contacts in diplomatic, academic, or government circles, subsidized non-communist publications like the newsweekly *Link* in India, careful embassy leaks to the right ears. Once in print, these rumors and "facts" can be picked up in other countries through normal press services, Soviet Embassy handouts, and replays in Tass or the Moscow radio.

The most effective form of the KGB's disinformation work is the forgery and distribution of "genuine" documents from inside the U. S. Government to highlight its aggressive intentions and interventionist policies. Concocted from whole cloth, or based on documents in KGB files with appropriate insertions, deletions, and distortions, these forgeries have had the greatest impact in the Third World, both on government elites and on public opinion.

India was not immune to this program that went into high gear in the late fifties and is still going strong. During my tour in New Delhi the theme of American plots focused, as I recall, on Washington's machinations in the Middle East. These assertions were buttressed by forged State Department documents that appeared in the left-wing sensationalist weekly *Blitz*. Once surfaced, the documents were replayed by controlled media contacts in the Middle East.

Some KGB operations made a distinct dent on their intended targets. Proof for American plots to assassinate undesirable third-world leaders ranged from Chiang Kai-shek to President Sukarno of Indonesia. Forged documents on an American plan to kill President Sukarno were transmitted through a (recruited) Indonesian ambassador who brought them to Sukarno's personal attention in 1964. He, and public opinion, were both impressed, and the accompanying orgy of anti-Americanism more than repaid the KGB for its efforts.

In the same year an extensive campaign was conducted by Czech intelligence in Latin America to convince the regimes that Washington had shifted to a hard line after President Kennedy's death. The "plan," purportedly devised by the assistant secretary of state, Thomas Mann, involved among other interventions CIA coups in several countries. The program was triggered by a forged USIA press release, fostered by a series of circulars produced by a notional anti-American organization, and bolstered by a letter under the signature of FBI Director Hoover (samples of CIA memoranda were apparently not available).

Other documents in these early years included forged issues of *Newsweek* for distribution in Africa through Hungarian service channels and several forged letters affording proof of an American conspiracy against the government of Tanzania.

Over a hundred forgeries of American documents have been circulated by the KGB and its sister services in the past thirty years. They have ranged from unclassified USIA reports to top-secret State Department cables and internal memoranda. Some have been totally bogus, others altered versions of genuine classified documents secured by KGB agents.

These anti-American operations were toned down in the early

stages of détente, but they flourished again after 1976. Some were now directed to a European audience.

A fabricated Army manual from 1975 was widely circulated to support Moscow's theme that the United States had started a campaign to support leftist groups in friendly countries to advance the American interest. The manual proved, among other items, that Washington was supporting foreign terrorists like the Red Brigades in Italy.

A genuine State Department airgram on the collection of overt economic information was altered to include a requirement for the collection of information that would be useful for bribing European officials.

Other forgeries have been designed to prove an American plot against President Sadat of Egypt, to promote Arab anti-American feelings by distorting American commitments to Israel, to delay the deployment of the neutron bomb to NATO forces, and to incite conflict within the NATO alliance by exploiting the differences between the Greeks and Turks.

The quality of KGB forgeries has improved in the past decade. The earlier forgeries, though full of errors of format and style, were good enough to make an impression on a receptive public. Recent forgeries like a bogus letter on NATO stationery with the forged signature of its secretary general and bogus letters on the letterheads of American ambassadors in Rome and Cairo reflect greater technical expertise. Not only has the KGB accumulated more and more genuine documents, but it has a supply of the correct paper with proper watermarks and of appropriate typefaces. It also appears to have more sophisticated political analysts who can make plausible inserts into original documents.

Forged documents can be very persuasive to the public and even to nervous heads of state. The KGB is unlikely to give up a game at which it has become expert.

Wars of National Liberation

The main covert action job of the KGB is to prepare the groundwork for revolutionary movements selected by Moscow as the nuclei of "wars of national liberation."

For almost forty years Moscow's program for revolutionary action depended on the use of Communist parties to seize power by force in "revolutionary situations" as defined by Moscow. Two periods of "the crisis of capitalism" announced by the Comintern in 1920–23 and 1928–34 led to Party-led putsches, insurrections, and local revolts that, without exception, failed.

In 1948, sensing another crisis in the postwar capitalist world, Stalin sparked revolutionary action in Greece, Malaya, and the Philippines. All eventually failed.

Under Khrushchev, as an adjunct to his New Diplomacy, the reliance on the parties and the broad-brush approach to global "situations" were very sensibly abandoned. The new approach was based on a country-by-country analysis of revolutionary prospects and a careful estimate of the prospects for a successful seizure of power by anti-regime groups. Native nationalists, not the parties, were to be the instruments.

Moscow's support of these national "wars of liberation" from the late fifties on was neatly timed to exploit the growing disintegration of the European colonial empires and the eruption of nationalist groups in Asia and Africa dedicated to the use of force to achieve their independence. Native insurgencies proved to be more effective than Communist parties.

The KGB's action role in supporting these "wars" is confined to their earliest stages. It must assist the Politburo, which alone determines when an insurgency is a "war of national liberation," by reporting on domestic situations and assessing the prospects of success for any one "movement." It must assess these prospects on the basis of the quality of its leaders, their political programs, and their popular support. The KGB accordingly plays a key role, especially when competing groups are vying with each other for outside support.

Once a decision to support a group has been made, the KGB plays an active role in providing paramilitary training on the spot or by secretly bringing select insurgents to the Soviet Union (or Eastern Europe or North Korea) and in supplying small-arms (it arranged for the smuggling of Czech arms to Patrice Lumumba's seccessionist movement in the Congo). If the Politburo, and the KGB, have made the right choice, and their group comes to power, the role of the KGB becomes secondary, for the Soviet government can then act openly and officially in supporting a friendly regime. It is part of the KGB's job to provide some assurance (there can be no guarantees) that Moscow will be able to maintain effective influence with the group's leaders after they have achieved civil power.

Angola went according to script.

Moscow committed itself to the support of the African insurgents in the Portuguese colonies from the late fifties on, not only in Angola, but in the other Portuguese colonies (Mozambique, Guinea) where Lisbon's unenlightened colonialism created the greatest native dissidence.

The establishment of an MPLA-created People's Republic of Angola in 1975 was the culmination of almost twenty years of KGB effort. Once in power, the MPLA became a de facto government, and Moscow's support became official: Soviet ships and planes openly supplied arms, military supplies, and Cuban troops. The KGB could now withdraw to its normal tasks of "advising" on the construction of an Angolan security service and, with luck, recruiting agents within the Angolan establishment.

There is, of course, no guarantee that the guerrilla leaders supported by Moscow will continue to "cooperate" after they have achieved power. Angola appears to be working, but Zimbabwe-Rhodesia is still an open issue for Moscow.

Robert Mugabe, who became the first prime minister of Zimbabwe in 1980, was the leader of the ZANU guerrilla army first backed by the Chinese. In 1976 he made an arms deal with the Russians, who had previously backed the faction of his rival, Joshua Nkomo, the leader of the ZAPU. He was, for the time being, Moscow's man in the fight against Rhodesia's white regime.

A Marxist-Leninist in his political principles, Mugabe's professed aims before gaining power were to establish a one-party state, to nationalize private enterprises, and to expropriate white-owned lands. These fitted Moscow's ideal formula for a new socialist state.

Once in power, however, Mugabe pursued a moderate line at the outset, abandoning all three policies.

Moscow has made its investment in a mercurial and unpredictable leader, and only time will tell whether Zimbabwe "goes socialist" and gives Moscow a political and economic return on its investment.

What every active guerrilla group needs is a safe base, preferably in a neighboring country where it can train, equip, and rest its fighters. Mozambique and Zambia were essential to the two Rhodesian factions, and Angola is now a useful base for actions against Zaire. Years before these recent successes the KGB entered on a grandiose effort to set up a regional base for the support of black insurgencies throughout the continent. It ended in the KGB's worst postwar fiasco.

Alarmed by an attempt on his life in 1962, Kwame N. Nkrumah, the first leader, president, and dictator of independent Ghana, turned to Moscow for help, and got it. Khrushchev's forward diplomacy of the time led to an almost reflex support of any African regime willing to seek Soviet assistance.

In the following years Nkrumah received substantial military and economic aid—and the assistance of the KGB in preserving his future security. KGB officers not only recruited, organized, and trained a presidential bodyguard for his personal use, but established a National Security Service to maintain control of the population on the model of the Second Chief Directorate in the Soviet Union. It selected the staff and, both in Moscow and Ghana, trained them in filing procedures, surveillance, and investigation. Under KGB guidance the new service established a nationwide network of informants in all sectors of society, an efficient domestic control system with one fatal gap—it did not penetrate the armed forces.

These actions satisfied Nkrumah's immediate needs, but the close ties between Accra and Moscow permitted the KGB to satisfy one of its major goals: the establishment of a regional base for action operations in black Africa.

A regional base in the heart of an operating area offers distinct advantages, as the Comintern had found out in Berlin and Shanghai. It permits recruiting and training agents almost on the spot, without the time-consuming and expensive process of sending them back to the Soviet Union or North Korea. Cutting down foreign travel also promotes the security of insurgent leaders, and a central training establishment increases the efficient use of staff personnel. Ghana had an ideal geographic situation, and the movement of agents into and out of the training and operations center was eased by the loose travel controls that exist on most borders of the African states.

It was a large-scale interservice exercise. The new "Bureau for Technical Assistance" was staffed by hundreds of instructors, specialists, and operational planners not only from the Soviet, East German, Polish, and Czech intelligence services, but from the Chinese, North Korean, and Cuban services as well. The Bureau, with its hundreds of staff officers, represented not only a heavy commitment on the part of the KGB, but a demanding organizational effort in coordinating the work of half a dozen other services.

The Bureau, broken down into geographic sections, handled hundreds of trainees in its classrooms and jungle training camps from more than a score of African countries (the list almost covers the map of black Africa), most of them still under European colonial regimes. Each of the "national" teams was shaped to become the spearhead of a guerrilla group to mobilize popular support for a violent takeover of the established regimes.

The base went the way of Nkrumah who, during a visit to Peking in 1966, was ousted by a military coup. The personnel and files of the Security Service and the Bureau were seized, its native staff arrested, its training camps destroyed. More than a thousand Russians, some hundreds of Chinese, and lesser numbers of the other overseas visitors were thrown out.

The KGB made something of a comeback in the seventies utilizing Cubans and East Germans.

This grandiose KGB effort in Ghana reflects Moscow's early impatience to gain an immediate foothold with new revolutionary regimes. Its ambitions were understandable, for black Africa offers an inviting prospect. It is a series of socially and politically primitive states, rent by tribal rivalries, containing scores if not hundreds of "anti-colonial" individuals and loosely organized groups. Small, well-trained insurgent units with propagandists and firepower hold high promise of success in countries with a simple security structure, poor communications and roads, and large unpopulated areas.

Given a few years the Bureau would have lit at least a dozen nationalist fires and perhaps have overthrown several European regimes. From that time on the KGB has given up the consortium, or group, approach to revolutionary action and worked one-on-one with individual national groups.

The KGB's work in Africa has been handicapped by the virtual absence of Communist parties and by the paucity of official Soviet cover installations south of the Sahara. As more and more colonies become independent countries with more or less stabilized regimes, the KGB requires intelligence sources rather than friendly insurgents, with the notable exception of the Union of South Africa.

Action South of the Border

For Moscow, Latin America has been a tempting target since the October Revolution. The Comintern paid it a good deal of attention (far more than Africa), and from the twenties until today organized Communist parties have operated in almost every country from Mexico to Argentina. In these semideveloped countries, most of them under authoritarian regimes, organized labor and the university campus offered practical opportunities for propaganda, demonstration, riots—and, potentially, insurrections.

The KGB now has a threefold task: to subsidize local Communist parties, to carry out some modest intelligence tasks, and to control and discreetly direct political action operations.

The Latin American Communist parties, many of them small, often working underground, could not have survived these sixty years without financial help. Comintern subsidies and training programs kept the parties going, and they played a useful role before the war in penetrating or taking over the maritime unions, a major Comintern target. Since the war the KGB has taken over the task of supplying money (sometimes via the wealthier European parties), of smuggling out Party members for indoctrination and training in the Soviet Union, and of encouraging their work among students and labor unions. Latin American universities are still the focus of Marxist thought and revolutionary actions throughout the continent.

In most countries of Latin America the KGB has no serious intelligence targets other than the Foreign Office, which offers the simplest means of keeping track of Brazilian or Argentinian diplomatic relations with the Main Enemy. The KGB's Spanish and Portuguese specialists systematically cultivate Latin American diplomats on their overseas assignments, and single out, so far as we can see, those diplomats who are to be assigned to the United States or the European capitals. The KGB specialists in Latin American capitals make friends with the local diplomats, not to recruit them, but to provide the basis for an introduction to a "colleague of mine" on his next assignment to New York, Bonn, or London. KGB officers in New York are particularly thick with Latin American diplomats assigned to the United Nations.

These third-country diplomats provide the KGB with another handle against the American target. Their minimum contribution is to report on their American contacts (they are useful "spotters"), but they can also produce useful political information and gossip from their social contacts with American or European colleagues.

Next to the Foreign Offices the KGB's main local target in each country is the domestic security services. Its recruitments of security and police officials cover the continent.

Friendly contacts over vodka have led to many direct pitches, for the most part financial. The KGB not only wants to keep track of what interest the security service has in Soviet, Cuban, or East European intelligence personnel, but an agent in a security service also serves a political purpose. In most cases of a planned military coup, not only is the service in the best position to see it coming, but in many cases the coup planners find it desirable to enlist the prior support of the security chief, both for the information in his files and for the action he can take to support the coup by locating and arresting key civilian officials. Military juntas would also prefer taking over security services intact rather than starting from scratch. In either case, the KGB will get early warning of a coup (a desideratum for Moscow as well as Washington), and it may end up with an agent who can report on the secret activities of the military junta.

It is in the sphere of political action that KGB practice has radically changed in the past twenty years. During the fifties, KGB officers in many countries, especially those with an inefficient security service, were freewheelers, constantly on the move around town making frequent open and secret contacts with radical elements, especially labor union and student leaders. Scores of KGB officers were thrown out—for putting out anti-government propaganda, for stimulating or supporting demonstrations, for handing out money.

These semi-open "cowboy" operations declined during the sixties as Soviet diplomacy called for the improvement of official relations with the Latin American governments—the resumption of diplomatic relations with many, the fostering of trade, cultural exchanges, etc. Charter flights still take scores of young and promising Latin Americans to Eastern Europe and Moscow to continue their education.

Moscow's urge to calm down revolutionary actions in Latin America for some years ran in a head-on collision with Castro's all-out program for revolutionary action throughout the continent, but Moscow's pressure finally brought Havana to heel in the late sixties. The uniform failure of Castro's adventures, in Bolivia and elsewhere, and the growing anti-communist sensibilities of military regimes made "peaceful coexistence" a prudent course.

The lessons of the past are not lost on Moscow. It was clear that, if pressed, Washington would take action to prevent the emergence of a stable leftist, Marxist, or communist regime in its own backyard. The "communist" regime of President Arbenz Guzmán was overthrown in Guatemala in 1954 with American help. American Marines prevented a potential "leftist" takeover in the Dominican Republic in 1965. The lesson of Chile was even more telling. American connivance in the overthrow of Salvador Allende's "Marxist" regime showed Moscow that not even a democratically elected government was immune to Washington's prophylactic surgery.

Moscow lost more than a Marxist regime in the overthrow of Allende. It lost a potential regional base for operating against the southern cone of Latin America.

Over 20,000 Latin American exiles flocked into Chile after Allende came to power. Individual national groups plotted and planned under the benign, if not cooperative, eye of the Chilean secret police who had been effectively taken over by Cuban intelligence. There are some indications that, when Allende fell, preparations were being made by the Cubans for the systematic training of non-Chilean revolutionaries. The opportunity was there but, as in Ghana, politics intervened.

The usefulness to the KGB of Cuban intelligence cannot be underrated. In Latin America itself it has natural advantages over the KGB—the absence of a language barrier (outside Brazil), the increasingly benign image of Havana in many Latin American countries, and the common anti-Yankee prejudice throughout the continent. All of these open many doors for the Cubans that are closed to the Russians. Cuban intelligence now has a working liaison with some security services, for example in Panama and Venezuela, and has its own quota of agents in such countries as Nicaragua.

In the past decade Cuban intelligence has also developed a good reputation in more distant areas, especially in the Far East, where its officers concentrate on developing access agents to government officials in the Philippines, Tokyo, and Indonesia. These proxy agents, like those of the Polish and Czech services, are a free gift to Moscow.

The Mexican Aberration

Moscow's general caution in refraining from direct Soviet action in Latin America (leaving the dirty work to the local Communist parties or to Havana) was violated in the sixties and early seventies by an extensive, long-term revolutionary effort to unseat the regime in Mexico.

Of all Latin American countries Mexico is the most tempting target to Moscow: a left-wing regime in Mexico would be even more irksome to Washington than the communist regime in Cuba, not only as a political and economic partner, but also, on the parochial KGB level, as a convenient base for operations into the shaky states of Central America and against the Panama Canal.

The arguments against such a venture were, of course, strong. A Mexican revolution, however disguised as a popular uprising, was bound to create diplomatic problems of the most urgent nature for Washington and probably lead to American intervention. In the early fifties the GRU chief, apparently on his own, had started recruiting Mexicans for a future action operation. When his actions were discovered by the Party authorities, he was fired —after being on the job for only a few months.

Yet, in 1963, the KGB began another action operation that went on for the next eight years under Brezhnev.

The KGB plan was clear: to establish a Moscow-directed terrorist-guerrilla group to lead a popular movement against the regime through violent actions.

The plan emerged out of the Soviet Embassy's efforts in Mexico City to recruit university students either through the Mexican Communist Party or the "Institute of Mexican-Russian Cultural Exchange." One of these students, a thirty-one-year-old named Gomez, was selected as the nuclear figure in the plan and sent to Moscow in 1963. After being trained for four years, he established the Movement of Revolutionary Action (MAR) among the Mexican students in Moscow. He went back to Mexico to recruit more members.

Then came a rather lame cover-up of the Soviet role. The men recruited by Gomez and others were brought to Moscow to be handled by the North Koreans, who got them to Pyongyang for several months of guerrilla training in the summer of 1970. Traveling in small groups, the forty-odd trainees were back in Mexico by September ready to recruit new members, set up training bases and safe houses, and organize the actions they had been trained for: "expropriations" of bank funds, procurement of weapons from the police and Army, coordinated bombings and terrorist attacks, raids to sabotage power lines, railways, and factories— all instruments of psychological warfare designed to arouse the populace, create an atmosphere of emergency, and provoke extreme government reaction.

Before their campaign really got under way, a purely accidental discovery of an MAR safe house by a village constable led to the arrest of several MAR fighters. Subsequent arrests and interrogations led to a complete exposure of the operation and the precise role the KGB had played. Five Soviet diplomats were implicated and expelled in March 1971, and a storm of anti-Soviet feeling broke out over the entire continent: Moscow, it was clear, was still playing the old game of revolution by violence.

Why Moscow embarked on this hazardous undertaking with détente in Europe already a fact is hard to gauge. It threatened their diplomatic position in Mexico (for the KGB a valuable base for operating into the United States), its image as a "peaceful" regime, and its incipient accommodation with the United States. The gimmick of having the revolutionaries trained in North Korea could only limit the knowledge of the MAR underlings of the Soviet role, but any one of half a dozen "leaders" would be able to incriminate them. As it turned out, plausible denial was impossible, and Moscow simply labeled the charges as another example of provocation and anti-Soviet propaganda.

How far the KGB went in "selling" this operation to the Party leadership is not known, but it cannot be ruled out that the KGB professionals were so taken with the brilliance of their own plan against a high-priority political target that they persuaded the politicians to go along. There can be no question that an operation of this extent and sensitivity could not have been mounted

without Politburo approval. Even Brezhnev must have been
tempted by the dream of a Marxist Mexico.

Notes on the Border States

In India (and in Indonesia and the United Arab Republic) the
KGB played a circumspect role in both its espionage and political
action operations, for Moscow's billion-dollar investment in
maintaining friendly relations with all three states could be jeop-
ardized by unfriendly secret games.

A similar caution has apparently controlled KGB work against
the countries on its southern rim: Pakistan, Afghanistan, Iran,
and Turkey.

Moscow's interest in Pakistan stemmed from its hostility to
India, its military alliance with the United States, and the location of advanced American military equipment on its soil, the
missile and communications listening post (and U-2 base) at
Peshawar, and from 1960–61 on its growing friendship with
China. Khrushchev's public hostility to Pakistan fills the record
in the late fifties and early sixties (Powers' U-2 flight in 1960
sparked Khrushchev's greatest virulence and heavy-handed
threats), but from 1957 to 1962, when I compared semiannual
notes with my colleague in Pakistan, the KGB residency was
curiously inactive.

There appeared to be two reasons. The Soviet effort in Pakistan was mainly diplomatic and political, and its political and
propaganda program focused on building up the strength of the
civilian political leadership and carrying out a steady anti-
American propaganda barrage. (Later it supported the East Ben-
gal separatist program which was to end up in the establishment
of an independent Bangladesh.)

The second reason was more pragmatic. The military regime in
Pakistan ensured a difficult milieu for secret work. The activities
of Soviet diplomats were closely, and easily, monitored. Their access to both the military and the Foreign Office officials was severely restricted, and the recruitment of an Army or Air Force
officer of rank in a disciplined defense establishment poses one of
the greater challenges for any intelligence service. Whatever the
reason, the KGB appears to have been slightly more active in
friendly India than unfriendly Pakistan.

Regarding the other border states, I can offer only a few snippets of fact and some speculation.

In Afghanistan the KGB (and the GRU) had a friendly neighbor, even under the monarchy, and the close relationship between the two regimes would have fostered easy access to any information Moscow wanted without recourse to secret agents. In any event, there have been no spy scandals in Kabul for a generation.

The events leading up to the revolution of 1978 are not completely clear, but there appears to be no evidence that Moscow, or the KGB, helped engineer it. On the other hand, the events under the succeeding socialist regimes must have been closely monitored by the KGB without, however, making it possible for the Soviet leadership to avoid the military invasion it finally decided was needed to stabilize a disintegrating society. With the invasion, Soviet intelligence can now place as many officers as it needs to keep track of Afghan developments. The KGB's main task in Kabul must be to organize and train an Afghan security service capable of developing a control system of some sort after the fighting has stopped.

The operating climate in Iran after the Shah's return in 1953 has been even more difficult for the KGB than for Western services. Restrictions on the movement of Soviet diplomats outside a limited zone around Teheran, and the constant watchfulness of Savak, the Iranian security service, for any Iranian contacts with foreigners, made the direct recruitment of agents in the military or government hierarchy both difficult and dangerous to the Soviet-Iranian political and trade connections.

The military target in a militarized society is naturally of major interest to the KGB and the GRU, with the latter in the better position to exploit its official contacts with Iranian officers for agent-candidates. In December 1978, before the Shah's flight, an eighty-five-year-old Iranian major general was caught delivering a secret Army document to a Soviet intelligence officer in Teheran. He had apparently been supplying information on U.S. military equipment and other items of interest for *nine* years.

Another recent case testifies to a strong Soviet effort to reduce the problem of communicating with senior Army sources in Teheran. Two-way communications within the city were carried out by the most modern techniques available. Instructions *to* the agent were sent by satellite from Moscow to his radio receiver. Reports *from* sources in Teheran were sent by burst, or high-speed, transmissions and were picked up by a small, special receiver that could be located in a parked car anywhere outside the Soviet Embassy compound.

Another source of information on internal Iranian affairs that cannot be discounted is the Iranian Tudeh (Communist) Party. Our first detailed study of a Communist Party in 2242 Que was one done in 1948 on the Tudeh, then most powerful within the armed forces. When it became illegal in 1953, its leadership finally ended up in East Germany, where it subsisted with subsidies from the Soviet and East German parties. Its sources of information from within Iran during these years cannot be traced, but even Savak could not entirely destroy its connections with the homeland. Being a secret communist under the Shah was no mild venture, but the reappearance of the Tudeh Party in some strength after the collapse of the Shah's regime testifies to the presence of some Party functionaries—and intelligence sources—within Iran during the dry years.

I have always had the greatest respect for the organizational continuity of an illegal Party apparat, with its political leadership residing on foreign soil. The persistence of the Spanish and Portuguese parties during decades of illegality affords two persuasive instances.

By the early seventies the KGB officers in Iran were, almost without exception, fluent speakers of Farsi, the native tongue of the nontribal Iranians. Since Farsi is also the language of the Afghan elite, the KGB's corps of Afghan-Iranian specialists moved with some regularity from Moscow to Teheran to Kabul and back to Moscow. As the situation in Iran develops in the coming years, these language-area specialists will give the KGB a head start over their Western colleagues, who are more addicted to English, French, and German.

The language requirement for effective operations is even more demanding in Turkey. The Turkish language is difficult, the Turks are difficult, and Turkey is a difficult country to enjoy. Here the KGB entices its younger recruits to become Turkish specialists by simply giving them a 25 per cent increment on their salaries.

Turkey is, for various reasons, a hard place for the KGB to operate in, but it has an understandable interest in the American monitoring stations and advanced U.S. equipment supplied to the Turkish armed forces. It is also, of course, an avenue into NATO.

A crucial border area of KGB interest has been the western stretch of the Sino-Soviet frontier occupied on both sides by Muslim national minorities. The KGB sponsors several organizations of Uighur refugees from Sinkiang Province (Eastern Turkestan), who are natural recruits for carrying out both propaganda and espionage activities within Sinkiang. The major émigré front, the Uighur National Liberation Movement in Exile, also has a paramilitary wing, the Movement for Free Turkestan, with some 80,000 troops under the command of a former Chinese major general who fled to the Soviet Union in 1961. These émigré groups have an ambitious minorities program: not only the reunion of Eastern Turkestan with Soviet Central Asia and of Inner Mongolia with the Mongolian People's Republic, but the independence of Tibet and Manchuria. They are well organized and well financed, and are in touch with Uighur communities in China, Taiwan, Turkey, and Saudi Arabia, but their "liberation" operations within China itself cannot be gauged from the heavy radio and leaflet propaganda they put out.

What other KGB operations there are inside China is not known. No KGB defector has reported on the Chinese sector of its operations, and no public trials of Soviet agents in China fill the vacuum.

ON THE USE OF VIOLENCE

The place of violence in revolutionary action has gone through a remarkable evolution since Marx. It has been the focal point of the *practical* ideological disputes within the communist camp for twenty-five years.

For Marx, armed revolutionary action was the final stage in seizing power in a highly developed capitalist state.

For Lenin, the place and timing of the armed takeover was directed at the weakest link in the capitalist system: it happened to be Russia.

For Stalin, who announced three "revolutionary situations" in his lifetime, the Party was the instrument for seizing power by violent means in both capitalist and colonial countries.

For Khrushchev and Brezhnev, Communist parties must seize power by peaceful means. Violence is reserved for "wars of national liberation."

Moscow's late conservative line on the use of violence has faced a series of challenges from the Left.

For Mao, the armed action of peasant guerrilla forces led by the Party can *create* a revolutionary situation. Political power comes out of a gun.

For the early Castro, and for Che Guevara, armed guerrilla units not only create the revolutionary situation, but create the Party in the process.

For many elements of the New Left that emerged in the sixties, violence is justified *per se:* it weakens the establishment (capitalist or communist) as an end in itself. Violence is the only means to a new undefined world.

It is these threats from the Left that have forced Moscow to work hard to keep up its image as the world leader of radical anti-capitalist forces at the same time that it promotes the image of a friendly nation-state prepared to cooperate with the West.

This pressure from the Left has been somewhat reduced in the past few years. Moscow worked for almost a decade to slow down Castro's precipitate call for revolutionary action in Latin America. Mao's death, and the shift to the right in China, now faces Peking with the same dilemma: inspiring the "Chinese" parties in Latin America and the Near East to revolutionary action, while promoting friendly relations with the American and European bourgeois democracies.

To employ violence in a nonrevolutionary situation has always been for (Moscow) communists the sin of adventurism. Violence must have a political purpose: the seizure of power at a "scientifically" determined moment in history.

What, then, is the Moscow view of terrorism, individual acts of violence directed against persons or institutions: murder, maiming, kidnapping, raids, hostages? What, if any, is the KGB role?

Moscow is adamantly opposed to terrorism except as one among many means needed for seizing power. It is, of course, essential in wars of national liberation, for in just wars all means are acceptable: bank robberies, raids on police and Army barracks, the murder of rightist politicians. These acts must be under the control of a leadership able to orchestrate the total resources of political action, propaganda, and armed units required for the seizure of power.

The terrorist movements that came out of the late sixties in the capitalist countries were native in origin and carried out their bombings, kidnappings, knee-cappings, and murders on their own. There were no signs of any foreign involvement, much less KGB contacts, in the work of the Weathermen in the United States, the Baader-Meinhof Gang in Germany, the Red Army in Japan, or the Red Brigades in Italy. In the recent clean-up (April 1980) of the Red Brigade leadership in Italy, for example, no evidence was found for any foreign involvement except contacts with other European terrorist groups.

These groups are anti-establishment in the broadest sense: not only against their own regimes, but against political parties of whatever coloration—and that includes the communists as well as fascist groupings as in Italy.

The terrorist programs of various factions within the Palestine Liberation Organization present Moscow with a more complex political evaluation than the purely anarchist European terrorists. The Palestinians as a whole are fighting a war of national liberation against the Israelis, and terrorism is one of their tactics: it has a political purpose. Yet the Soviet assessment must also be a pragmatic one: does PLO terrorism advance the Palestinian cause?

Moscow's secret assessment of PLO terrorism we cannot know, nor is there any evidence I know of that the KGB plays any role in the selection, training, or equipping of PLO terrorists. Moscow's support is, of course, not needed. The terrorist groups have adequate training facilities, arms supply, money, and false documentation available within the Middle East and in Libya. Even if the KGB played some kind of indirect support role, it would not be in a position to direct their action any more than would the moderate PLO or other Arab elements.

The political question that remains open is the extent to which the Soviet leaders, in their discussions with Yasir Arafat and other PLO leaders, express any views for or against the terrorist tactic. The issue must be a delicate one, for Moscow has to decide whether the terrorist tactic advances or hinders the PLO's progress toward a Palestinian State.

Whatever its role in PLO terrorism, the minimum KGB aim is to have sources of intelligence within all PLO groups (as in any politically significant group anywhere). It is active in recruiting Palestinian students studying at foreign universities, men who on their return to the Near East will become workers or functionaries in one of the groups under the PLO umbrella.

When the KGB participates in the training of *guerrilla* candidates or their instructors, these men are also candidates for recruitment as intelligence agents. The PLO is far too crucial an organization for the KGB not to have inside sources—and the KGB has had more than ten years to get in.

XII

BUNGLES, DANGLES, DOUBLES, AND DEFECTORS

Straight narratives of simple spying, fact or fiction, make dull stories. A man copies a document, delivers it to his handler, and goes home. The same routine repeated time and time again makes up the career of a spy. Good spies are quiet spies, and there are no stories of uncaught ones. The dramatic interest of a caught spy is in how he was caught.

Counterespionage, not espionage, is the high drama of secret operations: the lead, the chase, the search, the final exposure. The quiet sergeant in the Pentagon, the quiet secretary in the Chancellor's office, the ambassador's butler become public heroes or anti-heroes, their exploits admired or maligned.

The same rule holds for spy fiction. There are no good stories of straight espionage. Joseph Conrad's secret agent was a terrorist. James Bond is not a spy but a noisy adventurer. Le Carré's Smiley is a counterspy on the hunt for a mole.

More Soviet agents have been caught in the postwar world than have agents of all other services, Western or Eastern, combined. It is not ineptitude but the sheer quantity of Soviet secret operations that has led to this high rate of exposure. The more agents, the more likely some will be blown.

Secret operators, like surgeons, can be sloppy.

Even a professional Soviet intelligence officer, being human, can be careless or stupid. He sends his suit to the cleaners with a microfilm of a classified document in a trousers' pocket. Holed up in a Copenhagen hotel, he rapes the chambermaid, the police are called in, and a room search comes up with a clutch of false passports and cipher materials.

Sorge's colleague, Max Klausen, lost his wallet in a taxi en route from the German Club in Tokyo to the house where his transmitter was located: it had money, a driving license with his photograph, and the English version of a secret report to be radioed to Moscow. He was fortunate: the cab driver apparently kept the money and threw the rest away.

Sometimes the system of communications goes awry. In two cases, involving an agent in Switzerland and a U. S. Army clerk in Panama, packages containing microfilms of classified documents were not picked up by the addressee and returned to the bogus senders. Opened at the post office, investigation led to the culprit.

Simple accidents intervene in the secret world as in the open. A dead drop in a park is stumbled upon by children. A cigarette package with a secret message inside is secreted in a trolley-car shelter—and picked up by the wrong man.

The witting or knowledgeable wife is another danger.

Normally there is no need for the wife of an agent to know what her husband is up to, but a long-term spy can be hard put to maintain complete cover within his own family. Sergeant Johnson's wife played a role in his recruitment, and knew what he was up to. A highly emotional woman, she was a constant threat to his security, but it was only after he had pulled off his coup at Orly airport that she brought him to grief. Wives denounced their husbands during the spy hearings in Washington in the forties. The two assassins in Germany, Stashinsky and Khokhlov, were persuaded by their wives to give up their trade and turn themselves in.

It was perhaps fortunate for their careers that Sorge and Trepper were bachelors.

Minor bungles have tripped up several Soviet illegals.

The Canadian cover of Gordon Lonsdale, we have seen, broke down over a small piece of foreskin. Had the KGB been thorough enough to read the medical report of the original Gordon Lonsdale, they would no doubt have had him circumcised.

The exposure of another "Canadian" illegal was triggered by much greater sloppiness.

A Soviet illegal who had emigrated to Canada with his wife from Western Europe established himself in business in Montreal and lived his cover for two years. He vanished from Montreal and reappeared in Tokyo as an active Canadian businessman with a new identity and a new wife.

His new identity was that of a small-time native travel agent from central Canada. The travel agent's name and vital statistics had been extracted from his visa application for a trip to Moscow with other travel agents to assess travel opportunities in the Soviet Union. It was a stupid shortcut, for the real travel agent was still alive, and a simple investigation exposed his double in Tokyo.

Dangles and Doubles

The worst mistake any service can make is to recruit as an agent a man who has been "dangled" before it by a hostile service. The basic rule of thumb in the business of recruiting is to suspect anyone who takes the initiative in making contact with an intelligence officer.

The KGB is especially allergic to people who volunteer their services in capitalist countries whose security services are experienced enough with Soviet methods of operations to tempt them with attractive bait.

Soviet intelligence is genuinely concerned about the FBI in its American operations, for it is aware from experience that the FBI will occasionally recruit an American for the sole purpose of having him recruited by a KGB legal. The KGB manual I have cited earlier prosaically notes that "the person being dangled either attempts to interest us in his intelligence potential or he takes the initiative and offers to pass us certain secret materials." It also emphasizes that dangles display a "disproportionate interest in money . . . (there is every reason to assume that money received from our intelligence service serves as additional compensation for the plant)"—this is normally not true. It then examines several categories of FBI dangles, including not only visitors to Soviet installations to elicit KGB interest, but also "persons with liberal views who have contacts with Soviet installations." Only if the KGB officer himself takes the initiative in spotting, studying, and recruiting an agent-candidate, can he reduce the chances of being sucked in by the other side.

In spite of its sensitivity to dangles, the KGB has been occasionally sucked in, most recently in the case of Navy Lieutenant Arthur Lindberg, whose three Soviet contacts were arrested in Woodbridge, New Jersey, on May 20, 1978.

Under instruction, Lindberg had taken a Black Sea cruise at the end of which he had passed a note offering his services for money. Moscow took this seriously—it had successfully recruited other Americans who had gone on Black Sea cruises—and the New York residency was instructed to pick up the contact.

A diplomat in the Soviet Mission to the U.N., Vladimir P. Zinyakin, and two U.N. employees, Enger and Chernyayev, were assigned to the case and met Lindberg seven times from October 22, 1977, to the time of their arrest. The KGB interest focused on American underwater warfare projects, a perennial concern of Soviet intelligence since the late fifties. Zinyakin possessed diplomatic immunity, but the two U.N. employees were tried and sentenced to forty years. The pair was later exchanged for five Soviet dissidents.

A greater hazard for the KGB—throughout the world—is to recruit a man who then goes immediately to the police and announces the Soviet approach. Given the right man, and the right service, the KGB's "agent" can be doubled—he is actually recruited to work for the second service—and the KGB's agent meetings, intelligence tasks, etc., become an open book to the other side.

Since the early days of our doubling émigré agents into KGB/Karlshorst, literally hundreds of KGB agents have been doubled against their handlers by European and Latin American services. In countless cases these doubled agents have been used to catch the KGB officer in the act of receiving a classified document, a kind of frame which nonetheless gives a government grounds for throwing out the culpable KGB officer.

Many of these cases involve low-level KGB approaches, but

some aim fairly high. A direct cash offer for jet aircraft information was made to a British RAF officer who immediately informed his superiors and was instructed to play along. A similar offer reported by a worker in a British aircraft plant for classified drawings permitted the security service to establish a notional net of sub-sources, including one of its own staff men.

A recent case (1978) in Canada involved a direct cash offer to an RCMP official who reported the approach and was played back for a time until the Canadian Government threw out the KGB officers involved in his handling.

The KGB runs into other hazards harder to avoid. A legitimate and useful KGB agent can be caught in his spying and forced or bribed to continue his work under hostile control. If the agent is handled right, the KGB officer will not be able to detect any change in the agent's behavior or in the information he supplies until he suddenly finds himself declared persona non grata for improper behavior.

Dozens of cases run by the FBI into the KGB, often for years, are on the record. In 1967, for example, a man by the name of J. Huminik worked for the FBI for five years against a third secretary in the Soviet Embassy in Washington.

How the Center judges these errors of judgment by its field officers cannot be gauged. In some cases, as with Navy Lieutenant Lindberg, it is itself responsible for allowing the New York residency to be sucked in. In falling for a dangle, of course, the KGB is not losing an agent, for it never had one. What it does lose is one of its officers expelled—itself no great loss if he turns out to be a clumsy operator. He may do better in Minsk.

One blown agent can expose another, if he knows him, or knows of him.

Recognizing that the loss of an occasional agent is inevitable, every intelligence service does everything it can to insulate an agent from his handler and from other agents. For many KGB agents where live meetings are essential, his case officer is a man without a real name (Bill, Ivan, George do not help), without an address, with an unknown job or office. Where the operation simply requires the passage of reports or documents one way, and money and instructions the other, the agent knows only the dead drops or accommodation addresses he is instructed to use. He does not know where his documents go after he has turned them over. He does not know who his real boss is—nor, in many cases, even whether he is working for the KGB or the GRU or for Polish or Czech intelligence.

The Party nets in Washington, as we have seen, were comradely affairs in which many of the comrades knew each other. The KGB attempt to insulate one agent from another by separate handling came too late to save the net.

Yakovlev, as we have seen in Chapter II, made his fatal mistake in linking two sensitive operations (Dr. Fuchs and Julius Rosenberg) by employing Fuchs's contact to pick up Greenglass' report in Los Alamos. Fuchs led to Gold, and Gold led to Greenglass and Rosenberg. Without this cross-link, Rosenberg might never have been caught.

That accomplished but inactive operator, Colonel Abel, made a minor but crucial error in handling his assistant, Hayhanen. In spite of their frequent meetings Hayhanen did not know his boss's name or his address, but one day Abel took him to his room in a warehouse in order to provide him with a radio. No physical link between the two existed except for that one tie-in, and Hayhanen's recall of the warehouse's location was enough for the FBI to track Abel down. He might otherwise have reached the status of senior citizen in Brooklyn.

Defectors

Accidents or human error have rarely exposed top KGB agents: Dangles and doubles lead to news headlines, but do not uncover moles. Philby operated safely for over twenty years, the German Felfe for a decade, yet both barely escaped exposure from the most lethal threat to KGB operations: its own case officers, or trusted members of its sister services. Western agents within Soviet and Polish intelligence, and defectors from those services, have blown the majority of top KGB agents in the sixties, the high-water mark of KGB agent losses.

The most spectacular exposures of KGB operations have come from the defection of illegals. In many cases they are the direct result of bungling by Moscow Center: either picking the wrong man for the job or mishandling an otherwise competent man.

The choice of Hayhanen as Colonel Abel's assistant, we have seen, could not have been a worse personnel decision.

The Center's obtuse handling of its two most notorious assassins, Khokhlov and Stashinsky, also led to their defection in West

Germany. It simply failed to understand these two men well enough to assess realistically their psychological capacity to kill another man.

Another illegal in Germany, Lieutenant Colonel Eugen Runge, defected in 1968—mainly, it appears, because he was mishandled by his superiors.

Born of German parents in the Ukraine, Runge was carefully trained in Moscow for three years, and worked on practical assignments in East Germany before being assigned to West Germany, first in Munich, then in Frankfurt. Equipped with an East German wife designated by the KGB, he was given the funds to set up a dry-cleaning establishment that failed, and then took a job as a salesman for vending machines in which he prospered. He was a most inconspicuous little man.

Among the agents in his net was the hapless Leonore Heinz, the Foreign Office secretary who had been lured into marriage by Heinz Suetterlin, one of Runge's men.

The intelligence take from the Suetterlin operation was apparently so spectacular (almost three thousand secret and top-secret documents from the heart of the Foreign Office) that the Center became suspicious of the reliability of the whole operation. Runge and his wife were asked to come to Moscow for a discussion of the case, and after what must have been some disconcerting sessions, he was given a holiday at a Black Sea resort. It was there that he decided to give up his career. He secretly photographed his personal file at the Center for later use as proof of his bona fides.

Though his superiors were reluctant to let his wife return with him to West Germany, Runge appealed to KGB Chairman Andropov on the grounds that returning to Germany without his wife would ruin his security. Andropov agreed to let her go along. On his return he walked in to the German authorities, and blew the Suetterlins and several other agents he had been running, one of them a janitor in the French Embassy.

Perhaps the Center cannot be faulted for its bad judgment, for Runge was a shrewd operator able to cover up his personal reactions to the Center's unfriendly handling. It was nonetheless its error in taking too hard a line with a top field agent that cost the KGB one of its most valuable sources in West Germany.

Less spectacular, but far more extensive, has been the exposure of KGB agents by its legals in the West.

A KGB legal in the field not only knows the identity of the

agents he is handling or has handled during his career, but often has gleaned at least some tidbits of information on other active KGB agents—from indiscreet remarks of his colleagues, from the kind of great successes that become bruited about in the corridors of the First Chief Directorate, from intelligence reports he has read that indicate at least the Western department or office to which the reporting agent has access. A previous headquarters assignment, say in the North American or German-Austrian departments, gives a defector an even broader range of agent identities.

When Anatoli Golitsin defected in Finland in 1961, he furnished over a hundred leads to past and current agents. He underlined the sievelike quality of NATO secrets, for he had read scores of NATO documents during his Moscow assignment and was able to pick out the right ones from a collection of genuine and bogus papers.

A GRU staff officer run by the CIA for over eight years came up with scores of leads, including the arrival of a female illegal in New York, though most of them could not be systematically followed up while he was still in place for fear of blowing *him*. Yuri Nosenko, who defected in 1964, was less valuable since his career had been mainly in the Second Chief Directorate, but even here he gained some knowledge of the First Directorate's activities abroad.

One of the most valuable contributions to the exposure of high-level KGB agents operating in the West was made not by a Russian but by a Polish intelligence officer while on duty in the Warsaw headquarters of the Polish service (UB) in the late fifties.

This self-appointed mole offered his services in March 1959 in a letter signed "Sniper" addressed to the American ambassador to Switzerland. It contained enough information to confirm the writer's access to useful classified data. In the ensuing two-way correspondence (he wrote fourteen more letters) he further established his bona fides as a Polish intelligence officer by quoting from some secret NATO documents and giving details on UB operations. He also claimed that the KGB had several penetrations of Western intelligence services.

The cream of his reporting centered on his allegations that the KGB had penetrated the British intelligence service and other highly classified offices. Pressed for details, he supplied them: In a November 1959 letter he reported that the KGB was in possession of two British intelligence documents. The subsequent investigation in England led to the arrest of SIS officer George Blake, in 1961.

In April 1960 he alleged that British naval secrets were being leaked to the KGB through a British national recruited in Poland about 1950 by the UB and later turned over to the KGB for handling. This rather pointed lead led to Harry Houghton, an employee of the British underwater Weapons Establishment, and the arrest not only of Houghton, but of the three illegals, Gordon Lonsdale and Mr. and Mrs. Kroger, all of whom were tried and convicted in 1961.

An agent of even greater prominence was exposed as the result of a letter in March 1959 simply stating the fact that a delegation of officers from West German intelligence (BND) visiting the United States in 1956 had in its ranks two KGB agents. This rather precise lead came out of a briefing given in 1958 by a KGB general to an assemblage of East European intelligence chiefs who were discussing the penetration of a joint U.S.-BND office in Bonn operating against the Soviet Embassy. The trail, of course, led directly to two BND officials (already under some suspicion), Heinz Felfe and Hans Clemens.

At the beginning of the Christmas vacation in 1960, "Sniper" made a prearranged meeting in West Berlin and identified himself as Michal Goleniewski, a mid-ranking UB officer.

How did a UB officer get to know the intimate details of KGB operations far removed from his own professional sphere of interest?

He was himself a KGB agent within the Polish service. He had been recruited after Wladyslaw Gomulka's accession to power in 1956 to keep the Russians informed on activities within the UB. He was on intimate terms with several of his Soviet case officers (who were ostensibly carrying out a proper liaison with the UB), and they simply talked too much to their trusted "agent." Except for the lead to Felfe and Clemens, which came from a formal KGB briefing, Goleniewski's Soviet colleagues were vain enough to boast about their gold mines in the West. Shop-talk behind the Curtain was apparently looser than in Manhattan.

This case illustrates the price the KGB must sometimes pay for its close links with the sister services. The Polish and Czech services particularly often carry out KGB assignments which their own agents are in a better position to execute. Had the KGB not "commandeered" Houghton, he might still be in place, and the disgruntled Polish case officer who resented KGB high-handedness might never have grumbled.

Escape and Exchange

The hazards of spying in developed societies with an effective security service are well known to the KGB, and it takes every precaution to prevent the arrest of an endangered agent. The greatest profit the KGB gets from a penetration of a security or intelligence service is early warning of an impending investigation and of the possible arrest of one of its agents.

An escape plan is built in to every key operation from the start. In an emergency it can be triggered either by the KGB officer or the agent himself.

Richard Sorge activated his escape plan as Japanese security was closing in, but lingered in Tokyo for a fatal day or two to get his final report on Pearl Harbor—and perhaps to see a little more of his dancer girlfriend.

Léopold Trepper was on his way to disappearing from the land of the living beneath a false tombstone when he decided to get his teeth fixed before he "died."

Julius Rosenberg was equipped with an escape plan for himself and his fellow workers that started with a rendezvous in Mexico City. Money, documents, and cover stories were available, but the timing was late.

Burgess and Maclean, and later Philby, disappeared quietly and neatly at just the right moment to avoid disaster. The mechanics of their flight remain cloudy.

As soon as Sergeant Robert Johnson got his job at Orly, he was equipped with two sets of forged documents under other identities and given contact instructions for a meeting in Holland.

Scores of KGB and East German agents have fled to the East in the last ten years before they could be arrested. A single signal can start the agent in motion.

Even when he is arrested and jailed, the KGB does not forget a key agent. The loyal Soviet spy evokes paternal solicitude, just as the renegade merits retribution. Both attitudes make good business sense, clearly affecting the morale and confidence of working spies and possible recruits.

The most sensational escape of a top KGB agent was that of

George Blake, the British SIS officer who had been exposed by Goleniewski.

Born Behar in Holland of a Jewish father and a Dutch mother, Blake came to England, served in the Royal Navy during the war, and studied Russian at Cambridge. Assigned to the Foreign Office's Far East Department in early 1948 (Burgess became a member in the spring), he was appointed temporary vice-consul in Seoul, Korea, that fall. He was interned at the outbreak of the Korean War and recruited by the KGB before his release in April 1953.

For the next six years he worked in SIS (British intelligence) in London and in Berlin and transmitted to his handlers every document of interest that came across his desk. He was a worthy successor to Philby. Blake was sentenced in 1961 to forty-two years, the longest term ever meted out by a British court. His escape from the medium-security Wormwood Scrubs Prison in October 1966 was widely heralded at the time as one of the KGB's more brilliant secret operations.

Blake's cell was in one of four cellblocks surrounded by a twenty-foot-high wall in a London suburb. An exemplary convict, cheerful and well liked, he made friends with an Irishman, Sean Bourke, in whose eyes Blake was a "prisoner of conscience." Bourke agreed to help him escape after he himself got out, first on a work-release program, then on his own.

Blake and Bourke first worked out a system of passing written messages via a prison inmate. Since the escape depended on precise timing, rapid two-way communications were essential, and Bourke solved the problem with flair. He smuggled in a pocket-sized transistor walkie-talkie that Blake hid in his cell, and the two were able to chat at leisure, on one occasion for two hours, though Blake, like Trepper in the old days, objected to being on the air too long at a time.

Bourke went about his job in a businesslike way. He worked out a practicable route from one of the cellblocks to the wall facing the grounds of a hospital, reconnoitered the area outside the wall, plotted the best routes for a getaway car, and spotted desirable locations for a hideout. Bourke carefully rehearsed the getaway from the prison wall, noting the state of neighborhood traffic during the period of the break and the time required for police from the nearest station to arrive on the scene (he had a leeway of several minutes).

It was a low-cost operation, and Bourke managed to scrape to-gether the money needed for a secondhand car, the rent for a hideout flat, some clothes, and a false passport. A camera and film had been smuggled in to Blake to take the photographs required for the passport. The simple equipment required was the cheapest item on the budget: a car jack for breaking (quietly) an iron bar on the windows, a wire cutter, three clotheslines, and thirty steel knitting needles for the ladder.

The escape, as narrated by Bourke in *The Springing of George Blake,** was a close call, but Blake made it to the flat with a bro-ken wrist suffered on the drop from the wall, and stayed there, within a few miles of the prison, until mid-December, when the hue-and-cry of the search had calmed down. On the seventeenth, two of Bourke's friends bought a secondhand camper and se-creted Blake in a small cavity behind a wooden drawer in the back. The camper crossed the Channel by the Dover-Ostend ferry and delivered Blake to the East German border. He was taken to KGB/Karlshorst headquarters, where he was identified by his old Berlin case officer who had been flown in from Moscow.

Bourke followed a few days later, crossing over from West Berlin, and spent a few days in the Karlshorst compound before flying to Moscow to join Blake.

The revelation that Blake was a KGB agent pointed to a dis-maying fact about the much-touted "tunnel" in Berlin where Soviet military communications were intercepted in a joint British-Amer-ican operation. Blake had been in on the planning for the tunnel in London and was on the spot in West Berlin during the opera-tion. The KGB accordingly knew about the tunnel even before it was started, but did nothing to "find" the tunnel until April 1956 in order to protect its source, Blake. We can assume that some controls were put on the sensitive military information normally sent over the tapped wires.

The great KGB feat in springing Blake heralded by the world press also turned out to be a bubble. His escape was a one-man job by an ingenious alcoholic Irishman who did not require any help from the KGB professionals. Yet the KGB will always be given some credit for it in many minds, including the minds of other Soviet agents.

KGB/Karlshorst apparently did take some steps to arrange the escape of its mole in the German service.

In prison, Heinz Felfe managed to keep up communications

* New York, 1970. No one can vouch for the details.

with the outside. He had an easy life working in the library, look-ing at TV, and playing chess with his fellow inmates.

One of the prison projects was the wrapping and labeling of magazines for subsequent mailing. A willing worker, Felfe man-aged to insert secret-writing messages into magazines which he addressed to places that functioned as live mail drops for the KGB. The precise content of these messages we do not know, but they were without much question devoted to working out a plan for Felfe's escape.

Felfe's transfer out of the prison broke off communications and aborted any escape plans KGB/Karlshorst may have been con-cocting.

Christopher Boyce, who had been sentenced to forty years for selling satellite secrets from the Black Vault in TRW, escaped from Lompoc Prison in California in January 1980. Since many other inmates had broken out with little difficulty, Boyce ap-parently did the job on his own with a tin snip and a homemade ladder to scale the wall. In any event, his value and prior service would probably not have prodded the KGB to try to spring him, especially not from an American jail. The consequences for détente before Afghanistan would probably have been too great a price to pay.

The final resort to free a valuable agent in prison is to arrange a swap.

The first and most notorious Soviet-American barter deal was the swap of U-2 pilot Francis Gary Powers for Colonel Rudolf Abel.

Moscow's first response to Abel's conviction in 1957 was in tune with later practice. The Moscow *Literary Gazette* described the Abel affair as "lowbrow crime fiction," and labeled it an FBI "hoax."

In March 1960 the Supreme Court affirmed the judgment and thirty-year sentence on Abel. On the first of May Powers was arrested after his flight over the Soviet Union failed. Within a month Powers' father wrote to Abel in prison suggesting an ex-change. After Powers' show-trial in August and his sentencing to ten years' confinement, months of intricate private and official ne-gotiations led to the exchange of the two men on February 10, 1962, at the Glienicker Bridge between the two Berlins.

It was not an even exchange: a professional intelligence officer under a thirty-year sentence for a reconnaissance pilot with a ten-year sentence.

The swap not only rewarded a good officer for his past services, but permitted the KGB to debrief him in the fullest detail on his experiences in the United States, and to employ his talents in Moscow in the training division by giving lectures and briefing illegals.

After seven years in prison, Felfe was exchanged in 1969 for eleven routine prisoners in East German jails. He was still of value as a consultant on operations in West Germany, for he knew most of the officers in his old service, the BND, its techniques of communication, its thinking.

Swapping each other's agents has been a wholesale enterprise between the two Germanies for years. The British, the French, and the Americans have all swapped with Moscow or Prague. Swapping has become a minor industry in the world of espionage today, and professional intermediaries have grown up in East Berlin and New York.

Swaps are usually uneven. The Krogers were exchanged for a British college instructor, Gerald Brooke, who had smuggled some émigré propaganda material into the Soviet Union in 1965. The Czech-German MP, Alfred Frenzel, was swapped for a German woman archeologist and three men in East German prisons.

The prospect of a swap gives an added value to an arrested spy. Storing up hostages for future spy swaps is employed both in the East and the West.

In 1977 the FBI arrested two U.N. employees for espionage (the KGB retorted by framing several Americans in Moscow), and the two men were convicted and sentenced to an unprecedented fifty years in prison—a clear American invitation for a serious swap to come. It came in 1979 when the two were exchanged for five Soviet dissidents.

Two Soviet spies for five Soviet dissidents: a curious equation. There is no simple arithmetic for swaps even when both sides are exchanging spies, but the equations become even more mysterious when non-spies are exchanged for spies.

Profit from Loss

Soviet reaction to the capture of one of their spies is silence, a flat denial, or a wordy implausible denial. The report is dismissed as anti-Soviet propaganda or as a deliberate Western provocation.

The KGB does not want to lose a good spy, but when he is

caught, it can reap profit from his exposure. The bigger the spy, the greater the profit.

Captured Soviet spies of quality trigger an ambivalent response within Western security services or among the reflective public. There is pride and relief that the malefactor has been exposed. There is guilt and regret that he was not caught sooner. Every counterespionage success in some sense marks a failure.

Security services are very much a private club, insulated from the public, which often has an exaggerated image of their competence. They are, like the armed forces, a focus of patriotic loyalty as the guardians of the citizenry. Any public exposure of their frailty has a highly emotional impact.

There is therefore a built-in avoidance mechanism within any security or intelligence service that creates a reluctance to go all out in investigating a suspect in their own ranks. If there is no legal case against him, the safest solution is his dismissal. Actual suspects must be handled quietly. There may even be a reluctance to establish facts, for a rigorous investigation might leak within the government or to the press.

The exposure of Philby in England and Felfe in Germany were unmitigated disasters for the services involved and highly profitable to the KGB, for these men were standing testimony to the inefficiency of the Western services and the brilliance of the KGB.

The effect on the morale and efficiency of their colleagues cannot be measured. They are all in some way contaminated. To see five or ten years' work go down the drain, to recall the man they trusted, to run over in their own minds each personal or professional contact with the renegade, to spend months or years in assessing the "damage" he has done: these are hard experiences in any secret bureaucracy.

The public effects are less intense but more widespread. *Their* service, after all, is a poor service—it cannot catch spies even in its own ranks. And the query, of course, arises: What other Soviet agents are still operating safely in this, the heart of the government? Public outcries, journalistic fervor, legislative investigations all combine to continue the witch-hunt and shatter public confidence.

Any high-level penetration of any government agency can have the same effect: a spy in the British Foreign Office, in the German Chancellor's front office, in the NATO command. Who else is there?

These are domestic reactions. Perhaps more important to Moscow is what I have called the Philby effect: the shattering of confidence among allies. Exposures widen the cracks that are already there: the distrust of the British in American intelligence and military circles; the distrust of Americans, British, and French in the reliability of the Germans; the standing distrust of the British and Americans in French security. The political and diplomatic fallout from these cases cannot be measured.

On the other side, these recurring proofs of the KGB's effectiveness add to the image of the powerful Soviet state, an image that can only contribute to its interest both in the West and in the Third World. They have led to what has become a new game in the West: the search for "moles." It is an active game in the United States, the one country where no moles have yet been found. There *must* be a mole in the Central Intelligence Agency and in the Federal Bureau of Investigation: How can the KGB have missed out on their main target? The hangover from the European cases promises to be a long one.

ON MOTIVES

Why have scores of Soviet and East European intelligence officers come over to the West in the past thirty years?

In the black-and-white days of the Cold War it was easy to see such men opting with their feet for "freedom." They were allegedly men who changed sides out of principle, who saw in our side the good guys. My old chief, Allen Dulles, found the word "defector" a denigrating term for these men and preferred "volunteer." These men were voluntarily enlisting in the fight for freedom. They were, in using that vague term, "ideological" defectors.

In Allen Dulles' day, and later, boards and committees were set up to analyze the motivation of the men who had come over. They hoped to establish patterns of personality or background that would permit us to single out other potential defectors and work on them. The results were operationally worthless, for there were no patterns. There have been no strictly "ideological" defectors, only individual intelligence officers who defected for personal reasons.

The most common cause of defections in the fifties was a shake-up in intelligence headquarters that threatened the security, if not the life, of field officers. After Beria's execution in 1953, KGB officers in Tokyo and Vienna came over. After the Czech events of 1948 and 1968, and the Hungarian revolution of 1956, Czech and Hungarian intelligence officers defected in large numbers.

In the other cases I know of, there were pressing personal reasons for the men who gave up their careers, countries, and often families to flee to the West.

In the early fifties some intelligence defectors deserted from the Soviet Zone of Occupation because they fell in love with a German girl and were refused the right to marry a foreigner. More recently, in 1971, a KGB specialist with the Soviet Trade Delegation in London, Oleg Lyalin, fell in love with his secretary, and deserted both his service and his family in Moscow.

In the fifties and sixties many low-level intelligence defectors had money troubles of one sort or another. The Russians almost automatically charge defectors with embezzlement. In some of these cases the man had stolen company funds. In most cases they had not.

More complex personalities are not open to a ready analysis of their motivation: a man frustrated in his career with a deep resentment at his superiors' failure to appreciate his talents, a sexually insecure officer with a wayward wife, or a senior Jewish official threatened by the anti-Semitic drive in his service.

Defectors, as judged by their former employers, are traitors. Some are quite unstable, men who do not fit anywhere and who run out as a last resort in their search for stability. For some, defection was an act of revenge, getting back at someone for their failure to be successful: the boss, the service, the Party, or the regime. Several have changed their minds again and "redefected" to the Soviet Union.

Defectors are, for the most part, an unhappy lot. They have given up their home and country for an uncertain career in a strange society. The act of defection itself compounds their personal problems. From Gouzenko on, the rehabilitation of defectors has proved an onerous burden for Western services.

I am not suggesting that defectors are ignoble. They are simply human, and they act for human reasons. Men caught up in unpleasant circumstances, they seek a way out. It is deceiving ourselves to see them as heroic fighters for freedom, recurrent testimonials to the rightness of our cause.

XIII

THE ENEMY
AT HOME

The major domestic challenge to the Communist Party and the KGB for the past fifteen years has been posed by those of its citizens who dissent from or act against the control system.

A dissenter, in its Russian equivalent, is a "different-minded" person. He does not think the way he should (by Party standards) about the Party, Soviet society, foreign policy, or the role of the individual. It is an elastic term, and since it is defined by the Party, it can embrace a wide range of equivalents: "ideologically unstable," "bourgeois mentality," "anti-Soviet," "counter-revolutionary." "Difference" is a political crime. It is also a sickness, a malady that can be cured. If the society is "sane," difference is a form of insanity.

When the dissenter speaks out or acts on his differences, he violates the Party monopoly of thought and communications and becomes a threat to state security.

Stalin killed all expressions of open dissent within and outside the Party, and even in his postwar years dissent was confined to small, secret study circles among liberal Party intellectuals, religious sects, and ethnic nationalists. Strong pockets of resistance in the Ukraine, and lesser elements in the Baltic states, were wiped out by 1953.

Khrushchev's temporary thaw, and his de-Stalinization program, brought many dissenters into the open. The year of protest following the repression of the Hungarian rebellion in 1956 was shared in by secret student groups in Moscow and Leningrad, but the pockets of protest were small and isolated. Only with the trial of Andrei Sinyavsky and Yuli Daniel in 1966 did "dissent" as we now know it become an active element in Soviet society—complete with signed statements of protest, secret newsletters and journals,* demonstrations of support for dissenters—all outside the Party monopoly of the media.

The Party's growing concern with the increasingly active dissident groups led in 1969 to the establishment of a new and independent Chief Directorate within the KGB, the Fifth. It took over the files and personnel of the Second Chief Directorate concerned with the Soviet intelligentsia and university students, with religious organizations and groups, with ethnic minorities, and with Jews. Two years later, as "the Jewish question" assumed greater political importance, a special Jewish department was set up within the Fifth.

The Fifth Directorate is the final guarantor of Soviet stability by monitoring dissident activity and by breaking up those groups with serious potential for growth. The Party determines policy (on the Russification of the Ukraine or Central Asia, on the quotas for Jewish emigration, on the privileges of Lithuanian Catholics, etc.), but the Fifth tells the Party what is going on and takes whatever repressive actions the Party directs.

Public dissent reached its high-water mark in 1966–68, and the systematic Party/KGB efforts at repression began after the invasion of Czechoslovakia in 1968 and have gone up and down since. There was a crackdown in 1977, as the freeze started in Soviet-American relations, and again in 1979–80, apparently as a therapeutic operation before the Moscow Olympics. Almost a hundred trials took place between August 1978 and the spring of 1980.

Active dissent is concentrated in contemporary Soviet society in a small fraction of its educated class, in such ethnic minorities as the Ukrainians, Balts, and Crimean Tatars, among its Jews, and in a few religious groups like the Baptists and Jehovah's Witnesses who are not under direct Soviet administrative control.

* Much of this literature was distributed by *samizdat* (self-publication), privately typed and mimeographed articles, newsletters, poems, novels, etc.

Each group is "different" in its extent and organization, each has different goals, and each is handled by the KGB by different methods.

Organized ethnic and religious minorities face the KGB with the least problem of security control. Secret groups of Ukrainian, Baltic, or Central Asian nationalists are closely monitored and easily penetrated. When they go too far in their public protests or secret organizing, the leading activists are arrested.

The Ukraine has always been of great concern because of its size and location on the western border, its long and separate cultural and linguistic tradition, and its fiercely anti-*Russian* feelings, particularly in the western Ukraine. Moscow's suspicion of Ukrainian loyalty was intensified by the collaboration of many Ukrainians with the German occupiers during World War II and the continuance of local armed resistance to Soviet rule that lasted, as we have seen, into the early fifties.

Ukrainian dissent from the mid-sixties focused on one major grievance: the continuing Russification of the Ukrainian republic. It sought, not separatism, but the end of discrimination against Ukrainian education and language, the treatment of Ukrainians by the KGB, and the assignment of Ukrainian prisoners to camps outside the Ukraine.

Even pleas or movements for moderate reform of these grievances triggered drastic repression. Several waves of arrests, secret trials, and severe sentences have removed hundreds of Ukrainian dissenters since the mid-sixties. There is no reason to suppose that Soviet vigilance will lessen in the coming years.

Baltic nationalisms are less threatening. During and after the occupation of the Baltic states before the war, the professional educated classes were virtually wiped out, and the churches brought under Soviet administrative control. Lithuania, Latvia, and Estonia were stabilized by a combination of ruthless purges, absorption into military districts, and the appointment of non-Baltic administrators to the Republic government structure. Only the Lithuanian Catholics have displayed any impulse to open, organized dissent, and these the KGB is able to monitor and control.

The same vulnerability to KGB control applies to the other active, or potentially active, minority groups, principally the Crimean Tatars and Moslem dissidents in Central Asia. The problem of handling the national minorities is a problem for the Party, a serious policy problem, but in spite of the many discussions of the threat of separatism in the Soviet Union, it is an unlikely prospect. The Fifth Directorate keeps close track of any organized public or secret actions among all the minority groups, and the Party can adjust its policies to minimize grounds for dissidence. The steady bureaucratization, if not ossification, of Soviet society reduces, year by year, the prospects of any separatist tendencies.

The Jews are a special case for the KGB only because they act in the open and their treatment has special political overtones. Applicants for emigration visas are automatically "listed," dossiers compiled, and overactive applicants surveilled. They present the Party with a political and propaganda problem, and it is the Party authorities who determine who will be granted visas. The official rationale in selecting emigrants is not altogether clear, though applicants in high-priority or high-security jobs are for the most part rejected. Since Jews are legally permitted to emigrate only to join relatives abroad, the KGB dossiers are relevant to each applicant.

Who compiles the final list of visas granted is not known. Does the Party set up quotas and criteria for exit visas, and the Fifth Directorate forward its specific recommendations? Are certain Jews selected mainly from the large cities to minimize the organized efforts for emigration? Precisely what role do various considerations play in the Party's decisions: the legitimate security hazards involved, a reluctance to build up Israel against the Arab interest, the loss of services to the state by educated technicians and professionals?

The Party has already lost out on two counts. The publicity gained by ethnic or religious dissenters has exposed the failure of Lenin's minority policies, and at the same time the concessions made to Jewish dissenters has established a precedent for other minorities.

The Intellectuals

The Fifth Directorate faces by far its greatest challenge in dealing with dissident intellectuals. These are to be found among what the regime calls the *intelligentsia,* men and women with an advanced education, now probably numbering some forty million Soviet citizens. The Soviet term is too broad to be useful in talking about dissent, and I shall use "intellectuals" in the Western sense.

Those intellectual dissidents visible to the West come mainly from academic and literary circles: Andrei Sakharov, Aleksandr Solzhenitsyn, Roy and Zhores Medvedev, Vladimir Bukovsky, Anatoly Shcharansky, Andrei Amalrik (killed in November 1980 in Spain in an auto accident). How much dissent exists among university students, lawyers, creative artists, or the armed forces is unknown in the West.

These dissidents (including some Jewish, Catholic, and Ukrainian intellectuals who go beyond single-issue protests) have become known as the "democratic movement," a loose term for those who speak out or act against the system's undemocratic policies: fighters for civil rights, for humanism, for a respect for individual moral and intellectual freedom.

The "democratic movement" is neither a movement nor a coalition of "democratic" forces. There is no "movement" in the sense of a coordinated, much less organized, protest effort, and thus no unified target the Fifth Directorate is called upon to monitor or control, but rather a series of individuals and fleeting organizations that have to be handled by the Party and the KGB each on its own merits or demerits.

Nor are the dissenters uniformly "democratic." The spectrum of intellectual dissent runs from those who want to reform the system to those totally alienated who want to destroy the system. Men such as Leonid Plusch and Zhores Medvedev accept Marxist-Leninist principles and the legitimacy of the Party, but demand greater freedom within the system: the right to travel, emigrate, or read Western publications; the removal of restrictions on scientific inquiry; the freedom to speak out and enter into a dialogue with the Party. These are the loyal democrats, men who simply demand the full extension of the civil rights guaranteed by the Soviet constitution. These men are in effect addressing themselves to the Party leadership who alone can reshape the Party's repressive policies to achieve greater democracy within the system.

At the nondemocratic end of the spectrum are the outright opponents of the regime who want, in many cases, to restore a more authoritarian regime: a theocratic Russian state (Solzhenitsyn), or the neo-Stalinists and Slavic nationalists who stand for law and order, object to the mild Party line, and favor greater repression of anti-regime elements.

In controlling these intellectuals of the right or left the Party and the KGB exercise a wide range of techniques, both extralegal and legal.

Extralegal Measures

The formal KGB task is, of course, to monitor the activities and publications of all dissidents through surveillance and informants, to investigate secret or semisecret "political" contacts at home or through correspondence abroad, and to provide the evidence, when called upon, to government prosecutors for a civil or criminal trial.

Short of arrest, a series of graduated pressures on active or potential dissidents is employed:

—A reprimand by the Party or by an institution like the Union of Soviet Writers puts a man on the alert.

—Expulsion from the Party, or from the Communist Youth League, curtails his career prospects and can ostracize him from professional and social life.

—A writer or artist forbidden to publish or exhibit his work is forced to take low-paid manual labor to avoid the criminal charge of being a "parasite."

—Firing a man from a well-paid job in the establishment puts his family in a tight spot in a society where all jobs are establishment jobs.

—Personal harassment can wear a man down.

The techniques of personal harassment by the KGB are those open to any security service: conspicuous surveillance, house searches, tapping or cutting off the telephone, warning his colleagues against associating with him. The KGB has beaten up dissidents (commonly disguised as a mugging), and even threatened their lives. It can also put the finger on an honest dissident by spreading the rumor that he is a KGB informant.

To search out latent oppositionists, the KGB can secretly produce and distribute *samizdat* documents: false petitions, bogus programs of national groups, misleading proposals (a mild form of the provocation tactics employed in its global "disinformation" program).

All these pressures come to a head when a dissident is called in for a "chat" with the local KGB. Here the threats are made explicit: either shut up or take the consequences. The visitor has no uncertainty about the message, for the KGB can start a civil or criminal process.

Legal Measures

As a final recourse the regime can resort to three legal (if not judicial) measures: commitment to a psychiatric hospital, expulsion, or arrest and trial.

The "indefinite compulsory treatment" of a sane man in a psychiatric hospital, revived from czarist days, permits the KGB quickly and easily to silence the "criminals" who in an open trial might make a spirited (and bound to be publicized) defense of their "crimes." There is no clear indication what standards are followed in selecting candidates for psychiatric treatment.

The forced emigration of leading dissidents such as Solzhenitsyn and Valery Chalidze serves two purposes. It is not only a warning (of a dire kind to patriotic Russians) of their possible fate, but it is a sharp blow to the morale of the dissidents at home. There must be some awareness in the Party and the KGB that life as an emigrant can rob a writer or artist of his talent when it is rooted in his homeland.

Confinement to a psychiatric hospital or expulsion removes the most influential dissidents as centers of further infection without the incitement to further dissent provided by an open trial.

The Soviet legal system, like the KGB, is an instrument of the Party. The authorities decide beforehand who is guilty, the charges to be brought, the proper sentences, open or closed trial, and location.

Arrest and trial are, of course, the simplest solution to the dissident headache. Hundreds of men and women have been tried and sentenced for "political" crimes since the Sinyavsky/Daniel trial of 1966. It is estimated that some thousands of "political" prisoners now reside in prisons or labor camps. Yet the inhibitions on the regime are powerful. A trial today, even in the provinces, cannot be kept secret. Made public, it can promote another surge of dissent, as well as international support for the defendants. It is the most obvious index to the state of repression in the Soviet Union.

Incorrigible troublemakers are simply arrested and rearrested, even such internationally known figures as Major General Peter Grigorenko: one of the most militant and vocal "freedom fighters."

Minor figures in each subelite are put on public trial and given moderate (by Soviet standards) sentences as punishment and warning to others.

These are, in effect, show trials, the defendants deliberately selected to warn others of their ilk to tread softly. It was Stalin's old, and murderous, technique in the thirties, but even its milder, current form makes the same demands on the KGB in requiring a water-tight prosecution: by securing confessions, providing bogus witnesses, and concocting evidence of a foreign plot. The purpose, as before, is three-fold: to punish the "guilty," to provide a lesson to others, and to uncover sympathizers.

There can be no comparison between the show trials of the seventies and Stalin's show trials of the thirties—in scale, in the stature of the defendants, in the lethal outcome. Yet there are some common elements in the tasks assigned to the KGB then and now that are worth isolating.

The trials of the thirties were simple frame-ups. Stalin determined the cast of main characters and the broad outlines of the plots. It was the NKVD's job to fill in the plot, select the supporting cast, create the working script with confessions, witnesses, and evidence. It was a formidable job even for the task force of the most experienced operators and interrogators in NKVD ranks: each man knew that the trial was a frame-up, for had there been a real plot, he would have been the first to know it.

The alleged plots were, and are, a tribute to the subtlety and ingenuity of the conspiratorial mind. In the trial of Zinoviev *et al.* (August 1936), of Pyatakov *et al.* (January 1937), and of Bukharin *et al.* (March 1938), the NKVD drew on its files to create "nets" and "centers" based on *any* connection between any two people to extend the web of the conspiracy: a chance meeting, a casual remark, a distant cousin, spending the same night in the same town. No organization chart could map the intricate connections of the centers and nets. No one could understand the plots as they were revealed in court, nor does a patient reading of the trial transcripts help. Their very complexity created their power to persuade. It is a tribute to Prosecutor Vishinsky's mind and memory that he could keep track of what he was trying to prove.

Stalin's plots all originated abroad, mainly with Trotsky in exile, and the plotters purportedly had working connections with the German and Japanese intelligence services.

There are now no bizarre or complicated plots for the KGB to concoct against the dissident defendants, but one theme remains intact: the simple allegation of foreign connections.

Soviet xenophobia has survived Stalin. Dissenters are pictured as contaminated by "bourgeois ideology" transmitted from abroad; by Western journalists in Moscow, by anti-Soviet émigrés abroad, especially the NTS, and by Western intelligence services. The prosecutors still tag the defendants as "imperialist agents" and attempt to equate dissent with espionage wherever they can.

Since unauthorized contacts with foreigners are viewed by the KGB as having in them the seeds of disloyalty, secret foreign machinations are readily detected and easily believed—by Soviet citizens. The foreign threat and the remnants of the psychology of capitalist encirclement still pervade the mentality of the Party and the elites. It is an attractive rationale for many—since dissent is un-Soviet or un-Russian, it must be inspired from without.

"Confession" (or self-criticism) has always played a singular role in Party thinking both in the Soviet Union and in China. A public confession by a "sinner" not only supports the allegations against him, but is a living example to believers and nonbelievers alike of the power of the faith he has, through weakness of character or bourgeois contamination, temporarily abandoned. Repentance is good for his soul—and for the souls of others who might be tempted.

No aspect of Stalin's show trials impressed world opinion more than the spectacle of intelligent and powerful men such as Zinoviev, Pyatakov, and Bukharin fluently, often volubly, accusing themselves in public of outlandish plans to kill Stalin, restore capitalism, and cede Soviet territory to the Germans and the Japanese.

In today's show trials, confessions are a rarity. Whatever pressures the KGB may exert on arrested dissidents, it has, with four or five exceptions, failed to produce a confessional mood or true repentances. For the most part dissenters on trial have fought with the prosecutor, derided his "evidence," and pleaded not guilty to the crime. The prosecutors have come down hardest on those who attempt to rebut the charges made against them. One of the most vigorous resisters, Vladimir Bukovsky, was sentenced in

1971 to twelve years' deprivation of freedom (he was expelled from the Soviet Union in 1977).

Today the KGB no longer needs to frame the victims by concocting evidence to confirm the paranoid fears of a Stalin. The defendants have, for a fact, published their criticism of the regime abroad and have been members of human rights committees and these acts constitute the bulk of the evidence required by the prosecutor in recent trials. Nor do the witnesses they produce have to be steered into fictional statements about the accused: what they cite from their own experience is for the most part adequate to confirm the "crimes" of the defendants.

The Stalinist repression was essentially irrational. Any public or private disagreement or criticism of the regime spelled exile, imprisonment, or execution. Even suspicion was enough, and innocent people suffered. Punishments were often arbitrary, displaying no relation between the sentence and the "crime."

Today the active dissenter knows what is permissible, and he knows what the consequences of certain acts will be: whether it is signing a petition, writing a pamphlet, having a book published abroad, talking to foreign journalists, giving a news conference, joining a public protest in Red Square, or starting an unauthorized group.

The regime moves within the broad reaches of the criminal statutes by methods of "socialist legality." These statutes can be narrowly or broadly interpreted, but it is the actual violations of specific statutes that are punished. To that extent the prosecution of dissenters is rational: it is understandable.

It is not the individual dissident who poses a security problem for the Party. Men such as Sakharov or Solzhenitsyn are a propaganda liability to the regime, but they are not a serious security threat. A greater threat comes from any organized group outside of Party control that promises to become an effective organization. A small number of determined men openly or secretly banded together with a common purpose is the nucleus of a potential action-instrument against the regime—a lesson that Lenin and his small band of Bolsheviks learned and proved in 1917.

The organized, open group becomes an automatic target. The militant Action Group for the Defense of Human Rights, for example, was established in 1969; four years later all but one of its fifteen members were warned into inaction or tried and imprisoned. The Human Rights Committee organized in November 1970 by Sakharov and Chalidze became inactive by 1973.

Chalidze was deprived of his citizenship while in the United States, and Sakharov now speaks as an individual.

Secret groups are a greater challenge. The publishers, distributors, and readers of the *Chronicle of Human Events* were an elusive target for the Fifth Directorate. It must have been particularly noxious to the KGB for its reportage of KGB practices and (otherwise) secret trials, which received worldwide coverage when its issues were smuggled to the West. The *Chronicle* was closed down temporarily in 1972 when the KGB threatened to arrest and punish a number of innocent hostages.

The *Chronicle* group symbolizes the limited power any loosely organized group can achieve. Most of the men and women involved did not know each other—reporters, editors, mimeographers, distributors. They had no two-way system of communications, no forum for composing their political differences and creating a common political platform, no secret meetings for planning joint actions. Its loose structure both reduced its capacity for action and made it an elusive target for the KGB.

The more organized a secret group, the greater its capacity for growth and future action, *and* for penetration by informers or *agents provocateurs*. This is the scissors any rebel group faces in a closed society.

Why So Few?

Dissident intellectuals in the Soviet Union today are a minuscule fragment of the like-minded but passive intellectuals in Moscow, Kiev, or Leningrad. The intellectual activists number, at any one time, from several hundred to perhaps one or two thousand: signers of petitions, members of "committees," writers and distributors of *samizdat* materials, authors of manuscripts sent abroad for publication, holders of news conferences for Western journalists, etc.

Why are there not more activists among that special class of Soviet intellectuals who resent the system?

The reasons they give to their Western contacts and to their activist colleagues at home are very human reasons:

—They see no purpose in open dissent. Since it will get nowhere, the sacrifice of jobs or privileges will achieve nothing.

—The prospect of corrective labor camps is a chastening prospect.

—They suspect that many, if not most, groups of dissenters are penetrated, or can easily be penetrated, by the KGB. Active participation would then lead to immediate exposure.

—Dissenters are being exploited by anti-Soviet groups and nations abroad. This lesson is driven home by the Party and emphasized in KGB chats. For patriotic Russians, open dissent can be unpatriotic, if not treasonable.

—Some dissenters are crackpots ("possessed"), fanatic beyond reason and often stupid in their pursuit of human rights. Others are criticized for their messy personal lives.

Much has also been made of "the Russian mentality," a philosophical and emotional frame of mind imbued with a sense of fatality and futility. Thinking, talking, brooding, taking a passive and pessimistic view of events, and feeling guilty for not acting on their principles—and no more. As one Western observer put it, "The Russian intelligentsia is not made for action."

A less philosophical and far more concrete ground for inaction lies in the simple fact that the Soviet intellectuals, like the intelligentsia as a whole, are first and foremost bureaucrats.

The Soviet Union is a vast, closely knit, party-government bureaucracy, a large-scale federal civil (and military) service in which bureaucratic values naturally prevail: job security, promotions, seniority, pensions. The bureaucratic mind, in Moscow, Washington, or Rome, is marked by timidity, conservatism, and conformity. It is intent on personal security and promotion. A good bureaucrat does not rock the boat. The higher up he is, the more he has to lose.

In a communist society the pressures to conform are even greater, for if a man is demoted or fired, he has no job alternatives. Nowhere is the conserving force of the bureaucracy greater than in a society that is all bureaucracy.

However independent-minded the bureaucrat (scientist, professor, writer), however contemptuous of the Party, however alienated from his colleagues, the pressure is on him to lead a double life: to be a good man at the office, to dissent in the privacy of his living room.

There are substantial compensations for keeping his mouth shut in public. With a good job during the day, he can indulge himself at night in the way all educated people like to live. He can eat good food, have a private apartment, talk with his friends, read unauthorized publications, listen to Western records, tune in on foreign radio stations. The passive protestant need not suffer except in his conscience.

The choice of the vast majority of Soviet intellectuals for public conformity should not be denigrated. Because he lives in a society with special punitive measures for public dissent, his only alternative to martyrdom is to keep his mouth shut in public and indulge the very human urge for a good life.

Both the Party and the active dissidents are caught in similar dilemmas.

The dialectic of internal security ranges in every society between coercion and consent. At this stage of Soviet history, as the society gradually and painfully moves from a closed to a partly open society, the Party faces the dilemma of how much openness it can permit without weakening its own monopoly of power. The more intense its coercive pressures (harassment, arrests, trials), the more intense the protests, and the increasing need for coercion.

The self-interest of the dissidents calls for their pursuing a moderate line to avoid their removal. Yet the more moderate, the more palatable they are to the Party, the less impact they can have. All-out opposition is suicide. A loyal opposition spells impotence.

The democrats thus face a dilemma: if they stay small—a circle of friends in one living room or another—they remain impotent. If they "organize," or coalesce into any kind of group, they are easily penetrated and dissolved by the KGB.

ON THE MOSCOW OLYMPICS

The holding of the 1980 Summer Olympics in Moscow gave the KGB's Second and Fifth Directorates their greatest security challenge in Soviet history: the prospective influx of over ten thousand athletes, over five thousand journalists and TV correspondents and their crews, and several hundred thousand hard-to-screen fans and tourists. Though the American-led boycott substantially lowered those numbers, hosting the Olympics exacted a high price from the KGB as well as from the uniformed police and military guards.

KGB preparations for the foreign inundation began in the fall of 1979. Its first task was to prepare a cordon around Olympic Village, a temporary network of informants and agents comparable to the *agentura* it maintains around the permanent foreign colony of diplomats and journalists in Moscow itself. By screening and selecting the service personnel required to maintain the village, the KGB was able to monitor all entries and exits, all untoward incidents, personal relations between Soviet and other athletes, etc. It brought in hundreds of KGB staff personnel from provincial offices throughout the Soviet Union to handle this closeup surveillance with the assistance of the Polish, Czech, or Cuban security men attached to their contingents and of the special informants among the communist athletes and trainers.

The KGB's specific concerns ran the gamut from espionage to protest, from the misbehavior of the visitors to that of Soviet citizens.

Would the Western intelligence services or anti-Soviet émigré groups abroad use athletes, trainers, or journalists to make secret contact with an already recruited agent? Would anti-Soviet émigré organizations send in agents under tourist cover to distribute anti-Soviet leaflets and books, or smuggle in money for Soviet dissidents?

The paranoia characteristic of the Second Chief Directorate saw all these as serious threats to be neutralized only by close surveillance, especially against those foreigners who spoke Russian and who took the initiative in meeting Soviet citizens.

Then there was the problem of Soviet citizens who might approach a visitor on their own initiative.

A major KGB concern throughout the games was to cut off possible foreign contacts with the dissidents. Moscow is the main center of Soviet dissent, and the Communist Party took several therapeutic measures during the months preceding the games to minimize the danger. It arrested and tried some of the most active dissidents. It placed others under house arrest. It removed their most prominent spokesman, Andrei Sakharov, from the Moscow scene by exiling him to the city of Gorki. It warned other leaders to keep their mouths shut and intensified its surveillance among dissident circles.

The heaviest charge placed on the KGB was the avoidance of anti-Soviet incidents, demonstrations or placards that could disturb the peace at the games and be publicized around the globe. Here it was the thousands of journalists and their enterprising cameramen who posed the main problem.

Foreign journalists were officially assured that they would not be harassed by the security authorities in covering the games. A later edict made it clear that they were free to cover the games, but not to pry into the facts of contemporary Soviet society by interviewing Soviet citizens and photographing non-Olympic scenes or events.

What the KGB was most concerned about was the threat that the dissidents would take advantage of foreign cameras to stage a media-event of global reach: a demonstration carrying placards ("Human Rights," "Jerusalem Now"), or a man leaping from the stands in front of the starters and getting caught in the cameras' eyes for at least a few seconds before he is hustled off to jail. These are sudden events difficult to control.

A routine, but high-priority, task was to avoid any terrorist or political actions such as marked some of the earlier Olympics. A successful or even boggled terrorist attack would have been an ig- nominious disaster for the KGB and would fortify all those who argued against the holding of the games in the Soviet Union. Of all modern services the KGB is best equipped to foil a terrorist plot. Its coverage of border entries and of international airports and cross-border railroads is denser than is possible in the West. It has the richest central files on foreigners in the world, and its "lists" of actual or potential security threats include not only Western agents, anti-Soviet émigrés, and hostile journalists, but every known or suspected terrorist of any nationality or political persuasion, from the IRA to the PLO.

As it turned out, the KGB did its job well. Only a handful of news reports on non-Olympic events came out of Moscow during the games. No great TV spectacular was mounted by the dis- sidents. No acts of violence marred the peace.

Whether the KGB made useful intelligence contacts with any of the visitors, only time will tell. The last thing the Russians wanted out of their Olympics was a spy scandal, and a brake must have been put on the KGB to avoid any offensive actions against the visitors. The story of a dirty-picture frame-up would have blanketed the Western press and provided further testimony to the Russians' callous disregard for the innocence of sport.

XIV

DO SECRET OPERATIONS MATTER?

In its seventh decade the KGB is in a new ball game, or, as a serious Marxist would put it, in a new and rapidly developing stage of the global process. The opening of détente in the late sixties, the rapidly accelerating process of change in the Third World, the steady growth of Soviet industrial power and commercial interests, the widespread multiplication of socialist economies, the energy crisis in the capitalist nations, the sharpening focus of the Arab-Israeli conflict in the Middle East, the weakening of American power and influence around the globe—all these give the Party bureaucrats in Moscow more to think about than Stalin or Khrushchev could have imagined.

The growth of the Soviet-German connection, the American defeat in Vietnam, Soviet successes in Angola and Ethiopia, Castro's growing camaraderie with Latin America, the destruction of the Western bulwark in Iran, the "stabilization" of Afghanistan, the shakiness of the feudal regimes in Saudi Arabia and the Persian Gulf, might well convince the Communist Party that it is on the right course.

As the tempo of events picks up, greater demands are made on the KGB both for intelligence and action. The political and economic situation in each country, large and small, must be analyzed more frequently and in greater detail. Open diplomacy, from military and economic aid to propaganda and exchanges, must be bolstered by secret political action and by agents of influence. Impending wars of national liberation in Africa and Latin America must be recognized and assessed. The military capacity and intentions of the Main Enemy must be constantly reviewed. Preparations must be made for the eventuality of regional or global wars.

What *is* the role of secret operations in Moscow's forward diplomacy?

Security at Home

However dynamic Soviet actions in the outside world, the crux of Soviet security begins at home. However useful the work of the First Chief Directorate abroad, the Party's priority interest is to maintain a stable Soviet society under its control, and that is, as we have seen, the work of the Second and Fifth Directorates and their secret agents, or informants.

What is the future of national, religious, and intellectual dissent within the Soviet Union? Can it have an impact on the Party's monopoly of power?

Though there is much talk about separatist trends in the Soviet Union, they are in my view easily controllable by the Party. Ukrainian, or Baltic, cultural nationalism can be allowed within limits. Political nationalists seeking independence or autonomy can be nipped in the bud, for it is inconceivable that any *organized* group could reach the point of effective action within the present control system. As the Russification of the ethnic minorities proceeds apace, more and more of their brightest young men will take their place in the Russian-controlled Party and government bureaucracies and play ball with the system.

We sometimes forget how isolated most of Soviet society is from outside events. There is no evidence that the Muslim fundamentalism at work in Iran has spread into the Central Asian "Muslim" republics. Nor is there any evidence that the invasion of Moslem Afghanistan has caused unrest among the Soviet Moslem population. Though border controls have relaxed since Stalin's day, the Party's control of the media constructs a psychological barrier no less effective in avoiding contamination from the outside world.

Most religious institutions in the Soviet Union will continue under the administrative control of the Party-government, and groups like the Baptists and Jehovah's Witnesses can be infiltrated. The Jews are the most vocal dissenters, but the "problem of the Jews" in the Soviet Union is now self-liquidating. Once the Party made up its mind, whether or not under mainly international pressures, that the nuisance value of disgruntled Jews was greater than the value of their talents to Soviet society, it has systematically permitted their emigration, a policy that promises to continue until there are no more Jews who want to emigrate.

The dissident intellectuals, Christian, Jewish, or atheist, pose a greater and noisier problem, but not in my judgment any kind of serious threat to the Party.

The Western image of Soviet dissent tends to inflate its impact on Soviet society. It is perhaps the novelty of political protest in the Soviet Union that leads to its exaggeration. Dissenters make news. Western journalists and academics talk their language, and vice versa. They are reachable in Moscow and Leningrad. They are open and candid with foreigners they can trust. They are, for the most part, admirable "fighters for freedom," sacrificing their own interests for a higher cause.

Some observers predict that dissent will grow as the intellectual elite itself grows, and there is more education, more intercourse with the West, more available Western publications, more international conferences, more officials stationed abroad. As the Soviet Union becomes more porous, more non-Party thinking will spread.

On the other hand, the growing prosperity of Soviet society gives the Party increased capacity to reward those who play ball with the regime, especially the scientific workers essential to industrial progress. The New Class will expand. The elite will have increased status, income, and privileges. Dissent addresses itself to this elite, precisely those who enjoy and support the status quo.

If these positive appeals do not work, there is always the Fifth Directorate. The Communist Party cannot prevent dissent, but will monitor it and limit, hide, or punish active dissenters. As conditions change, the KGB changes. Émigré dissidents have noted the higher quality of KGB officers with whom they have had personal dealings. The obvious punitive measures open to the KGB are now bolstered by more sophisticated ploys. The so-called Andropov gambit pushes the line that many books and articles are not published for nonpolitical reasons: they are simply not of high enough quality. A more telling argument the KGB can use is that open dissenters, especially the authors of manuscripts sent abroad, strengthen the anti-Soviet propaganda campaigns of Western reactionaries—a form of collusion with the enemy that weakens the society they (it is assumed) wish to strengthen by reforms.

A difficult argument for the KGB to handle in its "sophisticated" dialogue with dissenters is their citation of the rights guaranteed by the Soviet constitution and by the official signing of the Helsinki Convention. The KGB rationale that these are meant for outside consumption, and not for domestic application, puts the KGB officer on a fairly weak wicket.

Soviet dissent is an embarrassment, not a threat, to the Party. As human rights have become an international issue, Moscow faces a sharp scissors: a dialectic between internal security and the Soviet image abroad. The Party must maintain a highly selective tactic of pressure and punishment if it wishes to project a more moderate image abroad. It must, at the same time, handle with care foreign pressures to relax its repressive measures. Here its Achilles' heel is the scientific intelligentsia. Philosophers, poets, and novelists are not essential to industrial progress, and the nonconformists are easily insulated from the rest of society. The scientists are indispensable. There will be other men like Sakharov and Medvedev, and with them the Party must tread softly. The threat of a total boycott by Western scientists after the Soviet invasion of Afghanistan would probably have hit Moscow far harder than the boycott of the Olympic summer games or restrictions on the transfer of high-level technology.

The dissenters may have no future, but their ideas do. The dissenters keep alive within the Soviet elite human and humane values the Party now ignores: freedom of protest, self-expression in the arts, an open science.

When, and only when, reformist ideas penetrate the middle ranks of the Party and new blood is injected into the gerontocracy of the Politburo, can the kind of substantial reforms be made that the dissident intellectuals want. And it will be their contribution to have kept alive, in whatever modest circles, the continuity of non-Party values that this or the next generation of Party bureaucrats may convert from theory into practice.

Does Soviet Espionage Matter?

In the past thirty years great-power espionage has become a large-scale enterprise enmeshed in East-West politics. Spy trials and spy scares have played an intermittent role in Cold War attitudes on both sides. Two acronyms, KGB and CIA, have become a focus for people everywhere as the sinister symbols of two warring imperialisms—secret threats are the greatest threats, for they cannot be assessed. Rosenberg, Philby, Guillaume, Penkovskiy: who are the others?

Various recipes have been offered in the West to cope with the problem of Soviet espionage since the disparity between Soviet and Western capabilities in secret operations is clear to all.

One recipe calls for the reduction of Soviet diplomatic staffs in the major capitalist nations to reduce the range of official cover. The ejection of over a hundred Soviet officials by the British Government in 1971 and a smaller number by the Canadians several years later are citied as desirable moves in this direction. Yet the complex political and economic relations that have evolved between East and West place a brake on such actions. Even during the height of the Cold War, Western governments were not inclined to take such drastic measures.

Another, more bizarre, recipe calls for a Soviet-American agreement to stop spying on each other and to give up covert action operations on both sides. Why, one may ask, should Moscow give up a uniquely effective instrument of national policy in exchange for the ending of the minor covert pin-pricks it is faced with from the West?

A more modest formula calls for alerting the citizens of the world to the Soviet secret threat by publicly identifying known Soviet intelligence officers in every capital. This game can, of course, also be played by the other side.

Granted the increasing number of Soviet agents in the open playground of the Western democracies, and the difficulty of catching the best of them, how important is it that they be caught?

The primary peacetime purpose of an espionage service before the technical age was to give early warning of impending hostilities: spies sought mobilization plans and Foreign Office and General Staff documents and communications. That purpose is now served, for both Moscow and Washington, by the increasingly open nature of both societies, by overhead satellite photography and sensing, and by the interception of virtually all of each side's electronic communications by the other. Human agents will not herald the outbreak of the next major war, if there is one.

What, then, is the major profit to Moscow from its expensive spy apparatus in the West?

It saves Moscow time and money in upgrading its technological capacity. The major focus of the KGB program in the United States is on industrial espionage: collecting information on commercially restricted or militarily classified equipment, manufacturing processes, research and development, advanced sectors of scientific research, etc. At a time when Soviet technology was at a low ebb in the postwar years, information on Allied A-bomb research and production made a vital contribution to Soviet security. Today, when Soviet technology has advanced to the Western level in many sectors, the requirements become less urgent and more specialized: electronic equipment, offshore oil drilling, atomic energy plants, car and truck production, etc. Moscow saves money when the KGB steals industrial secrets. It saves time by shortcutting development through exploiting Western experience.

It reduces apprehension in Moscow. Soviet and East European agents have systematically ransacked NATO files for the past twenty years. NATO equipment, contingency plans, inter-Allied bickering are—and are likely to continue to be—an open book. Spies in the Western political and military establishments, at lower or higher levels, can monitor secret plans for Western military action in the Middle East or intervention in Iran or Yugoslavia. Spies in the right places can induce a feeling of security by negative reporting or guarantee no strategic surprises by positive reporting. Their value in reducing the (normal) paranoid tendencies of the Soviet mind should not be underestimated.

It assists in the effective carrying out of political and economic negotiations. Any negotiator would like to know the stance and fall-back positions of the other side before the conference starts. Spies are one answer.

What is the profit to the West in countering Soviet espionage efforts?

Soviet technological advances can be slowed up in those limited sectors still classified secret by denying Moscow the ability to get them on the cheap. Since most of what the Russians want can be obtained openly from available literature or the purchase of prototypes, this slow up quickly narrows down to:

Keeping secret our technical military secrets. The precise importance to a nation's security of keeping its military secrets in a world of advanced technology and instant communications has, as far as I know, never been dispassionately analyzed. There is, on the one hand, the case of NATO. If secrecy were essential to its effective performance, it might best be scrapped, for its command must, to be sensible, work on the asumption that NATO secrets will continue to be available to the Warsaw Pact. On the other hand, although the impact of leakages from the Joint Chiefs or the NATO command *in peacetime* can easily be exaggerated, it is a simple fact that Soviet agents now in place will continue to function in time of war when the exposure of military secrets can be lethal.

There is an overriding, if intangible, drive for catching Soviet spies: a strong emotional compulsion to keep the nation's secrets *whatever they may be*. It is a violation of national pride, as well as of security, when a hostile spy is exposed—be he a desk man in the Department of State or a researcher in a West Coast laboratory. A Soviet spy is an enemy in our midst; the American spy-fever in the early fifties and the British reaction to Philby's flight to Moscow in 1963 are only extreme forms of this basic patriotic reaction to proof of foreign hostility.

Another, longer-term factor should not be discounted.

The KGB (and the GRU), like the Soviet General Staff, take contingency planning for war very seriously. Both its legals and illegals devote some of their effort to identifying and reporting on sabotage targets, and Moscow Center collates this information much the same way as the Air Force builds up its bombing-target dossiers. The illegals, however, are the ones who have an action as well as an intelligence mission in wartime.

Even though we have no clear notion of how many illegals are in the West on "sleeper" missions, and how many of them will be activated only in war, each year that passes permits the KGB to get more of them in place. In a protracted all-out war, a handful of trained illegals can carry out selected sabotage missions that will have a serious impact on the Enemy.

Does Influence Matter?

From its inception the Soviet regime has devoted a great deal of effort to increasing its influence in the world outside its borders. For thirty years it worked mainly on the political Left: through the Comintern and its national sections, its international fronts and friendship societies, and a vast array of international media—radio, books, pamphlets, periodicals.

Since the late fifties it has worked mainly on the elites of the decolonized nations of the Third World by the conventional methods of Western diplomacy: military and economic aid, treaties of friendship, propaganda, state visits, student scholarships. In a handful of cases it has supported guerrilla groups and wars of national liberation.

From the late sixties on, it has concentrated on developing its influence in capitalist societies, working mainly on the political Center and Right, the parties and social groups that make up the elites of the current establishments. Its aims are clear: to promote the most rapid possible development of the Soviet economy through capital investment and technological advancement and the extension of the Soviet economy into the world market.

Under the roof of SALT diplomacy and other military negotiations today, the main business of détente for Moscow is business: favorable trade terms, desirable capital investments, joint or solo banking, insurance and sales ventures abroad. This business goes on at the level of foreign trade officials, industrial executives, and bankers. It is here that such agents of influence as the KGB can recruit will pay off in hard (foreign) currency.

Influence *does* matter. In fact, the major positive task of any senior nation-state today is to increase its influence with other nations within the limits of its capacity. And today that influence is directed by both East and West toward economic rather than national security goals. For most nations the world has become more and more an economic world as the Cold War died down, as the shortage of fuel has affected the shaky economies of the West, and as the competition between the West German, Japanese, and American economies has sharpened.

Concern for Soviet espionage can blind the West to the developing clout of the KGB as an adjunct to Soviet diplomacy. Competent, aggressive, with something to sell, the KGB activists in New York, Bonn, and Paris work hard day by day to advance the Soviet interest without (in most cases) committing any felonies or even misdemeanors. The overall value of their work can only be assessed in Moscow.

This wide-ranging effort is worthwhile in itself. Even without the recruitment of an espionage or influence agent, Moscow comes to know more about the personalities of the capitalist elites, the people in and around the policy-making apparatus in the government and business world. As Moscow's official representatives move into wider circles of legal, business, and political interest, they often know beforehand whom they are talking to. And the Central Index in Moscow can prove valuable even in legitimate business. A new government official or negotiator can be checked against the Index: Have we met him before; do we have a handle on him; will he be a "productive contact"?

The rationale of influence operations in the West is simple and sound. As Moscow's relations with Western nations become more intense and more complex, the call on Soviet diplomacy to affect the Western elites in Moscow's interest becomes ever more demanding. In London, Bonn, and Paris their steadily growing contacts run across the spectrum of the establishment: government and political party leaders of the Center and the Right, labor leaders of all political complexions, key editors and journalists of all hues, and prominent members of the corporate and banking communities.

Making friends with American bankers and industrialists, protecting the Soviet interest in truck-assembly or petrochemical contracts, developing receptive ears in government officials, dissolving anti-Soviet prejudices in corporate boardrooms and editorial offices: these are the marrow of competitive coexistence.

ON THE DECAY OF ALLEGIANCE

I cannot avoid a final and cheerless comment on one aspect of Western society that promises to ease the KGB's future recruitment of agents.

Personal allegiance in many nations of the Third World are not to the state, but to the family or tribe, to a charismatic leader, or to an ethnic or political party.

Allegiance in the West is to the nation-state: a patriot is loyal to his country. When patriotism weakens, the self-interest of the individual citizen takes precedence.

The so-called Me generation marks the decline of national allegiance, a weakening of emotional and moral ties to the community. The individual puts his own interests first: for self-fulfillment, for money and status, for relief from boredom or anxiety. He seeks personal gratification, and the focus on self makes him vulnerable to appeals to his ego. Money, recognition, adventure become stronger needs than the impulse to be loyal to his community. As the number of such people increases, the reservoir of agent-candidates for the KGB increases. The KGB prides itself on its study of the bourgeois psyche, and its more than a thousand gregarious officers in the West are in a position to single out the most susceptible.

Money and sex become even more effective tools. Money, above all, as Western economies falter, money for the editor of a failing newspaper, for the businessman desperate to make a good deal, for the American GI who has overused his credit cards, for the little man who wants to live it up, for the member of parliament who wants to keep a mistress.

I have been struck by the number of oddballs the KGB has found helpful in recent years: in Bonn, in California, in Rome, and Paris. Perhaps the quota of neurotics in Western society is increasing with the growth of a pervading anxiety as political lines are blurred, economic institutions are questioned, and government itself becomes suspect.

Both the narcissist and the neurotic are prime bait for the KGB.

Viewed in this light, Soviet espionage becomes part of the psychodrama in the meeting of East and West, a minor but symbolic element in their confrontation.

INDEX

Gilbert, Jean (alias of Léopold
Trepper), 14, 18, 19
Goebbels, Joseph, 8
Goering, Hermann, 2
Gold, Harry, 38–40, 55, 124,
240
Goldfus, Emil R. (alias of
Rudolf Abel), 53
Goleniewski, Michal, 243, 245
Golitsin, Anatoli, 242
Golos, Jacob, 31–33, 36, 70
Gomez (Mexican student),
226–27
Gomulka, Wladyslaw, 243
Gorbunov (alias of Lt. Gen.
Gribanov), 92–93
Gorki, 265
Gottfried, Dr. Harold, 157
Gouzenko, Igor, 25–26, 37, 50,
58, 72, 112, 132, 251
GPU (Soviet security service),
6n
Great Game, The (Trepper),
18n
"Great Grain Robbery," 198
Greece, 143, 156, 219
Greenglass, David, 38–40, 48,
240
Greenglass, Ruth, 38–39, 40
Greenland, 171
Gribanov, Lieutenant General,
92, 93
Grigorenko, Major General
Peter, 259
Gromov, Anatol, 28, 33, 49, 72
Grossvogel, Leo, 14–15
GRU (Chief Intelligence
Directorate of the Soviet
General Staff), 51, 67, 68,
110, 111, 129, 174, 175, 177,
180, 191–92, 204, 205, 240,
242, 273; Canadian network
of, 25–27, 40–41, 47, 49, 50,
58, 62, 133, 199, 213; and
Chambers net, 30–31, 35, 50,
60, 62, 70, 179; and KGB,

21, 24, 47, 63, 64, 71; KGB
security control of, 64;
"material incentives" to
recruits, 168–69, 179; and
NATO installations, 156;
originates system of "illegals,"
62; and Sorge, 6–14, 21–22,
24, 50, 62, 70, 205; structure
and scope of, 61–63;
telephone espionage by, 197;
Third World operations of,
62, 211, 226, 229; and
Trepper, 14–22, 23, 24, 50,
62, 64, 70, 85, 199
Guatemala, 225
Guest, David, 120
Guevara, Che, 232
Guillaume, Guenter, 149–51,
271
Guinea, 220
Guzmán, Arbenz, 225

Hague, The, 166
Hamburg, 6, 8, 13, 41, 68, 209
Harbin, 7
Harvard University, 3, 41, 130,
210
Havana, 186, 225, 226
Havas, 10
Hayhanen, Reino, 54, 57–59,
240
Heidelberg, 171
Heinz, Leonore, 146–47, 241
Helmers, Carl, 146
Helsinki, 54
Helsinki Convention, 270
Herrmann, Col. Rudolph
Albert, 205–6
Himmler, Heinrich, 6, 20
Hiroshima, 27
Hiss, Alger, 33–34, 35, 36, 40,
131, 132, 133, 137
Hiss, Priscilla, 36
Hitler, Adolf, 4, 5, 6, 7, 11, 14,
15, 16, 17, 18, 20, 22–24, 41,